TEST TEAM
of the century

TEST TEAM
of the century

Edited by Garrie Hutchinson

Harper*Sports*
An imprint of HarperCollins*Publishers*

Cover photographs: *Front cover, top half, clockwise from top left:* Arthur Morris, Bill O'Reilly, Bill Ponsford, Neil Harvey, Don Bradman, Keith Miller, Ray Lindwall. *Front cover , bottom half, clockwise from top left:* Shane Warne, Ian Healy, Greg Chappell, Dennis Lillee, Allan Border. *Back cover, clockwise from top left:* Clarrie Grimmett, Victor Trumper, Sid Barnes, Doug Walters, Stan McCabe, Don Tallon, Alan Davidson, Warwick Armstrong, Steve Waugh, Lindsay Hassett, Richie Benaud, Jack Gregory.

The statistics published in this book are correct at the time of going to press.

Every effort has been made to contact the copyrightholders of material contained in this work, in some cases details are missing, illegible or insignificant. The publisher welcomes any information in relation to missing credits or acknowledgments.

Harper*Sports*

An imprint of HarperCollinsPublishers, Australia

First published in Australia in 2000
by HarperCollins*Publishers* Pty Limited
ABN 36 009 913 517
A member of the HarperCollins*Publishers* (Australia) Pty Limited Group
http://www.harpercollins.com.au

HarperCollins*Publishers*
25 Ryde Road, Pymble, Sydney NSW 2073, Australia
31 View Road, Glenfield, Auckland 10, New Zealand
77–85 Fulham Palace Road, London W6 8JB, United Kingdom
Hazelton Lanes, 55 Avenue Road, Suite 2900, Toronto, Ontario M5R 3L2
and 1995 Markham Road, Scarborough, Ontario M1B 5M8 Canada
10 East 53rd Street, New York NY 10022, USA

National Library of Australia Cataloguing-in-Publication data:

Test team of the century.
ISBN 0 7322 6854 0.
1. Cricket players – Australia – History – 20th century.
2. Cricket – Australia – History – 20th century.
I. Hutchinson, Garrie, 1949– . II. Title.
796.3580994

Cover photographs: All photographs from Ross, Hutchinson & Associates collection, except the following cover photographs from Allsport: Dennis Lillee, Shane Warne, Ian Healy, Greg Chappell, Don Bradman, Steve Waugh, and Richie Benaud.

Produced by Ross, Hutchinson & Associates
52 Cambridge Street, Collingwood Victoria 3066 Australia

Printed in Australia by Griffin Press Pty Ltd on 79gsm Bulky Paperback

7 6 5 4 3 2 1   00 01 02 03 04

CONTENTS

INTRODUCTION

by Garrie Hutchinson

Like most Australians born in the first half of the twentieth century (males anyway), I would have given any part of my anatomy to have bowled one ball for Australia in a Test match. There is no other activity that demands such sacrifice, no other sport which calls up such dreams. Not even Australian football. Early on it was clear to me that I didn't have the prowess, or the physique, to be good enough to play football for my school team (chockablock with VFL players) – but it was more than possible to imagine bowling for Australia.

This was at University High School in Melbourne, where the footy team was replete with Carlton greats such as Gags Gallagher, and where, two years after we matriculated, one of the cricket team actually did earn a baggy green cap. That was Les Joslin, who didn't become a champion, but has earned my undiluted envy because he dreamed the dream, and made it come true.

Until I was well into my forties, not so long ago, I could seriously (but privately) imagine a situation where I was travelling in the backblocks of Zimbabwe, say, when the Australians were there, each bitten by a virulent mozzie while on a visit to Victoria Falls inspecting the statue of Livingstone, and stricken with malaria, the day before the Test. The call went out, beaten on jungle drums, and carried to all Aussies not mozzie infected. Leggie needed! Report to Harare, pronto!

And there, on a stretcher beside the dusty nets Steve Waugh rises on one delirious elbow, and says, 'Dr Hutchinson I presume!' He tosses me the cherry, and I whirl a few down on a length to a wobbly Ricky

---

Garrie Hutchinson co-edited 200 Seasons of Australian Cricket, *and watched the University High School First XI of 1965 (pictured, Les Joslin, front row, second from right) with undisguised envy.*

Ponting, thinking – there! Older than Bert Ironmonger! (who first played for Australia aged 46 years and 237 days, pictured opposite).

As for the rest, that is a private imagining, but as in a lifetime of summers playing social cricket with writers, actors, artists and historians (including some marvellous beings who had been trained properly as lads) it is possible to bowl, accidentally, one or two, perhaps a grand total of six, perfectly pitched and spinning leggies, so I know what they feel like, what they look like, and can endlessly bowl them in my mind when listening to the radio in the summer.

But I can say that if I had been called upon in Harare, or Manchester, or on the mat at Lahore I would (in my dreams) have bowled those six perfect deliveries, received a nod from the captain, and would have scurried off to have that spinning finger surgically removed, and mounted as a piece of memorabilia before I turned into David Sincock.

Cricket is *the* Australian game, of course. It was the game that united the nation 24 years before Federation at the first Test at the spiritual home of Australia, the MCG. Cricket is the game which sent a team of original Australians to England 99 years before the referendum that allowed them to be Australian citizens. Cricket is the only team game which unites Australians, except for, with rare exceptions, those Australians who were here before cricket, or who have come here since Bradman retired.

That caveat aside, cricket is the national game. Which is why the events involving match-fixing and its relationship to betting have been so distressing. We accept that the greats of cricket are human, that is part of the game's attraction, and we know that gambling on the game was one of the original traditions of the game in the nineteenth century. Fast bowlers are fiery, batsmen are elegant or sloggers, spinners are cunning and deep, but all of them (in our case) are Australians. They might be larrikins, as were many World War diggers, and they might have taken a crazy thousand-to-one bet against Ian Botham (and won the bet and lost the Test), or taken a bookie's money in exchange for weather reports (taking money from bookies is a legitimate sport after all the money they have taken from us). Cause for uneasiness – but not entirely against the spirit of being an Australian, which fixing or throwing matches, however unimportant, is.

The players of the century are all characteristically Australian, many of them irredeemably and loveably so, and none of them, not even the contemporaries – I stake my spinning finger on it – will be found to have been less than good sports in all the meanings of the word.

The Team of the Century is the one officially chosen by selectors assembled by the Australian Cricket Board in early 2000, and, like every cricket follower who saw it, I sympathised in the impossibility of the task, and picked my own team whom I thought might give the 'officials' a run for their money.

While the official team includes a number of well-known larrikin-types, what with Lillee's aluminium bat, Warne's soap operatic life, Miller's flamboyance, O'Reilly's eccentricities – I believe 'my' team makes up for it in all-around Australianness, and contains some of the most tremendous players ever to pull on a baggy green.

Perhaps my team isn't as well balanced as the official one, partly because it was chosen for some non-cricketing reasons. I had another couple of teams to choose – the writers – and sometimes they made a strong case for a particular player.

The writers were asked to write about players in their own way, according to their own lights. I have also selected pieces from three players' contemporaries – as great in the writing field as the players on the cricket (which a pair of them also graced): Jack Fingleton, A. G. (Johnnie) Moyes and Ray Robinson. The result is, I trust, a very entertaining collection of history, memoir and cricket fact and fiction which illuminates aspects of a century of cricket in Australia, and the astonishingly varied careers of the immortals who have played it.

ARTHUR MORRIS

The Civilised Opener

by Gideon Haigh

On the table next to Arthur Morris is a new biography of him, by Sydney's Jack McHarg. Very flattering to be judged worthy of such a publication, he reasons, but it does have disadvantages. 'Good thing about getting older is that you forget all the ridiculous ways you got out,' he says, puffing quietly on a Davidoff. 'But now I read that I had a few failures, too. The chairman of the board I'm on at Trust Company, he always introduces me as "the man who never scored a duck". And I say: "Perfectly right, too". Truth's out now.'

So it is. But the truth is that the ridiculous ways Morris found to get out in 46 Tests were vastly overshadowed by the handsome ways he stayed in to acquire 3500 runs. 'He plunders bowlers tastefully and changes rubbish to cultured art,' Neville Cardus rhapsodised. 'I never tire of watching him.' Morris' batting was, moreover, true to the man, civilised, courteous, unaffected. From his verandah, he returns the salutes of Cessnock passersby, and acknowledges the car horns that sound in greeting. 'Lovely town really,' he says. 'Everyone's so friendly.' To the little girl on her mother's hand walking past: 'Give us a wave, Kelly Jo.'

There's a streak of self-mockery, too. The den is trophy-lined, but he first reaches to show you a coffee mug, a favourite gift from his former opening partner Ken Archer. It shows the pair coming out to bat with the caption: 'Who's the Old Bloke next to KA?' Friendly? Morris supposes he is, but then you should have met Arthur Mailey: 'You'd say to Arthur: "Arthur, isn't there anyone you dislike?" He'd say: "Well some people do disappoint me".'

Only occasionally – when a car backfires, or he hears voices raised – is Morris's composure slightly disrupted:

Gideon Haigh is a Melbourne journalist and author. Portions of this story first appeared in his book One Summer, Every Summer.

I suppose that when I hear voices raised, even today I remember my parents. God alone knows how they ever got together; they were such different people. The old man, being a schoolteacher, he lived a pretty monastic life: didn't drink, didn't smoke, didn't go out with sheilas. My mother liked a party. Smoked a hundred cigarettes a day from the age of 15 till she died at 91. They'd have a big argument and off we'd go.

Cricket was a happy refuge from his parents' estrangement. Morris joined St George at 14 as a left-arm spinner, where the club captain was Bill O'Reilly, whom he watched in a dramatic SCG Test when Allen's Englishmen overthrew Bradman's Australians just before Christmas 1936. Morris recalls:

I always enjoyed watching until Bill bowled. It seemed that all the beautiful strokes stopped when he came on, and I couldn't understand what he was doing to make the batsmen prod and miss. It was only as I got older that I learned what a great bowler he was. That Test was the first time I realised that first-class cricketers swore, actually. I was down there on the third man boundary, as naive as they come, and Maurie Sievers came running down towards the fence but the ball just beat him. And he goes: 'Fuck it!' I'd heard the word before but, with a very proper upbringing, I was quite shocked.

As a 16-year-old first-grade cricketer firmly under O'Reilly's spell, Morris slipped snugly into the nook of number one and never looked back. At 17, he was a state second XI opener in a team led by Ken Gulliver and including Colin McCool and Ron Saggers tackling a Victorian second XI incorporating Ian Johnson and Keith Miller. At 18, Morris was opening the batting for his state and scoring an unprecedented brace of centuries against Queensland. 'Bloody terrified I was,' Morris says. 'It turned out all right.'

It was December 1940, however, and white uniforms were being swapped for khaki. Private Morris of the AIF spent his war at Finschafen and Lae in PNG, fortunate that his movement control unit came no closer to the Japanese than sporadic bombings, but unfortunate in that cricket was virtually out of the question. For the next six years, he played only once with his St George compadre Ray Lindwall, and then in a softball game against the US Army. Their roles for once were reversed, Morris pitched while Lindwall prowled the deep field in front of the tree line. 'This big Negro came in and hit it so hard that it was headed for the jungle and we would never have found it,' Morris recalls. 'And Ray flew up in the air and took this great bloody catch. If he hadn't taken it, that would probably have meant the end of the game.'

A belated demob returned 24-year-old Morris to Sydney just in time for the first postwar Ashes series against Wally Hammond's Englishmen, reuniting him with a character first spied from the far side of an SCG fence almost a decade before: the mercurial, monstrously gifted right-hander Sid Barnes.

I can still remember Siddy the first time I played him. He played a long innings while O'Reilly went through Petersham, and this whipper-snapper rolls up to Bill in the showers and says: 'Well bowled, Tiger. That was some of the best bowling I've faced.' I'd've walked up to Bill and said something like: 'Excuse me Mr O'Reilly, may I have a word?' But Siddy's going: 'Yes Tiger, you bowled very well out there.' Bill just about swallowed the soap.

Barnes proved an inventive, unselfish and agile ally. 'More than anybody, Sid lost his best years to the war,' Morris says. 'He was such a great player before it; afterwards he was more calculating, didn't take any risks and stayed on the back foot, got himself in a bit of a hole. But you've never seen a stronger player through point.' The pair succeeded almost at once. Having failed in his first couple of Tests, Morris greeted 1947 with consecutive innings of 155, 122 and 124 not out. 'Is that right?' he asks. 'All I can say about that first century is that there was a big bloody sigh of relief at the end.' Then characteristically, there's the tribute to a rival: 'I tell you who bowled marvellously at me, did me all the time, did all of us: [wrist-spinner Doug] Wright. He'd jump and he'd go over the stumps; he was too quick. But because of his run and his jerky action he'd bowl a couple each over you could get at.'

The Morris–Barnes alliance was ratified and validated when the pair went to England as part of Donald Bradman's unchallengeable 1948 side, rooming and opening together for four months and averaging 87 and 82 respectively. Both scored hundreds in their maiden Lord's Tests – Barnes having staked £8 on himself to do so at 15–1 – as Australia won by the small matter of 409 runs. The tour's pinnacle was Morris's triple-century partnership with Bradman at Leeds, underwriting a successful Australian last-day chase of 404. Now that was fun, Morris assures you. There's an almost mischievous glint in his eye.

All the press'd said: 'Thank God, this is the day we've been waiting for, where we finally beat these Australians'. And suddenly you get that perverse feeling that you want to stop them and, before you know it, you can take on the world. They weren't bowling at all badly but, when you're batting well, you make your own rubbish, and we just kept going. [England captain Norman] Yardley, he had to go for a win so the field was always in, and I hit 20 fours in my first 100.

At lunch Morris decided that the bowler he most needed to neutralise was Denis Compton, who had beaten Bradman several times and had him dropped at slip. 'Denis was a pretty handy left-arm bowler, but he wasn't regular,' Morris says. 'So I thought that whenever he pitched up I'd get stuck into him and loft.' In a famous photograph of them resuming after the adjournment, the Don is imparting some advice, but Morris appears preoccupied, tight-lipped, staring ahead, perhaps finally resolving on his forthcoming contest with Compton's chinaman. 'He was bowling like a batsman,' Morris recalls. 'Trying to do too much: if I started coming down, he'd throw it up further. So I'd keep coming.' Compton's first two post-lunch overs yielded Morris seven boundaries, a pivotal period that restored Australian momentum. Morris made 182, his stand with Bradman yielding 301. 'Bradman earned the better part of his knighthood on that day,' wrote Denzil Batchelor. 'And Morris was surely unfortunate to have missed … an OBE.'

Morris rounded out the tour at The Oval with 196 in what was known to be Bradman's last Test and – thanks to the disintegration of his relations with the Australian Board of Control – also proved Barnes's swansong. Their last stand was 122 – dwarfing England's all out 52 – and though Morris had fruitful alliances with the likes of Jack Moroney, Ken Archer and Colin McDonald, he never attained quite the same simpatico as he had with Barnes. Morris recalls:

When Siddy went I lost a lot of support because he'd always get ones. Jack was a good player but, well, you had to get a two before Jack'd come one because he didn't back up. Then I ended up with Ken Archer who was a beautiful batsman to watch but played very firmly: mid-off, mid-on, bang, all the time. You'd look up the scoreboard after 20 minutes or so, and you'd had six hits or something. Ken says – and I deny it completely of course – that I came up to him after twenty minutes of one Test match and said: 'Ken I don't want all the strike, but can you at least give me 50 per cent?' I'm sure I could never have said such a thing, but he swears that I did.

Morris also came to know a constant English thorn: Alec Bedser. Bedser dismissed Morris 18 times in Tests; Morris scored eight of his 12 Test centuries against Bedser. Their subsequent correspondences and communications – for they became lifelong friends, in faith with the spirit of their rivalry – still freely refer to both.

Some days, it was Morris's nerve and judgement that prevailed. In one Test at Old Trafford, Morris was paired at the top of the order with stand-in opener Ian Johnson. Johnson watched from the non-striker's end as Bedser bowled a wicked first over, moving the ball one way then the other at the very last instant. Morris met every ball in the middle of the bat, then conferred with Johnson in mid-pitch. 'It's doing a bit,' he confided, deadpan. 'We better stick around.' For the next hour, Morris took every ball from England's master of medium pace, absorbing him like a punching bag.

Other days, of course, it didn't go according to plan. Bedser achieved an incontestable edge by eclipsing Morris six times in eight innings worth 60 runs while touring with Freddie Brown's Englishmen in 1950–51, the nadir an anticlimactic duck in the SCG Test. 'Bloody ridiculous really, on this beautiful wicket,' Morris says. 'Alec bowls a long hop, at quarter rat power just to get his arm over, I walk inside to touch it to leg, and it goes "flick". And there it is, before all these people, bowled for a blob. I started to laugh halfway back because I came in to just dead silence.'

The tide then turned in Adelaide. On the morning of the fourth Test, Morris came down to breakfast to find he'd been allocated a seat at table 13. He paused superstitiously, then sat down anyway; what would be, would be. For the next day and a half, Morris was occupied with making 206; 'watchful, phlegmatic with hardly a hint of mortal error' commented E. W. Swanton. Finally, with the last man at the crease, he donated his wicket to finger-spinner Roy Tattersall; a photograph of the dismissal shows Morris smiling cheerfully as if released from the cares of solemnity.

Among contemporaries, there was always the feeling about Morris that he could summon resources as he wished. Ken Archer recalls a meeting one morning before a Shield match at the 'Gabba, where his friend advised: 'Not feeling too well, dear boy. Don't think I'll want to bat too long today.' But when a couple of wickets fell early, the New South Welshman flashed Archer a long-suffering look, and proceeded to blast 253 out of 400, the last 50 in 17 minutes.

Yet Morris seldom gorged himself at the crease. Batting was a pathway to pleasure, not a road to records, and dismissal merely postponed enjoyment rather than thwarted ambition. He was philosophical even when run out for 99 by partner Neil Harvey in the fifth Test at the MCG against South Africa in February 1953. 'Last ball of the over I was at the bowler's end, so I was really thinking about getting my hundred next over,' says Morris. 'Tayfield was on to Neil, and he hit it to cover and took off. It was his call, so I had to go, and I probably hesitated because I wasn't expecting it. And that was the difference between being run out by four yards rather than six!'

Perhaps the yen for big scores had faded by that stage. When Morris was back in England as Lindsay Hassett's vice-captain a few months later, he passed 50 a dozen times but only transited once to a century. But how could anyone describe this as a disappointing tour? Why, Morris met his future wife, Valerie Hudson, a willowy showgirl appearing with Bud Flanagan and Teddy Knox's 'Crazy Gang' show *Ring Out the Bells* at the Victoria Palace. When she took an assisted passage a year later, they married at the Sydney Registry Office.

Morris hadn't thought of himself as the marrying kind. 'Would you have been with the example of my parents?' he asks. 'Ian Craig says that the first time we met, when I was driving him and Richie Benaud after a game, I really ripped into them: "Whatever you do, don't get married. It'll be the end of you." Because, me, I'd seen it all before, hadn't I?' But there he was, married. Funny how things turn out.

It was destined, though, to be a tragically brief union. They'd been together only five months when Morris joined Australia's first tour of the West Indies in March 1955. Morris opened the trip with 157 then scored 111 in the first Test at Port-of-Spain, batting with all the brio of his early years and completing a notable record collection. Ray Robinson's chapter on Morris in *On Top Down Under* is called 'Saying Hello With Hundreds': an allusion to Morris's uncanny facility for immediate acclimatisation, for he scored centuries on his first appearances in Australia, England, South Africa and the West Indies. But when Morris returned from the West Indies, he learned that Valerie had been diagnosed as suffering breast cancer – she had refrained from informing her absent husband – and would live less than 18 months. Morris's playing days were over at 33.

'I had to retire,' he says. 'I knew we wouldn't have long together, five years at the outside. The one thing I wanted for her was to take her to England a last time, which wasn't easy because we had no money, but

I was a very lucky man.' One of Valerie's former impresarios, Windmill Theatre proprietor Vivian van Damm, sent a cheque for £1000 to the 'best showgirl I ever had', and an envelope arrived from Lindsay Hassett containing another £500. 'He'd written this ridiculous letter,' says Morris. 'Lindsay says: "I'm building a house and I don't know where the money's going. You just pay me when you can."' Morris paid his way in England by writing cricket for the *Daily Express* during Australia's 1956 Ashes tour, at the conclusion of which Valerie died.

Arthur Morris remarried, to Judith, in 1967. Behind his neat front garden and the brass plate at the front door for 'A. Morris', he lives for his competition tennis and intermittent bus trips to Sydney. One other thing: like his father, he's always voted Liberal. He was even approached during 1949 to run for a safe seat, but refrained: the disdain of Labor voters on the Hill would've been too much to bear. Sir Robert Menzies was a friend and familiar during and after Morris's cricket career, though – as if to ward off any suggestion of political partisanship – the player refers warmly to Arthur Calwell and 'Doc' Evatt. The deputy prime minister, Evatt, took Morris, after his first-class debut, to Stan McCabe's sport store in George Street and told him to choose a bat.

Morris adds that he also found Paul Keating 'quite charming' at a charity breakfast before a Prime Minister's XI game. He adds:

Actually I was sitting next to Sir James Balderstone. And I said to him: 'Do y'know? I'd love to have seen Keating and Menzies at it in Parliament together. They'd score off each other beautifully.' Keating goes over the top but he's a first-rate politician. And Menzies, of course, was just about the finest debater you could wish to see. It would have been better than the bloody Tivoli, it would! Front pages every day!

Ah, yes, but you can't compare champions of different eras, can you?

MORRIS, Arthur Robert

Born: 19 January 1922, Bondi (NSW)

Bats: Left-handed
Bowls: Left-arm slow 'Chinaman'

First-Class Career

Debut: 1940–41 New South Wales v Queensland, Sydney

M	Inn	NO	Runs	50	100	Ave	Ct	St	Runs	Wkts	Ave	5	10
162	250	15	12614	46	46	53.67	73	–	592	12	49	33	–

Highest Score: 290 Australians v Gloucestershire, Bristol, 1948
Best Bowling: 3/36 Australian XI v Tasmania, Hobart, 1952–53

Test Career

Debut: 1946–47 Australia v England, Brisbane

M	Inn	NO	Runs	50	100	Ave	Ct	St	Runs	Wkts	Ave	5	10
46	79	3	3533	12	12	46.49	15	–	50	2	25.00	–	–

Highest Score: 206 Australia v England, Adelaide, 1950–51
Best Bowling: 1/5 Australia v England, Manchester, 1953

BILL PONSFORD

How Did Ponny Sleep?

by Jack Fingleton

Ponsford was a true product of the monopolist age. He guided records and runs into his own exclusive cartel by hooking, driving and cutting for hour after hour with the precision and certainty of a machine. His bat looked twice as broad as any other batsman's; his appetite for runs appeared as if it would barely be appeased when Judgement Day sounded.

Four of his first-class tallies were 437, 429, 352 and 336. In four successive innings in first-class cricket in Australia in 1926–27, Ponsford made 437, 202, 38 and 336 – a total of 1013 runs.

Ponsford, more so than any batsman in history up to his time ignored the simple merits of a century or a double century. Ambition sought Olympian heights of satisfaction. Like Bradman, who was to follow closely in his steps, Ponsford did not know the meaning of the word pity in its application to bowlers. The lore of mercy with Trumper was rich in legend. It was said of him when he had made a century he looked about for a deserving bowler, one who had tried bravely or, perhaps, a youngster in need of encouragement, and he gave him his wicket so unostentatiously not even the bowler was cognisant of it. Ponsford and Bradman, contrariwise, lived in a materialistic age. They were realists who tempered their batting with no mercy.

Ponsford humiliated the humble Tasmanians in 1922–23 to make the then world record score of 429. He sharpened his bat on the Queensland grindstone in 1927–28 to make another world's score of 437. Once in Australian cricket he performed the magnificent feat of 11 successive first-class centuries.

Jack Fingleton (1908–81) played 18 Test matches at a very respectable 42.46, and wrote 10 equally stylish cricket books. 'How Did Ponny Sleep?' is reproduced with the permission of Malcolm Gemmell.

Ponsford was a popular player with his fellows. Away from batting creases he had a good sense of humour, but he religiously put that off when he put on his pads.

The story is told that when he made 352 of Victoria's record score of 1107 against New South Wales, Ponsford looked as if he would bat on into eternity; but at 352, enough runs for any team's total, Ponsford played a ball from outside his stumps onto the wicket. As he turned to see that his ears had not played him false he made this remark in a most doleful voice: 'By cripes, I am unlucky.'

Though in itself a tribute to Bradman, it was in essence unjust that Ponsford's really magnificent performances should have been practically forgotten in the rise and reign of Bradman. Sporting glory is as hollow as all earthly glories, but it is well to note that Ponsford retired from cricket at 34, an age at which Dr Grace was cutting his second teeth in the game.

O'Reilly, whose opinions were moulded in the blistering fire of experience, considered Ponsford the greatest batsman he bowled against, superior even to Bradman.

'I always gave myself a chance against Bradman,' O'Reilly once told me, 'but Ponsford seemed to be a different proposition. Like the elephant, he never forgot. He was ready for every little trick up your sleeve.'

It is of more than passing interest that Grimmet also thought Ponsford more difficult to bowl against than Bradman.

As with Bradman, wet wickets upset Ponsford. He did not like them and took no pains to hide his dislike. On coming to breakfast on tour, players never asked whether it had rained during the night. The question was, 'Did "Ponny" wake during the night?' If he did, it was assumed to have rained, for it was reputed that the merest trickle was sufficient to rouse Ponsford and cause him to toss uneasily on the thoughts of a sticky wicket for the next day.

Like most Australian youths who rise and decline much more quickly than their English contemporaries, Ponsford began to play competitive cricket at an early age. He was 14 when he first pitted his skill against Melbourne district players, but his youth would have earned him no compassion.

Australian sport is not like that. I remember playing competition cricket against an uncle when I was 15. He was a magnificent all-rounder who never wanted for runs or wickets, and I had vain thoughts that family pride would have made him pleased to see me succeed

PONSFORD, William Harold

Born: 19 October 1900, North Fitzroy (VIC)
Died: 6 April 1991, Kyneton (VIC)

Bats: Right-handed

First-Class Career

Debut: 1920–21 Victoria v MCC, Melbourne

M	Inn	NO	Runs	50	100	Ave	Ct	St	Runs	Wkts	Ave	5	10
162	235	23	13819	43	47	65.18	71	–	41	0	–	–	–

Highest Score: 437 Victoria, v Queensland, Melbourne, 1927–28

Test Career

Debut: 1924–25 Australia v England, Sydney

M	Inn	NO	Runs	50	100	Ave	Ct	St	Runs	Wkts	Ave	5	10
29	48	4	2122	6	7	48.23	21	–	–	–	–	–	–

Highest Score: 266 Australia v England, The Oval, 1934

against his bowling. I actually thought I might even get an easy one first ball! But not a bit of it. To him, the sight of me was inflammatory.

'The confounded cheek of this,' he seemed to snort as he ran up to bowl against me, and his roar for lbw, which could have been heard chains away, sent the umpire's finger skyward. (I am pleased to say that I had my revenge on Uncle some years later.)

The average Australian youngster learns in a hard school, and so it was with Ponsford. He once told me that he always followed advice received when a youngster. That was to get as many runs as one could on every occasion, because one would never know when a spin of misfortune would come along. Ponsford was no dreamer. It is an axiom that every first-class cricketer has had his run of outs, his spell in the doldrums.

'I don't think I had the intention of big scores at the start of an innings, but when runs did come along I guess I thought that this same opportunity might not happen along again and I would do well to make the most of it,' he declared in describing his big-scoring motives. 'I played on those principles. I did not think at the time that scores took much out of me. Now I am not so sure, for I certainly suffered after-effects.'

The task of keeping himself on the pinnacle to which he climbed undoubtedly took its toll of Ponsford. It exacted heavy nervous energy and prematurely killed his love of the game. At the time he felt that he never wanted to see a bat or a cricket game again.

Ponsford was a magnificent cricketer and I pay him homage. Justice will see that his worth is not forgotten, but, stupendous as Ponsford's deeds were, they paled when Bradman made his entrance.

Bradman did not allow Ponsford even a few short years to bask in a rightful glory. The true perspective of Ponsford's deeds had barely dawned on the game when Bradman ruthlessly thrust him from public thought with the most stirring string of big scores ever known.

Ponsford's wounds of 437 against Queensland had barely healed when Bradman reopened them and rubbed in salt with 452 not out – if you please – at the end of 406 minutes at the crease, with 49 fours!

The mere single centuries in Bradman's first-class career seem poor meat for him. He made over 50 of them, but it is his scores of 200 and over that tell the tale of his supreme mastery in first-class games. They are: 452 not out, 469, 357, 340 not out, 334, 304, 225, 254, 232, 252 not out, 236, 205 not out, 223, 258, 220, 299 not out, 226, 219, 238, 200, 253, 244, 206, 233, 270, 212, 212, 278, 258 and 202.

DON BRADMAN

Our God Substitute

by Don Watson

In the galactic era of my growing up we dominated every sport that mattered. We won Davis Cups and Wimbledon, we ruled the pools, we won gold and broke world records on the track. Hoad, Rosewall, Emerson and Laver; Cuthbert, Strickland, Matthews; Fraser, Rose, Konrads; Landy, Lincoln, Thomas, Elliott – what ecstasy it was to be alive and have their sweat mingling with our own!

In cricket, meanwhile, we won many more than we lost and the team abounded with near legends like Harvey, Benaud, Craig, Davidson and Grout. But there was a hole in the galaxy. First Craig was meant to fill it. When he couldn't, O'Neill was thrown into the breach. Later Walters: but, good as he was, Doug wasn't that good. No one was. It wasn't fair. In no other sport were such comparisons made. Only in cricket did the world await a second coming. In cricket no one escaped the memory of Bradman or the shadow he cast.

Of course he was not God, but in a country where sport was a religion and the Ashes like a holy war, Donald Bradman was a God substitute. It makes no sense to call him a great player. Allan Border was a great player. Legend is the wrong word too. Victor Trumper is a legend. Phar Lap, Bernborough and Ned Kelly are legends. Legends have something capricious at their centre – a fatal flaw in their character, a vulnerability to Fate. It's in this, as much as in their ideal qualities, that we see ourselves. Unlike Bernborough, who always left his run to the last minute, and Phar Lap and Ned who died leaving us wondering why and what if, Bradman left us very little to wonder about.

Don Watson is a Melbourne historian, author and speech, screen and comedy writer, and is one of Melbourne social cricket's most respected leggies.

In the late 60s a racehorse called Vain did a brief imitation of Bradman. A glowing chestnut colt, it won 12 of its 14 starts, and but for human error would have won them all. It won its last three in the space of a week, leading from go to whoa and getting home by prodigious margins. Vain was never off the bit. He ran the others off their legs. Bert Bryant, the great race-caller, said after one race, 'that's not a horse, it's a machine', as if the beast transcended nature. He was onto something there. Vain was a horse of annihilating powers, of godlike invincibility and perfection. I developed a mild obsession with the animal, and so long as I still put money on his increasingly distant – and invariably inferior – descendants, I have to acknowledge the derangement lingers.

There were greater horses than Vain, more legendary horses, horses which, in their struggles against handicappers, injury and age, gave punters a heroic view of their own lives. But Vain was no people's horse: Vain held out hopes of something beyond. That's where he met Bradman – on a celestial plane. Met him and passed on, while Bradman settled down there.

It is entirely possible that this Vain worship expressed some kind of primal need which established religion and politics failed to meet. Australians have never been beguiled for long by charismatic religious or political leaders. Billy Graham seduced them briefly during a very dull patch in the 50s and, using similar techniques, Bob Hawke mesmerised them for a while in the 80s. The young Queen Elizabeth, even more than Di, excited rapture and imitation. But none of these – much less Deakin, Hughes, Curtin, Chifley or Menzies – was ever accorded transcendental qualities. Hinkler and Kingsford Smith got up there for a while, then crashed. As, in our hearts, we expected them to. As we expect everyone and everything to. Not that we don't admire them: they're all fit inhabitants of museums – but not of Olympus. The Australian Olympus is an empty, echoing place in which a few horses clatter about. And a ball hits a bat repeatedly and a solitary voice calls in a nasal twang – 'Yes! No! Wait!'

In common with God, according to an old philosophical proof of His existence, Bradman was 'something than which nothing greater can be conceived'. On all the other proofs, Sir Donald has by far the better of it. His reality is fixed with pedantic certainty. Every single run, every dot ball, every four and six. The time he went in and the time he went out; the lesser beings who fell around him. It's all in the score books. You can imagine him presenting them at the pearly gates.

It is the average which sets him apart. Take Bradman out of it and cricket is a game in which no Test player can average more than 65. Bradman averaged 99. A three-minute mile might be roughly equivalent. Anything comparable in the 100 metres – 8.5 seconds, for instance – we'd say must have been hand timed by a close relation and assisted by a gale. But Bradman's average was accumulated without assistance of any kind, and very often against the odds, over 20 years, all over the world. It is superhuman. And anyone who thinks the duck he made in his last innings was a last-minute proof of his

mortality has got it arse-about. Bradman's last duck was the most Godlike thing he ever did. Any self respecting deity – and anyone passingly familiar with the behaviour of the Almighty over the years – will know that to have scored the four runs he needed to push his lifetime average past 100 would have been an unholy folly. It would have been a confession of mortality, a hint that he had something to prove. Jesus chided his disciples for harbouring similar thoughts.

Bradman was a sort of Cromwell among cricketers, a relentless, irresistible Protestant presence beating his enemies into dust – as if every bowler was the Antichrist and every ball a graven image he must dutifully pulverise. Every day was a Drogheda. In (Keith) Stackpolese, he played each ball on its merits and punished the loose one; but in Bradman's eyes hardly any ball had merit, hardly any deserved to escape punishment. He not only made extraordinary scores, he made them extraordinarily quickly. He regularly made more by himself in a day than we are accustomed to seeing whole teams make in a day and a half.

From the figures and the photographs we can imagine the range of his strokes, the coordination of his hand and eye, the sharpness of his vision, his reflexes, his lightning feet, but all those things together don't give you Bradman. They give you a Pollock, a Sobers, one of the

Richards or a Harvey – even some in the ranks behind them, like the Waughs, the Chappells, Gower. They give you people who are invincible on their day or even in a season, but not Bradman who was invincible across a 20-year career.

You don't have a Bradman until you add to the illimitable skills a stainless steel mind. The Don did far fewer of the human things which undo everyone else so regularly they become cliches: he played fewer careless shots; he did not seem to have bad patches, runs of outs, dips in form or confidence; he was less often distracted, including by his own reflection. Bradman's average tells us less about his skills than his self-control, his will to dominate, the fanatical dimension of his psyche. Viv Richards, the 'black Bradman', showed just how different he was every time he allowed his boundless talent to express itself in suicidal assaults. Bradman's genius encompassed an imperviousness to self-destructive impulses. He never let boredom fill the gap between the game and his mastery of it, his sublime skills and his opponents' inferior ones. Trick shots never tempted him.

He was both an artist and the epitome of the work ethic: tireless, ordered, methodical and shrewd; grasping everything that came his way, wasting nothing, deferring the gratification of a four for the safety of a single, accumulating, constantly accumulating, like a business entrepreneur. To the people who watched and read about him he must have seemed the very model of the rewards that hard work and application alone can bring. Leave nothing to chance. Show no mercy to rivals. Bradman is at least an honorary member of the club of twentieth century Australian nation builders. Essington Lewis would make a congenial companion in eternity.

Yet Bradman's star also vied with Hollywood and Ealing Studios. It's difficult to say if the men and women who milled through turnstiles to see him bat harboured the same fantasies which Ronald Coleman and Cary Grant inspired. Some women still glaze over when they remember Keith Miller at full stretch. Miller might have been an exception. The sexuality of cricket is subtle, not to say quite absent in many cases. At least, until recently, the etiquette of the game did not encourage speculation about the contents of a man's creams. In Bradman's day all exhibitionist instincts were, like the wedding tackle itself, salted away in a box. His expression seems always to have been assured and guiltless. No one could ever call him a wanker. But then, that was Cary Grant's appeal as well. Cary Grant and Don Bradman both knew that narcissism and crude display are for mere mortals, that standing in front of a mirror makes it harder for others to admire you. We cannot expect Michael Douglas or Shane Warne to understand this. How could they, growing up surrounded by their own reflections? These days it is probably not understood by anyone with his own teeth.

Forty years ago, when John Landy failed to win the 1500 metres at the Melbourne Olympics, it seemed that something in our insides broke and a cloud of darkness engulfed us. Yet, on reflection the next day, it almost felt right – even to a seven year old. Landy, after all, was not the God of running, but of decency. He was the embodiment of what we took to be the greatest virtue after mateship – sportsmanship. If athletes had been permitted advertising, John Landy would have had embroidered on his shorts what many of us had framed on our mantlepieces: 'For when the one Great Scorer comes to write against your name, he writes not that you won or lost but how you played the game'. Not Bradman: Bradman will meet the Great Scorer pretty much on equal terms, as one Great Scorer to another.

Today's pectoral-twitching cruds tend to make the heroes of those days look like innocence itself. They weren't innocent of course. Lew Hoad, Herb Elliott and Dawn Fraser weren't innocent. They were just better brought up – without television and with fewer mirrors. If they seem now to have been gloriously unaffected it was because they thought that grace was the natural and proper demeanour for people who habitually blitzed their opponents. It was part of being a hero. John Clarke once described how the great New Zealand middle distance runner, Peter Snell, broke world records before crowds of politely clapping dairy farmers who had knocked off early from the evening milking. Snell would stand there sweating in his singlet at the end and thank them all for coming, no doubt aware that when they got home they'd have to feed the calves.

Australian cricketers used to be like that. Some of them, like Ken McKay, played with a kind of world-weariness. Lindsay Kline looked almost shy. Even the macho types – Benaud and O'Neill played with shirts undone to their navels – could never be accused of actually showing off. Perhaps it was because they were closer to the days when the Almighty watched with an unforgiving eye for skites, for anyone putting on the mantle of invincibility.

Or perhaps it was because they knew Don Bradman was watching.

Bradman was not shy or, for a country boy, even particularly laconic. He was exploiting the commercial value of his talent when most of his contemporaries still hadn't seen the connection between the two – or had and thought it sacrilegious. He was certainly not modest, nor averse to publicity. He might not in all circumstances have stopped to help a fallen opponent, as John Landy did.

Yet he could never be mistaken for anything other than a chip off the national block. He had the walk, the gimlet eyes – the look Steve Waugh took on – which, like his voice, made him unmistakably Australian. He played the right game too. Hubert Opperman was a phenomenon on a bike, Heather McKay a freak at squash; Lindrum beyond compare at billiards; there had been world-beating runners, swimmers and boxers, footballers in all codes – but none of these sports were of the same account. Beating the Poms at cricket was the one true national passion, not surprising in a country which could not bring itself to cut the colonial ties. We did not draw pride from being members of the British Empire or Commonwealth of Nations without conceding some of the normal means of mature self-expression. Sport and war were useful substitutes.

It was essential to our self-esteem that the First AIF had performed better than the British on the Western Front, that Monash outperformed their generals, that Melba showed them how to sing. Not necessarily true, but essential. It was essential that we beat them at all their own games. Above all, it was essential to beat them at cricket. A cricket game could straddle the extremes of the national sentiment – the loathing of Britain and the love of it, the strut and the cringe. Bradman sailed right down the middle – triumphant proof that we could get the national rocks off without doing anything silly. Like other Gods, he was in general a consoling and conservative force, as well as an inspiring one.

His effect was immeasurable. It helped that he came from the bush and that the Australian legend was alive and well. Bradman was perhaps the most persuasive evidence that something in the air and open spaces, the dust, sweat and eucalyptus, something in the experience of Australians, turned ordinary folk from the British Isles into matchless athletes, poets and sopranos – not to say soldiers, aviators, innovators and irrigators. It was a heroic age. The *Bulletin* used to put us on a par with Ancient Greece. When Keith Hancock in his short history pointed out a few shortcomings, the *Bulletin* said the professor had been too long at Oxford. Depression and all, it was still Australia's glad confident morning and, year in year out, Bradman was its proof and herald.

The experience of the half century which has passed since Bradman retired tells us that there will be no Second Coming. We will go on seeing hopeful signs in the genius of other players. People will always say, as they've been saying recently about Tendulkar – 'that must have been how Bradman batted'. And Bradman might agree, but he'd only need to wink in the direction of the scoreboard to put it in perspective. Tendulkar has already played more tests and he's made half as many centuries; his average is not two thirds of Bradman's.

For intimations of Bradman the best place to go is not to Test matches, but to the lower grades of cricket. Anyone who has played the game in its rustic or suburban forms has run into these characters: the ones who will not go out, who punish what, by the lights of fairness and reason, does not deserve to be punished, who have no sympathy, who take no visible pleasure in anything short of total annihilation. The ones who chat amiably about horses at tea-time then stroll out and thump you again until dusk. You'll find similar types among fishermen, hotel pool players, rose growers and ladies who play solo. You get intimations of Bradman whenever you meet the person who you can't beat.

We think of the gods when we contemplate Bradman because his deeds suggest the conquest of mortal limitations. He beat his opponents by annihilating the barriers between mind and body, science and art, prose and poetry. He took a cricket bat and with it forged a marriage between Australian pragmatism and something unconquerable and sublime.

BRADMAN, Donald George

Born: 27 August 1908, Cootamundra (NSW)

Bats: Right-handed
Bowls: Right-arm leg spin

First-Class Career

Debut: 1927–28 New South Wales v South Australia, Adelaide

M	Inn	NO	Runs	50	100	Ave	Ct	St	Runs	Wkts	Ave	5	10
234	338	43	28067	69	117	95.14	131	1	1367	36	37.97	–	–

Highest Score: 452* New South Wales v Queensland, Sydney, 1929–30
Best Bowling: 3/35 Australians v Cambridge University, Cambridge, 1930

Test Career

Debut: 1928–29 Australia v England, Brisbane

M	Inn	NO	Runs	50	100	Ave	Ct	St	Runs	Wkts	Ave	5	10
52	80	10	6996	13	29	99.94	32	–	72	2	36.00	–	–

Highest Score: 334 Australia v England, Leeds, 1930
Best Bowling: 1/8 Australia v West Indies, Adelaide, 1930–31

GREG CHAPPELL

Effortlessly Upright

by Kate Fitzpatrick

From 11 a.m. Friday morning, until sixish on Monday evening, I watched the Sheffield Shield Match between Queensland and New South Wales. I was supposed to be interviewing Greg Chappell when he wasn't fielding or batting.

But, as Mum says, 'the road to hell is paved with good intentions'. All we did was reminisce. I went into a four-day trance – watching cricket is as near as I'll ever get to meditating – and was swamped by waves of nostalgia. I guess it had something to do with being the same age as Greg and coming from South Australia.

Greg Chappell's old school, Prince Alfred College, had the same maroon colours as Queensland. It was strange last weekend, a time warp back to school matches between PAC and the blue and white boys from St Peter's.

When I was at school, PAC boys were considered a bit fast – glamorous Protestants who were not forced to confess experimenting with the 1, 2 and 3 minor mating league steps out of a possible (but unthinkable) 10. SAC (my old school) girls were considered a bit fast themselves, but anything more than 3 (or 4ish) was beyond the pale and *we* had to confess.

I was safe. Apart from never getting any offers, I was far too busy chaperoning my friend Viv to muck around. She had a crush on a tall, blond, handsome PAC football star with a red MGA. Simon was *very* glamorous. At Victor Harbour over Christmas he took us for 100 mph (160 kph) car rides with the roof off. This was before breath tests, seat belts and kilometres. Wherever he went, Viv went and so did I.

Kate Fitzpatrick is one of Australia's leading actors, and once had a famous stint in the Nine commentary box. Her article first appeared in the Sydney Morning Herald, *26 February 1983.*

The 'Gidget goes sporty' romance lasted for two years. We watched all the PAC cricket and football matches and attended every dance. I don't remember seeing Greg Chappell. I know he was there. We probably even danced together … but made absolutely no impression on each other.

I can't imagine why, he's pretty impressive these days. Tall, lean, erect, proud, dark, strong and silent. He looks broody and mysterious.

He has an absolutely wonderful back, completely straight without being rigid and no wings. Ray Robinson described him as a poplar, upright in growth with little spread. Effortlessly upright, he gets taller as you watch him.

It's hard to imagine him ever joining the rest of us as we curl, curve and collapse back to the all fours of our beginnings. He bends in all directions, even falls backwards, and instantly returns, springs back to an absolute centre. Even leaning on his bat he is perfectly balanced.

The hand on his hip corresponds with the leg crossed in front. The straight leg echoes his stiff arm, with its bat extension. Exactly half of him is either side of a plumb line. And he's resting!

He was probably carried, and then walked, never crawled. He has thick, dark, very curly hair, and big, deep blue eyes that miss nothing. 'I have an American friend who is amazed when I can tell him what time he arrived at the ground and where he was sitting. You can see a lot out there. You get used to it.'

He can tell you if (and when) you nodded off, or wrote something or cracked a joke. 'I don't miss much – just the odd ball …' He thinks he's pretty good at reading people and situations.

He has long legs, arms, small wrists, and very beautiful long-fingered hands, which he uses economically, deftly, like a good mime artist. They are very strong and quite tough looking. One has a permanent scab that he keeps worrying and knocking. And the other a bone broken taking an amazing catch to dismiss David Gower.

Occasionally they become side flippers which he raises to acknowledge a 'Hey Greg' or 'Good on you Chappell'. Nothing else moves, just his hands – from pointing down to parallel to the ground, wrists still attached to his thighs.

It's great fun trying to work out his field-placing signals. To watch him and Allan Border practising what seems to be fly casting or elegant tennis forehands, and wonder if it's a trap. On the opposing team his brother Trevor seems to turn away as if he doesn't want to see them and feel obliged to tip off Dirk Wellham at the other end.

His mood on the field changed from day to day … lean boyish jumping around, head butting the ball, one day … still, severe, tougher, older, meaner looking the next.

Going to a Shield match is a bit like attending a school play or sports day. Most of the audience are players' friends, or family on comps. Waiting for guest tickets to be brought down to the Members' gate, you can pass the time by trying to guess which cricketer and what relation. 'I bet that's Dirk Wellham's brother.'

On the third day, huge white clouds behind the empty Hill looked like snow-covered mountains, and the idle, suspended, cable cars like a ski-lift … Cricket in Switzerland … Edelweiss, Leiderhorn, the Matterhorn, cow bells and red balls. As my mind wandered off, my companions joked about feeling like cricket groupies and discussed the other regulars there permanently positioned under the players' window, and the 16-year-old down the front today featuring a plunging white bathing suit top, and modest skirt ensemble. Suddenly he's with us again, jumper on, towel around his neck like a thick scarf, and would not be drawn into a conversation about cricket bats.

We start on childhood again. 'I didn't grow much until I was 16. I was very short, then all of a sudden, over the Christmas holidays. It probably has to do with the fact that I never ate much. Not much at breakfast, still don't. And I never ate lunch. I used to throw my Vegemite sandwiches away behind the shed. Mum'll kill me when she reads this.

'It was a waste of time. I was too excited to eat. I wanted to play cricket. You had to stay in the shelter, *sitting down* for 15 minutes! I couldn't stand it. I was exhausted at the end of the day. I'd ride my bike home and on the way stop off at a friend's place to do a bit of boxing. I was fine, until he hit me in the stomach. Then I was history.'

Half joking, he says: 'I sometimes think I started to grow when I started eating lunch.' His son, Stephen, is the same. 'Only not sneaky like me, he brings his home untouched.'

CHAPPELL, Gregory Stephen
Born: 7 August 1948, Unley (SA)

Bats: Right-handed
Bowls: Right-arm medium

First-Class Career
Debut: 1966–67 South Australia v Victoria, Adelaide

M	Inn	NO	Runs	50	100	Ave	Ct	St	Runs	Wkts	Ave	5	10
322	542	72	24535	111	74	52.20	377	–	8717	291	29.76	5	–

Highest Score: 247* Australia v New Zealand, Wellington, 1973–74
Best Bowling: 7/40 Somerset v Yorkshire, Leeds, 1969

Test Career
Debut: 1970–71 Australia v England, Perth

M	Inn	NO	Runs	50	100	Ave	Ct	St	Runs	Wkts	Ave	5	10
88	151	19	7110	31	24	53.86	122	–	1913	47	40.70	1	–

Highest Score: 247* Australia v New Zealand, Wellington, 1973–74
Best Bowling: 5/61 Australia v Pakistan, Sydney, 1972–73

International Limited-Overs Career
Debut: 1970–71 Australia v England, Melbourne

M	Inn	NO	Runs	50	100	Ave	Ct	St	Runs	Wkts	Ave	5
74	72	14	2331	14	3	40.19	23	–	2096	72	29.11	2

Highest Score: 138* Australia v New Zealand, Sydney, 1980–81
Best Bowling: 5/15 Australia v India, Sydney, 1980–81

He says he doesn't hold grudges, but remembers *every* mean thing ever done to him, from the age of three, in the most astonishing detail. Mrs Boxer, a grade three teacher, hated smelly little boys, and accused him of passing a rude note. 'I was at cricket practice, not even there.'

He was supposed to tell his mother, didn't and sweated for 10 days waiting for a parental showdown after the PTA meeting. Nothing happened. Either Mrs B forgot, or his Mum ignored it. 'Anyway, none of us were very smelly.'

Another teacher, Mrs Thompson, kept him in after school and forgot him. His worried parents arrived at the school and found him still sitting, alone, in the dark classroom.

He was 'pushed' off a fence at seven, by someone he remembers, but won't name, and hurt his arm. His mother said it looked all right and to stop whingeing … just the way my Mum did to my sister after a game of Rockets to the Moon.

After three days of little weeps under the tank stand, and less sleep, a doctor announced he had a greenstick fracture. Momentary triumph that something really was wrong with him changed to frustrated boredom when he wasn't allowed to bat. 'It drove me crazy. I kept arguing that it'd make things better, like wearing an arm pad. But my coach wouldn't wear it.'

Queensland declared at 405. I glanced back at him behind the glass and never found out what he meant. The pitch is being flattened by a dear little motorised roller, squeaking slowly up and down, missing the stumps. Two other groundsmen with buckets, spades, and brooms come out to fix the potholes. They look like the gravediggers in *Hamlet* … rough, very casually dressed, leaning on their spades, cracking jokes.

He didn't like school. Never read a play or finished a book, and still passed. 'It wasn't hard. The teachers relied on a few of us getting through to keep their jobs. They usually gave you the questions, went over and over the main points until something sank in. I'm not proud of it, but I didn't want to be a doctor or lawyer. I just wanted to play cricket. Anyway, after cricket practice I was too bloody tired to read.'

He reads a lot these days, novels, autobiographies, golf magazines. Currently *A Retreat from Radiance* by Ian Moffitt. 'I thought he was showing off to start, but as I get more towards the climax I'm loving it.' Before that, *An Indecent Obsession* by Colleen McCullough. 'Didn't bother with *The Thorn Birds* … everyone else had. Didn't go for The Beatles much either. I never wanted to do or like anything just because everyone else did. It put me off. I'm still the same. I liked the Dave Clark Five and the Hollies.'

The men in green coats seem at a loss – powerless to stop guests sitting in front of the Members' Stand. They give up finally and decide to join their families, cushions and Thermoses, and watch. Very shiny, clean men with red faces, and brilliantly oiled short back and sides, with a perfectly combined breaker wave in the front. They are much nicer on slow Shield days. It's a bit Hitler's Dad's Army during Tests or the Benson and Hedges games.

Allan Border comes to the door, baulks when he sees someone, backs off inside, has a *good* look, and then comes out with a cup of tea. Greg's back. He says he's not demonstrative, overtly affectionate or emotional. Wasn't encouraged to be. 'We were told to win and lose gracefully, that's it really. Ian's the most volatile. Says what he thinks. Trevor's had the advantage of learning from both of us.'

Warm hands, cold heart. 'I try not to hurt people. I'm amazed how people can hurt others. I'm sure I've done it. Mine'd be acts of omission more than anything else. I think of sending my wife or my mother flowers when they're ill, for example, and remember late at night, or on a plane. I've got a great memory, but forgot my shoes on my wedding day, had to borrow my brother-in-law's. They hurt.'

He loves his family, his brothers, his wife, all children, especially his; cricket and Dennis Lillee. He was very upset by a newspaper report about a two-year-old girl drowning in a backyard pool. He lives with the natural parental fear of something happening to his kids.

The only time he remembers crying (described as 'near to tears') was the day his first child, Stephen, was born. He was at Lord's in England, batting. His wife was in Australia. When drinks were brought on the twelfth man handed him a wire service photograph of his wife, Judy, and his brand new son. It made me teary hearing the story.

Cheating? 'I cheated a little bit at school, but I was dumb – only from kids who knew less than me – or were wrong. And I was usually found out.'

Cricket? 'If you call appealing for an lbw or a caught behind when you aren't sure, but hope you'll get away with it, cheating … I've done a bit of that, everyone does.'

He is adamant that money or a 'win at all costs' attitude had nothing to do with the Melbourne underarm incident. He was frustrated and annoyed. It was a protest about bad conditions. The administration was taking no notice: 'Nothing's wrong.'

'Would actors go on with holes in the stage and a leaking roof? There was no consideration for players. We had no right to an opinion. Look, six off the last ball was a one in one million chance … a three or a four wouldn't have helped them. Winning for us meant a couple of days off, a luxury, that's all.

'It was wrong. I regret it. I wouldn't do it again. I was shattered at the outrage and screaming chaos that followed. I'm stuck with it … but it wasn't illegal.' So he went to New Zealand the following year and was voted man of the series.

He is very pleased that his children are musical and artistic like his wife. 'The only thing I regret is not learning to play the piano.' When he has finished playing cricket he intends taking it up full-time and playing golf. He says his son is the best seven-year-old cricketer in the world. 'He's had a bat in his hand since he was born. If that's what he wants I'll help him – but I won't force him. I'm happy he's learning the piano.'

On the afternoon of the fourth day while New South Wales batted, an old man had a heart attack – the Members filled up with police, doctors, paramedics and ambulance men with respirators, injections and little flat-iron, heart-starter jumper leads. Elderly spectators moved away and looked steadfastly ahead, cricket wiping out fears of mortality. The players turned every now and then to check progress.

When I announced that I was interviewing Greg Chappell I dimly remember various people saying, 'He's difficult, taciturn, secretive, humourless or hard.' He must have hated those people or been bored witless.

'I feel I'm quite misunderstood – that's okay.' Somehow I didn't believe him. He admits to being determined, ambitious, going after and getting most things he wants. He says he's not much of a businessman, just good at picking partners.

He likes writing but thinks too fast and gets frustrated. On the other hand he can't stand being ghosted. He does have a phenomenal memory – long and short term – quotes conversation verbatim and remembers in detail what happened and what everyone wore. He'd be a great witness.

He is very grateful for the encouragement, help and sacrifice of his parents and refutes the story of his grandfather's (Victor Richardson) apparent lack of interest. 'That's rubbish – he was very keen on us playing and doing well – I remember playing with him once on a turf wicket behind his house. It must have been when Trevor was born.'

The only time Sir Don Bradman ever spoke to him was to tell him to change his grip. 'I was strong on the leg side – not the off. Sir Don was a South Australia selector – he didn't speak to anyone really except Ashley Mallett, the best spinner I've seen. Anyway, he walked through as usual. I said, "Good morning, Sir Donald."

'He stopped, turned and said, "You'll never be a good player with a grip like that." I asked if he had any suggestions. He did and showed me and said it'd feel uncomfortable at first but it would be easier with practise. He then walked off, stopped at the door, turned and said, "I've only given this bit of advice to one other player. He didn't take it. He's no longer in the team."

'I rushed to the nets. It was uncomfortable but it got easier. It's the grip I use now. I've used it ever since.'

He has ears that join without lobes – like mine. It's supposed to indicate criminal tendencies. 'I think I would have been a criminal if I hadn't been a cricketer.'

Yeah, I bet – a hit-and-run merchant no doubt.

He is warm, friendly, charming, well-mannered, humorous, sensitive, devoted to his wife and family, earthy, honest and a lot older and younger than 34.

He's a very Aussie hero, a bargain whatever way you look at it. Mrs Chappell is a lucky woman. I didn't ask about the ducks. May he never have another.

NEIL HARVEY

An Eternal and Exuberant Mollydooker

by Barry Dickins

From a big family of all right-handed natural cricketers and baseballers, Neil Harvey belongs to the Pantheon of what used to be called mollydookers – famous left-handers, that is. He seems to come from another, and possibly kinder, sporting world, before Packer-contamination, the death by cancer-of-the-conscience in today's world of betting upon the match outcomes – the skullduggery of making the Devil's bob by betting on, and even praying for, a loss.

What was Australian cricket in Bradman's time but appearing dead-set for one's country in a violent short-back-and-sides haircut, preposterous or holy floppy green cap, your box over your old fellow and thoughts of carting Jim Laker over long-on?

Neil says cricket's been kind to him, that he owes it a debt he can never possibly hope to repay, for it has taken him to every conceivable climate and country and loved him for his contribution to brisk boundaries. Centuries have come to him as unconsciousness comes to drunkards in the Outers of our world's giddy stadiums.

He has snicked and late-cutted and sixed and foured and leg-glanced and even clean-bowled an Indian. In India. He has fought off delirium and diarrhoea in Dacca and shaken the tiny Queen's paw when he was presented to her at Lord's, where he was shy, as well as charming of course.

Here is an athlete who knows the drama and disillusionment of dud wickets, rigged turf and multitudes gnashing their gums for a glimpse of greatness. And he has been a great before them – an ambassador of the willow who has been called the best cover fieldsman of all time.

Barry Dickins is a Melbourne writer whose books, plays and interviews with Diggers and police have illuminated some dusty corners of the Australian character.

Here I am on my way to meet him, nearly choking inside the Harbour Tunnel, thinking about breath and Preston Cricket Club Fifths, who I played for in the 60s. Coached, I was, by one of Neil's brothers, Ray.

One of Ray Harvey's fielding practice routines was to chuck elongated 'Compo' balls at cast-iron grass rollers so they could ricochet and brain you if you weren't paying due attention. I remember my brother John getting concussed down at Preston oval once, when he looked up at the sky for something to do. Luckily he wasn't too badly hurt, poor chap.

Now my cabbie takes me to the North Shore. It is a stunning day to listen to a legend from my old stomping ground, Fitzroy. We go right into the bush in Sydney. Drongo brickies' labourers are catching bricks on bendy planks to the emphysemic chuckle of cement mixers and occasional curses over the road from Mr Harvey's tranquil residence. But is he in? Has he forgotten? I yell out to the coarse workers: 'Who lives here, mate?' 'Neil Harvey', is all they yell back. He's a myth.

He opens the door and is just the same, only old. Precisely the same as the grainy newsreel footage I saw him in 40 years ago. He still looks fit with hooky sort of brawny sharp-angled arms that are blotched and powerful still. He smiles at me as if he wants me in slips or extra cover. He is 72 in October; but is merely a boy with lots of fun in him.

I settle in a cosy armchair and go back in cricketing time immediately, as he speaks mostly of couch-grass, grass seeds, various batting surfaces around the world and lists on his tough fingertips the Christian names of his brothers, who were all cricketers. But first off he explains just why he is left-handed in the first place.

'It was just the way I picked up the bat as a kid. I always liked to have the left hand right down low just above the blade, it just felt okay that way.' He gives a few left-handed swishes from his armchair.

The Harveys bowled and batted. 'All six of us brothers played first Grade cricket. Merv, he was the oldest. Then came Clarrie, the second one. We called him Mick because he was born on St Patrick's Day. Harold was the next. Then Ray, then there was Brian, he died at 35. He wasn't a bowler. Then there was Rita, my sister.'

Was she a decent bat?

'Yeah, too right. She wasn't a bad sort of a bat.'

He is putting up with Tony Lock's spinners in his mind as he grins, as he gets pretty serious, as he remembers everything – and his memory is prodigious, I have to say.

What he has to say about the terrifying Typhoon Tyson or the quick-change-mood-artistry of fiery Freddie Trueman coming in at him from Old Trafford? Wes Hell and Charlie Griffiths, did they upset him?

Nothing has upset him, except rigged Pom wickets, like those he cursed under his breath on the miserable and disastrous 1956 tour. A mysterious substance known as marl was fiendishly added to all kinds of bulldust the Poms used to construct Hell wickets in a bid to conquer us after the previous caning they received during the 1948 tour, when

Harvey and Bradman did what they wished with the whingeing Pommies. The dust wickets were so bad they couldn't see a thing on the last three matches of the '56 tour. A man stepped out to clout a Pom and saw nought but caked-up dust and particles of dehydrated rubbish.

'We won at Lord's on green-top, though, when the wicket was fair dinkum. Peter May, the English Captain, said "That's the last wicket you'll see like that." It wasn't the English players' fault. It was their ambassadors. The fault was not the players' at all. They commiserated with how bad it was. Even Laker said "You've got to get in when you can," in a shrugged-shoulder way. He bowled me twice, Laker. You couldn't acclimatise, not even after three days.'

His friendly expressive face shows determination, resolve, how to fight. It is a Fitzroy face. A world face. Familiar to me as Saint Georges Road, Scotchmer Street, all the back lanes and milk bars of Fitzroy, where blokes got born with guts. They don't give in, Harveys. Stuff that.

We speak of the world's most annoying barrackers. He doesn't mention Brisbane, Sydney or Melbourne, surprisingly, I thought. But the eyebrows narrow as he says 'Lancashire's pretty crook'. No more to add at the moment. Just a slight look of disgust dances over his temple.

Why were they so bad do you think?

'Oh, they're so sarcastic. "You'll be back inside after an over." Lancashire and Manchester are historical enemies, you know, the White

Rose and the Red Rose. It goes back hundreds of years. I tell you what, English grounds are spongy, not fast like ours. And their light is spongy.'

The slightest chuckling going on. 'When I played at Lord's there was no sightscreen. Leeds had two. Old Trent Bridge didn't have one at the dressing end. I played in '61 at The Oval; Les Flavel bowled me a full toss. I didn't see it. I didn't see the full toss! The dullness and all the dark brickwork made me miss it!' His mouth is agape.

He is really put out at being cheated out of having a proper go at the Poms. I asked him what score he was on when the sombreness made the pill hard to see. He leaps up out of the easychair and heads for his bookcase. 'I'll just look that up if you don't mind!' He comes back. 'I was on 13.'

He looks not so much tired as world-weary for a minute. Moving into extra cover to recall old times. 'In '48 Sam Loxton (he only calls him Sam) and I were room-mates. Lord's, this is. You share everything. You get close. You learn how to fight together.

'Batsmen are spoilt these days. They never get a crook wicket. They're pampered. Big sooks. Look at the new mowers of today. None of them are any good. They don't cut the grass right. Old Jim Reid back in the old Fitzroy days – by gee he used to pull the concrete roller with the horses. Got out the old draught horse he did. Put leather boots on him and everything, to make it right. He loved his cricket, too, that old horse!' He laughs till he cries, going back to the suburb he was born in. Good old Fitzroy. He's back in Argyle Street where he was born. The eyes fog up.

I ask him the difference between the captaincy style of Bradman and Benaud, to which he makes the point: 'Bradman never gave me any advice. He was 20 years older than me in '48 on that first tour. I was off to a slow start. I wasn't going too good on that first one, to tell the truth.'

He gazes down, the first time he has looked away from me. But the sparkly eyes soon rise up again, thinking of them. Seeing them.

'So I went up to Sam and I said to Sam, could you please ask Don what I'm doing wrong? And Don said "You can go back to your little mate and say to him: If you keep the ball on the ground you can't get out."' He laughs.

Neil tells me of The Don's famous remoteness: 'He's aloof, you know, was always that way. He's crook now, Don – now his wife's gone it must be tough. He gets a lady in to cook and clean up, but it must be hard. I don't think he's got long, Don, the way he is. It's a great pity. Back in England when we played as friends and team-mates together, he wouldn't have a beer or anything with us. We'd ask where he was and they'd say with his friends of England. They were people like Brian Valentine or Walter Robbins. If we were playing in England sitting around in our jock straps, having a beer, Bradman'd be gone, you know.'

How about your coach at Fitzroy, Joe Plant, what about him? Was he an inspiration or what?

'He taught me a lot about slow bowling. He and Arthur Liddicut were outstanding. Joe was off spin. Show me how to get out and hit it on the half volley, he would. He used to put down a coin – a penny – and got me to dance out and hit where the penny was. Then he'd leave the penny where it was and chuck cricket balls at me where I was, saying "Never mind the penny now. Just keep on hitting those balls."' Looks at me as though to say 'You couldn't miss in the end.'

'I was 20 when I came back from England. I went up to practice at Fitzroy and Joe'd say "Put the pads on, son. I'm going to have a go at yer. To see how you've improved!" A chuckle, with relish for old encouragers like Joe and Arthur.

'My first butterflies in England? I suppose it was due to all the strange conditions. I was twelfth man in Worcester. I found Sam was very, very good to me. He was seven years older than me. He used to say if you keep your feet moving (points to his shoes) you won't get self-conscious.'

How about your old team-mates? Do you get about and keep in touch?

'Alan Davidson I see a lot. We went to swimming together at the Olympic Trials. Black tea we used to drink in the old days; especially in India. It's safer than the water is. At Dacca I had tum worry.

We lost the toss. They can cheat on the coin over there. And on the way the matting is put down, they cheat on that, too, at times. They put it down on an ant-bed. If you don't supervise the Indians you get into strife. You supervise the watering of the ant-bed. And the tautness of the straps to keep the matting nice and tight. The Indians can cheat with matting and keep it slack on you so it won't bounce.'

He says Australia made 'Two hundred and twenty-five at Dacca. I got 96 out of it. It's the training and the concentration you need. You fall back on that. In Karachi in '56, and this is on coir matting, Fazal bowled us out coz the matting was sloppy. Here it is in the book. He got 6/34 and 7/80!'

He glares. He hates crooked cricket. He shows me an impression of Alec Bedser's hand with a hidden cricket ball in it. 'Alec Bedser was not

HARVEY, Robert Neil

Born: 8 October 1928, Fitzroy (VIC)

Bats: Left-handed
Bowls: Right-arm off spin

First-Class Career

Debut: 1946–47 Victoria v New South Wales, Sydney

M	Inn	NO	Runs	50	100	Ave	Ct	St	Runs	Wkts	Ave	5	10
306	461	35	21699	94	67	50.93	229	–	1106	30 36	86	–	–

Highest Score: 231* New South Wales v South Australia, Sydney, 1962–63
Best Bowling: 4/8 Australia v Middlesex, Lord's, 1961

Test Career

Debut: 1947–48 Australia v India, Adelaide

M	Inn	NO	Runs	50	100	Ave	Ct	St	Runs	Wkts	Ave	5	10
79	137	10	6149	24	21	48.42	64	–	120	3	40.00	–	–

Highest Score: 205 Australia v South Africa, Melbourne, 1952–53
Best Bowling: 1/8 Australia v India, Madras, 1959–60

hard to read but hard to play. He had such a big hand you couldn't tell what he was going to do with the ball.'

How fast was Typhoon Tyson?

'He was the fastest in '54; Hall in '60.' He suddenly remembers his greatest catch and gets into the past by coiling up his stocky body and miming it on the carpet floor. It is an uncanny re-enactment.

'My best catch. I didn't hold it. It held me. All through me it went until in the end it caught me! The ball hit me right in the middle of my backside! I went into a crouch, see? It hit me in the fleshy part of the bum. Talk about laugh!'

What sort of money did you get in '56 in England?

'Well you could sort of draw on it as you needed it. The '61 tour of England we all got 31 quid a week. That's what we all got. There was no difference. Not like Warne who gets what he wants or does his stack till they give it to him.'

He goes and gets several trophies, the first of which happens to be a very light, like balsa wood, bat – light as an incredible feather, it is. He absolutely beams as he hands it to me for a feel. Its handle is all eaten away and decomposed with black funny rubbery stuff shrivelling away. I squint my eyes and wish I had my glasses on to read the following inscription, for its lettering is sort of burnt into the back of the bat, half sepia ink; half time. It seems to weigh an ounce. Don't dreams weigh an ounce?

'This bat is a symbol of a great innings to my friend Neil Harvey in Australia's finest Test victory. Leeds, 1948. Don Bradman'. We look at the lettering for a very long time.

Is it holy?

'What do you think?'

He makes me black coffee and we nibble together three chocolate Teddy Bears.

KEITH MILLER

The Golden Nugget

by Ashley Mallett

Keith Miller was cricket's swashbuckler: larger than life, Miller leapt straight at you from the pages of *Boy's Own* paper. Miller was very much the people's cricketer. To many, he was the embodiment of some ancient god of war here on earth not just for a short time, but for a good time. Miller enjoyed life too much to worry about the batting or bowling strength of the England XI. He was a carefree soul with that cavalier touch which made him an instant hero with the fans. Every red-blooded British male in 1945 wanted to be like Keith Miller.

He had film-star good looks and was a war-hero. Miller flew night-time missions over Germany and occupied France in his Mosquito, bombing and strafing V-1 and V-2 rocket bases. If those missions affected him, the sporting public knew nothing of Miller's nervousness. However, he was often heaving in the dressing room just as he was about to walk to the wicket. When he entered the sunshine, Miller had found his stage. He loved the attention. He beamed as he strode to the wicket. As he stood relaxed and upright in his stance, Miller could well have been in Ancient Greece surveying his subjects from some exalted seat atop the Acropolis in Athens. He possessed an imperious quality. His very presence on the field demanded attention.

The British were nursing their wounds in 1945. England was desperate to get back to the tradition of cricket. Some of the old guard were back: Len Hutton, Wally Hammond, Denis Compton, but the Yorkshire spinner Hedley Verity had fallen in battle. England was crying out for a brand new hero. Their hero came in the guise of Keith Ross Miller, a young, brash Australian in England on loan for the war.

Ashley Mallett played 39 Tests for Australia and took 139 wickets at 29.85 with his offies, and is a journalist and author of biographies of Trumper and Grimmett.

Miller was destined to wow the ladies and seduce cricket crowds. He was like a runaway colt as a bowler, yet he assumed an almost aristocratic air when he batted. Ex-Australian Prime Minister Sir Robert Menzies saw the artist in Miller's play and he likened his explosive run and bowling delivery to that of Jack Gregory. Both men emerged as ready-made potential Test champions from the ravages of war. Gregory took part in the 1914–1918 conflict and Miller was an RAAF night-fighter pilot. Peril and excitement was the wartime mix. Those in the services socialised as if there was no tomorrow. The prospect of sudden and violent death was ever present. Friendships were made and torn apart in an instant. The war was both surreal and all too tragically realistic. Miller always had an adventurous spirit. His love of classical music compelled him on one mission to turn his Mosquito back to the war-zone. Taking a slight detour, Miller over-flew Bonn, Beethoven's birthplace. He copped a dressing-down from his squadron leader, but the officer was also careful not to dampen Miller's spirit, for in war there are times when taking a risk wins battles and saves lives. Ever the daredevil, Miller once flew up the straight of Royal Ascot one clear afternoon and another day he buzzed the Goodwood track.

But war is deadly serious. It respects neither friend nor foe, nor flesh and blood. Miller lost many of his mates during the war, including his boyhood close friend Ross Gregory, however, Miller's war was a charmed war. One fateful weekend, Miller was given time off to play in a match at Lord's. He usually met up with a group of mates for drinks at the Carlton pub in Bournemouth. When he returned he found the town barricaded off after a German raid. A Focke-Wulf had bombed and strafed it, causing the church spire to collapse onto the pub, instantly killing his eight mates.

Every year he has returned to England since the war, Keith spends time with a relative of each of his eight mates killed on that tragic Friday night.

As with many who journey to their cricket field of dreams, Miller thought Lord's to be 'a crummy place'. But there's something intangibly special about Lord's. It grows on you and it grew on Miller. You find yourself drinking a heady cocktail of atmosphere, history and tradition. Lord's was a place to have a bet on the cricket. Walk from the Lord's Pavilion in 1825 and you descended a flight of stairs. If you happened to turn left within a few paces you would happen across Mr Gully, his two 'legs' concealed by bushes. You couldn't see them but you could hear them calling the odds. It was inevitable that the Lord

Frederick Beauclerk would, at some stage on that very day, pass by, his ear cocked for odds that might attract. But it was at that precise moment that Mr Gully and his two 'legs' fell silent. The Lord Beauclerk, who was the Vicar of Redbourne in Hertfordshire and a doctor of divinity, was perceived as being a bit of a tyrant and opposed to betting. Yet he was a stalwart of the church and a chieftain at Lord's.

In reality, the Lord Beauclerk was both tyrant and compulsive gambler, given to outlandish bursts of bad temper. He often said privately that 'for me cricket [betting] is worth 600 guineas a year'.

There is no evidence that players from his era were 'on the take'. Perhaps Fuller Pilch and Co. were having enough trouble with the 'fast and ripping' Samuel Redgate with his shooters and fliers.

Miller has always enjoyed a bet, but all of Miller's betting was to do with the racetrack. Miller has always had a love of horses. As a kid he yearned to become a jockey, but when his mother (Edith) took her young Keith along to the Victorian Racing Club's Melbourne office, they were informed that Keith was 'too big' to become a jockey. Despite his being a small and slight kid, the VRC was quite right. Perhaps they saw in Miller's frame what the Millers could never have envisaged, for Keith Miller developed a playing weight of 13st 7lbs (86 kg) and he grew to six feet two inches (1.88 m). He could bet on Phar Lap, but never sit on him. And the Lord's of Miller's cricketing days did not have the betting tent, so Miller was never tempted to bet on cricket while still a player.

But Lord's itself will always hold a special place in Miller's heart and if Lord's is truly cricket's spiritual home, Miller has become its most pious 'convert'. His portrait now adorns this place. In 1993 Miller spent hours in 15 sittings for his portrait, commissioned by the MCC. By choice, Miller wore his RAF tie for the artist Michael Christopher

Corkrey (appropriately with the initials MCC), who lived his early life near the Bedfordshire village of Cranfield, near where Miller served. Miller, playing for Dominions at Lord's in 1945 and under the captaincy of Learie Constantine, hit a ball high over bowler Eric Hollies' head, which landed on the roof of the old broadcasting box above the England dressing room. Lord's has always revered its heroes and the Miller portrait is a fitting tribute.

He was plagued by back trouble throughout his cricket career. One day, returning from a mission over Germany, Miller crash-landed his Mosquito in a Kentish field. While his recurring back problems could be traced back to this crash, within an hour of having clambered out of his wrecked aircraft he dashed off to play soccer.

Paradoxically, Miller loved tradition but he hated convention. Even as a bowler he didn't stick to the tried and tested method of measuring out his approach to the wicket. Miller would simply walk back and turn at any point from two to 15 paces from the wicket. His statistics are good. (55 Test matches for 2958 runs at 36.97 and 170 wickets at 22.97. In 226 first-class matches for Victoria, New South Wales, Nottinghamshire and Australia, he scored 14 183 runs at 48.90 and 497 wickets at 22.30.) He scored 41 centuries all up, including seven in Tests, and took bags of five wickets or more in an innings 16 times, once grabbing a match haul of ten or more wickets.

The figures, however, do not reflect Miller's greatness, for the all-rounder played as a he fought the war, by impulse and mood. When the mood took him he bowled with extraordinary pace and hostility. Len Hutton, the England opener and arguably one of the two best opening batsmen of the twentieth century, told me in 1980 that the England players worried when the word went round the dressing room that Miller had been out on the town the previous night. 'His cure for a hangover was to bowl flat out. He accepted a single, or a two or a three, but never a four. Hit him for four and the next one would be an absolute fizzer.' Hutton reckoned Miller needed a challenge to bring the best out of him. 'He once told me that batting was more important than bowling, because they "always remember the batsmen".'

As a kid, Miller was my hero. He was the cricketing equivalent of film star Errol Flynn, the big screen's resident swashbuckler.

As with Bradman, Miller is a legend in his own lifetime. Stories abound about him, which are both true and apocryphal. There's the celebrated occasion when Miller turned up at the SCG, still in his tux. His New South Wales team was starting to file on to the ground as

Miller rushed into the dressing-room, tearing off his bow tie as he passed through the door. He whipped on his creams, the starched white shirt stayed, and, with bootlaces dangling, he arrived on to the field just as Alan Davidson was about to bowl. Miller was happy with his men. He thought, 'good, they're organised. I'm late and they've got things in order.' But Miller was never one to look a gift horse in the mouth. As he walked towards slip, he discovered through the barely opened louvres of his eyes that the wicket was decidedly green, complete with the unmistakable imprint of a 'road map' of little black branches. The wicket was a horror patch. He walked back towards Davidson, who was at the top of his mark, eager to bowl. 'Ahem, Davo. Sorry, Davo. Don't worry, I'll take it.' Miller bowled that first over, Davidson having been 'banished' to gully. Miller then proceeded to bowl as Hutton knew he could bowl. This was any batsman's worst nightmare, Miller with a hangover, bowling flat out on a green track. The nightmare did not last. Miller got 7/12 and South Australia was skittled for 27.

Miller was my hero. I thought him special, as indeed he was, but it was not until 1969, when Miller was aged 50, more than a decade past playing his final first-class match, that I saw close up just what a magnificent athlete Miller must have been. We tend to think of our era as the best in whatever sport. Human nature. And the kid's hero is not only the best of that time, but the best of all time. We met at the SCG No. 2 Ground, brought together by Alan Davidson, who was organising a cricket coaching film. I stood at a spot about seven paces from the stumps when Miller walked past. He puffed out his chest and said, 'Ahem … pitch leg to take off!' I could not believe my ears. Here was this 50-year-old legend announcing that he was about to deliver what some fast bowlers never achieve with any ball over years and years of practise and toil. Miller was about to do it first ball. Miller walked back, and with a toss of his head he turned and bounded in. There was a sense of urgency in his gait. Again I saw the magnificent high action. At that time Eric Freeman, the South Australia fast-medium bowler, was Australia's first-change trundler. Miller's delivery had a good deal more pace than Freeman's stock delivery, at least it appeared to have, and if it was illusory, the magnificence of Miller's high action did the trick.

The ball pitched on the line of leg stump and whipped to the off alarmingly to hit the top of the off stump! Miller, the consummate showman, beamed, his chest puffed out. 'Not this time. Give me another couple and I'll do it again.' Ball number three saw Miller redirect his delivery. Out of camera shot was Davo, holding a ball,

MILLER, Keith Ross

Born: 28 November 1919, Sunshine (VIC)

Bats: Right-handed
Bowls: Right-arm fast

First-Class Career

Debut: 1937–38 Victoria v Tasmania, Melbourne

M	Inn	NO	Runs	50	100	Ave	Ct	St	Runs	Wkts	Ave	5	10
226	326	36	14183	63	41	48.90	136	–	11087	497	22.30	16	1

Highest Score: 281* Australians v Leicestershire, Leicester, 1956
Best Bowling: 7/12 New South Wales v South Australia, Sydney, 1955–56

Test Career

Debut: 1945–46 Australia v New Zealand, Wellington

M	Inn	NO	Runs	50	100	Ave	Ct	St	Runs	Wkts	Ave	5	10
55	87	7	2958	13	7	36.98	38	–	3906	170	22.98	7	1

Highest Score: 147 Australia v West Indies, Kingston, 1954–55
Best Bowling: 7/60 Australia v England, Brisbane, 1946–47

showing a camera assistant his grip for the out-swinger. 'Have a look at Davo,' Miller said grinning, 'Let's give him a bit of a hurry-up.' Miller approached, turning his left shoulder at delivery straight towards where Davo was standing. The ball whistled towards Davo and the cameraman's assistant. They instinctively sensed danger and fell prostrate on the turf, the ball screaming just over their heads. Ball four, Miller's last delivery, was identical to his first: it pitched leg and hit the top of off. With a puff of his chest and a clearing of the throat, Miller turned on his heel and marched off into cricket history, his hero status intact.

After Bradman, Australia's greatest cricketer of the twentieth century is Keith Ross Miller. He was named after a great Australian airman (Keith Ross Smith). Miller was born to fly at dizzy heights.

In the wake of the 1969 SCG No. 2 experience, I needed no convincing of how good Miller must have been at the zenith of his career. Every now and again our paths would cross. I learned quickly not to be unduly influenced by others. Our vice-captain on the 1968 tour of England, Barry Jarman, told me to have nothing to do with Miller. I put that down to Jarman taking exception to Miller's hard-hitting comments in the *Daily Express*. Miller wasn't too hard on the Aussies, but some get a bit touchy. Miller never felt the need to pander to any Aussie cricketer. He was unafraid to say what he thought. Miller didn't need an after-play press conference to be able to 'read' a match. He knew a helluva lot more than our 1968 captain.

In 1989, long after I had retired, Miller and I found ourselves breakfasting in a hotel in Hong Kong. We were headed for Johannesburg, although our itinerary dictated that we catch a South African Airways jet in Taiwan. We faced a 14-hour flight to Johannesburg. I sat next to Miller. I asked him a variety of questions about cricket. One answer I shall never forget. I asked whether Geoff Boycott was as good as Len Hutton as a batsman. Miller said he thought Hutton to be a far better attacking player, but 'in terms of defence, purely defence, Geoff Boycott is as good as Len Hutton ... but for God's sake don't tell Boycott!'

The Victory Tests of 1945 paved the way for Miller. He scored 437 runs at 63.29, highest for either side, and he took 10 wickets at 27. It was in the Victory Tests that Miller became the Golden Boy, with his dashing batting, his blistering, unpredictable pace bowling and ability to take blinding catches at slip. From then on they called him Nugget.

Keith Miller was indeed the Golden Nugget of cricket.

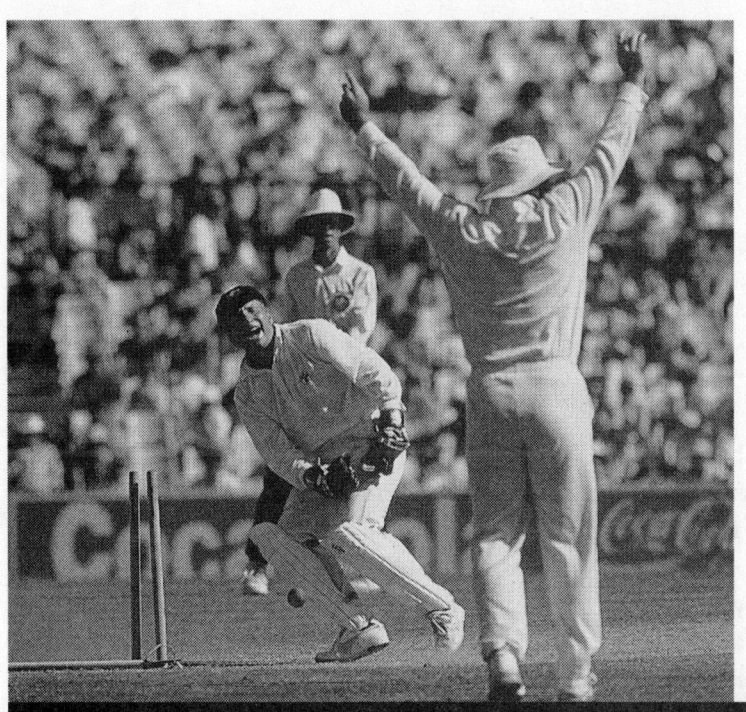

IAN HEALY

He Came from Nowhere

by Greg Baum

In the beginning, it was as if Ian Healy didn't exist. He came from nowhere and as a nobody into the Test team. In his first series, in faraway and mysterious Pakistan, the ball frequently went through him as if he wasn't there, and so did the looks of his new team-mates.

Healy exists now, in life and legend, still much the same height and weight as then, but a figure of substance, indeed a giant of the wicketkeeper's peculiar craft, and of the game of cricket. Some who cast those early, contemptuous looks are now proud to call him friend.

The quality that bowling colleagues cherished most about Healy was his presence. Some 'keepers catch the ball and mutely throw it back. Healy made batsmen feel as if they were being attacked from behind and along the flanks as well as in front.

He and the bowlers created the effect of jaws, closing in inexorably on the isolated batsman, until he was suffocated and crushed. He augmented his siege with nasally notations in a voice that Peter Roebuck memorably said was like a chainsaw. He was always *there*. He is still.

What was most remarkable about Healy was the way that early, ethereal figure filled out before our very eyes. He was not like Ricky Ponting or Brett Lee, preceded by handsome reputation, nor was he like Mark Waugh, arriving after many seasons of bounteous achievement. He had no shape at all; he had scarcely played a first-class game. Not so long before he was picked to keep wickets for Australia, as he toiled away in that least enviable of roles as his state's second-string gloveman, Healy was not even sure he still wanted to be a wicketkeeper.

Wicketkeeping had appealed to him as a boy in Biloela, 150 km from Rockhampton, because of its constant sense of involvement in the

Greg Baum writes for the Age *and is one of Australia's leading cricket writers.*

game. He pursued it to Brisbane, flirting with and then forgoing a career in schoolboy rugby league and a separate career as a batsman good enough to have been picked for an Australian Under 19 tour of England in that capacity. But his way forward was blocked by Peter Anderson, a dapper and much-admired 'keeper in the English tradition, who, at a time of much volatility in which six men had been tried and discarded following the 1983 retirement of Rod Marsh, was widely expected to be the next picked for Australia. That would have sealed Healy's fate; he would have been forever a shadow.

But when Anderson broke his hand in the 1987–88 season, Healy became Queensland wicketkeeper, and in Sheffield Shield matches in Launceston and Melbourne at the end of that turbulent season, Greg Chappell, a national selector, sensed the kernel of a tough nut. Allan Border, evidently, had also been impressed. Healy thought his selection was a mate's April Fool's joke, but no last laugh was ever longer.

Healy learned from the improbable circumstances of his Australian selection two lessons that he never forgot. One was about even breaks and suckers. He had been 'keeping for Queensland only because of an unfortunate injury to Anderson, his elder and better, and was chosen for Australia on little more than Chappell's whim. Subsequently, though he broke fingers as regularly as do all 'keepers, he made light of injury. When he fractured a finger taking a leg-side catch from England's Mike Atherton in 1991, he was told he needed six weeks rest. A week later, he was defiantly on his way to the West Indies. For six weeks, he played in unmitigated agony, yet easily rationalising that it was still more tolerable than the pain of not playing for Australia.

Healy missed only one Test match in his time, after breaking a finger on his second visit to Pakistan in 1994. He prided himself on his indestructibility, but also on his integrity. He would never have played, he always said, if he thought he would let Australia down by it. At career's end, he tallied up the damage blithely. 'A little creaky in the knees, back feels the pinch, one or two dodgy fingers,' he said. Others said he played with and through 10 fractures. 'A small legacy,' rejoined Healy. But he did make a particular point at his retirement press conference of thanking all his various physiotherapists.

The other seminal lesson was about work ethic. Confounded, but not defeated, by his early experience in Pakistan, and determined to keep his place, he applied himself more industriously and methodically than any 'keeper before him to fitness of mind and body. He began then, and maintained throughout his career, a routine on match mornings of donning his inners and bouncing a golf ball endlessly against a wall in a hotel carpark until he was satisfied with his feel. It is now the second most famous golf-ball routine in Australian cricket legend. He became colloquially renowned in the Australian team for his enjoyment of the treadmill. He also began to keep a daily diary that was intensely and sometimes painfully honest. 'I am so depressed

about my batting and general persona … negative, internal and quiet,' read one entry from a Test series against the West Indies, published in his 1996 autobiography. Then: 'So what? I failed with the bat. Get on with it … be a positive influence on all. Don't take the easy option of giving it all up.' You can feel his catharsis.

So Healy began to grow, into his job, into a force, and in the estimation of the cricket public. He never won its unqualified affection. A wicketkeeper, even a champion wicketkeeper, is not naturally a crowd's hero. No one goes to the cricket to watch him specifically. He rarely wins man of the match awards. He is a functionary who is noticed only when he is in some way remiss. He does not have the luxury of being graceful and gracious. Roebuck once observed that Healy prickled like a cactus on the field.

Warts-and-all television coverage has only exacerbated this effect for modern 'keepers, showing in close-up the blemishes that for past 'keepers were sentimentalised out of existence. Changing social mores meant that the streak of larrikinism that was so celebrated in Marsh was decried whenever it showed up in Healy. Wicketkeepers necessarily all come from a hard school. Healy kept in mind throughout his career a piece of advice he once read from former Australian 'keeper Bert Oldfield, who said that no one understood the 'keeper's craft and that if he ever got a chance to make a production of his skills, he ought.

Healy took his art to another plane, elevating an essentially prosaic business to the level of a spectacle. Statistics are crude, particularly concerning wicketkeepers, for they show only what was taken, not what was missed. There are plenty in Australia to say that Don Tallon,

Wally Grout and Marsh were better 'keepers, and plenty worldwide to say Alan Knott was the best of all.

But it is doubtful if any of them went two years without dropping a Test match catch, and in the meantime turned leg-side half-volleys into wickets. Healy did. Who will easily forget the stumping he made of England batsman Mark Butcher at Old Trafford in 1997? Butcher's merest mistake was to overbalance in his crease as he looked to flick away a wild Michael Bevan delivery, only for the unsighted Healy to gather the ball on the half-volley a metre wide of leg stump and in the same instant swish away the bails? The third umpire was called, but batsman and 'keeper both knew already that it was out.

Healy was a stickler for technique. He prided himself on the fact that he kept in a distinctively Australian style, moving late, keeping his feet and taking the ball as often as possible 'on the inside', rather than constantly diving hither and thither. He kept to and created wickets for many good, great and lucky Australian bowlers, but undoubtedly it was his work with Shane Warne that set him above all who had gone before him. It was not so much a partnership as a kinship; in Australian lore only the Marsh–Lillee coupling could equal it. Healy always insisted that he was the junior associate, yet though batsmen were forgiven their befuddlement when met with another piece of Warne sorcery, no such concession was ever allowed to the wicketkeeper who stood just one further metre away, often was unsighted, and did not have a bat for a first line of defence. Even when conditions were so treacherous that Healy had to don a helmet – it happened at least twice – he was meant to take every ball, and the half-chances, too.

After his retirement, Healy gave, in a column for the *Age*, an absorbing insight into the challenge of 'keeping to Warne. It was his gig, and so can only be told in his words. 'Down I'd go into my crouch early enough to watch Warne's visible cues, but not long enough to get leg-lock,' he wrote. 'I'd position myself outside the off stump so that the batsman couldn't obscure my view easily, and I'd go through my cues. Every ball, my mind says: "Watch the ball, move, stay down".'

Healy watched as Warne walked in his theatrically deliberate manner towards the crease. 'The flipper would have been detected two strides earlier, and this is not it,' he wrote. 'Leg-spinner coming, last seen leaving the hand, but how much will it turn? Looks like he's just rolled it out rather than ripping it, but it's heading straight for the big hole outside leg stump. "Stay down and move late", I keep telling my legs. This could do anything off the pitch, and by then it will be behind the batsman. Must ignore the batsman as he will only further distract me as I strive to isolate the ball. It should slide down leg, but will it? That's the dilemma, and I must wait and watch before deciding to move low and strong. Gloves low and relaxed enough to give with the ball, and in it goes, cleanly. Pat myself on the back, take a deep breath or two, and settle in for the second delivery of a captivating 30-over spell.' It was Warne's warm-up ball.

Healy's attention to the ball was infamously distracted for a fatal split-second in Karachi in 1994 when, with Pakistan nine out needing four to win, Inzamam-ul-Haq moved out to try to clip Warne through a gap at midwicket purposely left to lure him into the shot. He missed, but amid the shuffling and scuffing of Inzamam's feet, and through the puff of dust, the confusion of exclamations and the seeming certainty that the ball would hit the stumps, so did Healy. It skittered away beneath him for four byes. Australia then had not won a Test match in Pakistan for 35 years, and it would be another four before that record was redressed. In the American Embassy that evening, Healy cried.

Tours of Pakistan were the punctuation of his career. His first in 1988, with all its fumbling and bumbling, he was sure would be his last. His second in 1994 featured that miss at Karachi, and the breaking of a thumb at Rawalpindi which forced him to miss a Test match for the only time in his career. His third was famous for Australia's long-awaited victory at Rawalpindi, and for the moment in that match when Healy surpassed Marsh to become the leading Test wicketkeeper of all time. Amends can rarely have been so comprehensively made. A year later, Healy was gone from the game.

Sometimes, Healy's presence was too formidable for the game's delicate sensibilities. He clashed often and heatedly with opponents, umpires and officials. Most infamously, he clashed with the West Indies after a botched attempt to stump Brian Lara was given out anyway in Brisbane in 1992, an incident that reverberated down the seasons. Healy was from then until the end of his career estranged from Lara and indeed from the whole Windies team; when he sought to enter their rooms to proffer an olive branch in Sydney soon afterwards, Keith Arthurton greeted him thus: 'Do you want your arse broken, man?'

Healy was mortified at the time, and has said frequently since that if he could change one thing in his career, it would be to take back the appeal. To his retiring day, it remained his only regret. He seriously considered giving away cricket at the time, such was his anguish, until, in his typically methodical way, he sat down with a piece of paper, tallied up the pros and cons and discovered that he still loved the game much more than he hated it. But he never apologised for his intensity, feeling that it was his duty to be in the game constantly, and in the craw of opponents. Upon the occasion of his 100th Test, he said: 'I'd like to think that most oppositions find me a pain, regularly.'

Healy grew, changed, matured, had a family, broadened in his outlook and hardened in his temperament throughout his dozen years in Test cricket, but it would not be right to say that he mellowed in his middle sporting age. Rather, he learned. An associate once said that Healy's mean streak sat just above the surface of his playing persona throughout the first half of his career, but was concealed just below the surface in the second half. Perhaps that is true of us all. At any rate, his reputation grew. At Lord's in 1997, Healy scooped up a low offering from Graham Thorpe and promptly signalled no catch. Really, with his history behind him and television cameras all around, he could do no other. Yet such was his standing in the cricket world now that umpire David Shephard led the crowd in applauding his sportsmanship.

Of course, there was more to Healy's cricket than his wicketkeeping. He was, as 'keepers generally are, a batsman without fuss or complication, whose pugnacious manner seemed to ask the top order what was their drama. He was no stylist. His stance was unnaturally wide, and he crouched low as a crab over his bat, until it seemed he must overbalance. His inclination was always to get on with the game; he played the hook compulsively. But later in his career he discovered the perverse pleasure in some situations of playing no shots at all. All four of his first-class centuries were in Test matches, and all in the first match of a series, when terms and conditions are laid down. He could change the tempo of a match, and sometimes its course. At Port Elizabeth in 1997, Australia was seven wickets down when Healy hit a six to win a crucial Test match; it remains a favourite memory.

It was the decline of his batting rather than his tending of wickets that propelled him towards, and then into, retirement. In 1997, as Australia began to pursue a policy of separate Test and one-day teams, he was dropped from the one-day team in favour of Adam Gilchrist. It was a decision that was at once easy to rationalise and difficult to understand. Healy called to congratulate Gilchrist upon his selection, and again when the West Australian made his maiden century one night in Sydney, and took to greeting him, not in the least facetiously, as 'maestro'. He did not like life as a half-international, but he did not sulk about it. For a season, he was everyone's favourite cricketer; it was as if only in his absence we came to appreciate fully his presence. Nonetheless, somewhere a bell had faintly tolled.

Healy throughout his career described himself as 'the drummer in the band'. He said he never aspired to the captaincy, and always thought that wicketkeepers, with their constant engagement in the game, were by calling natural vice-captains anyway. He was Australia's, for three years. He was a team leader anyway, and at length an elder statesman. He inherited from David Boon the honour of leading the team in its triumphal anthem.

Like Boon, he straddled old school and new. After the Sheffield Shield match in Melbourne that thrust him into Test cricket, Ian Botham led both teams in shotgunning beer cans, and at dusk in a challenge to see if anyone could hit a golf ball over the MCG's old Southern Stand. Healy learned, and dutifully, even zestfully, practised the many stringent disciplines that govern the life of a modern cricketer. But he also celebrated Australia's wins harder and longer than any of his contemporaries. The first four nights of a Test match were rigorously Australia's, but the last was his.

Throughout, Healy prided himself on rising above adversity. The Karachi miss would have destroyed a lesser man, yet within months, he was back and monstering England. Hurt to lose the vice-captaincy in 1997, he rejoined with a brave Test century. He had to adapt all his career to new countries, pitches, bowlers, irritations and standards of performance and behaviour. He had to rise to new demands on 'keepers, particularly to make themselves at least useful with the bat and exemplars of good grace in the field. He was rarely confounded.

At his retirement, he characterised his career as 'a series of bouncing backs', and was not entirely convinced even then that he could not do it once more. Healy lost his enthusiasm for the routines of travelling and training, though never for playing. His 'keeping remained high class; on his last tour to Zimbabwe, the ball still seemed merely to flutter into his gloves like a butterfly into a net. But his batting fell away wretchedly, and he had been dwelling on retirement for a year before he announced it at the start of the 1999–2000 season. He had half-hoped to play the first match of that summer, on his home ground, but was rejected; in matters Healy, the head had always ruled the heart.

Since, Healy has worked as assiduously at a range of roles as he did at wicketkeeping. As a commentator, his growly voice is every bit as insistent now as in his playing heyday. And still nothing gets past him.

HEALY, Ian Andrew
Born: 30 April 1964, Spring Hill (QLD)

Bats: Right-handed, wicketkeeper

First-Class Career
Debut: 1986–87 Queensland v West Indians, Townsville

M	Inn	NO	Runs	50	100	Ave	Ct	St	Runs	Wkts	Ave	5	10
231	342	66	8341	39	4	30.22	698	69	22	0	–	–	–

Highest Score: 161* Australia v West Indies, Brisbane, 1996–97

Test Career
Debut: 1988–89 Australia v Pakistan, Karachi

M	Inn	NO	Runs	50	100	Ave	Ct	St	Runs	Wkts	Ave	5	10
119	182	23	4356	22	4	27.39	366	29	–	–	–	–	–

Highest Score: 161* Australia v West Indies, Brisbane, 1996–97

International Limited-Overs Career
Debut: 1988–89 Australia v Pakistan, Lahore

M	Inn	NO	Runs	50	100	Ave	Ct	St	Runs	Wkts	Ave	5
168	120	36	1764	4	–	21.00	194	39	–	–	–	–

Highest Score: 56 Australia v England, Melbourne, 1994–95

RAY LINDWALL

Studying Ray Lindwall

by Steven Carroll

The wooden fence at the back of the yard is already splintered and broken above where three white lines representing the stumps have been painted. From where Michael stands he can see through the opening onto the green lawn of next door's backyard. It is a late afternoon in early spring, and for the next hour and a half, while the light still holds, he will bowl against the fence.

From the moment he first saw the game played it was the fast bowler that caught his eye. Michael thinks of nothing else but fast bowling through the long school days, and dreams of fast bowling at night. Just one dream. And always the same. In this dream he bowls the perfect ball. He experiences its perfection from beginning to end. It is a delivery so perfect that it becomes known all over the suburb as the ball that Michael bowled. The scene is always the same. The red train at the local station is just pulling out from the platform, the mill cats are tumbling over each other in the Saturday afternoon sun, a vase of flowers at the base of the war memorial bows to the footpath in the heat, the milk bar owner in the main street pours milk for a lime spider, while on the dusty schoolyard oval in the shade of the great pines, Michael bowls the perfect ball and everything stops. The train delays its departure, the milk bar owner turns from his lime spider to the front window of his shop as if noticing a sudden hush and the mill cats look up from their games as word ripples through the suburb that Michael has bowled the perfect ball. And the witnesses, those who were there, will grow in number throughout the day and through the following weeks, till everyone will claim to have been there and witnessed the

Steven Carroll is a right-arm quick who has published two top-order novels. 'Studying Ray Lindwall' is an extract from the forthcoming The Art of the Engine Driver.

ball that young Michael bowled. And all will agree that, from the moment the ball left the boy's arm, to the moment it lifted the off stump from the ground, that it was the perfect ball and that the boy had a gift for speed.

It is his ambition that one day he will live that dream. That one day he will feel the ball leave the tips of his thumb and fingers, know from the moment it does what is about to happen, and look up from his

delivery stride to see the schoolyard crowd and everybody on the street that runs alongside the oval, pause in wonder as something of distracting perfection enters the everyday world of school bells and midday shopping. And even those who don't care for the game will nod to each other on the footpaths, acknowledging that it is an event.

But before that moment can be lived he will spend his days bowling against his back fence, until that part of the fence upon which the three stumps have been painted will shatter completely and a new set of stumps will need to be drawn in.

Michael kneels on the spring lawn with a small house-painting brush in one hand and draws a white line across the grass. When he is finished he gives the line a second coat and puts the brush down.

On the lawn two opened books lie in the sun. The opened pages of one contain a series of eight photographs, a series of newsreel stills that show, frame by frame, the great Lindwall's action. Lindwall is shown approaching the crease. Michael can see the great bowler gathering himself for the delivery stride. Lindwall hits the delivery stride, sliding through on the point of his right boot, then transfers his weight to the front foot. The next frame is the boy's favourite. Lindwall's arm is high, his back is arched, and the ball is about to be released. It is in that moment, in the split second before the ball is released, that the bowler is privileged. His balance, the feel of his feet on the ground, his rhythm, his aim, the arch of his back, the movement of his shoulders and the snug sit of the ball in his fingers will tell him in advance about the quality of the ball he is about to deliver. And already Michael is living for that moment when he feels the ripple of the perfect delivery passing through him and he tastes that perfect moment just before it happens. When it is his and his alone, before sharing it with the crowd. In the next frame the ball is released and the remaining two photographs show the smooth, even pacing of Lindwall's follow-through.

Michael has studied these photographs again and again, he has read the great Lindwall's book on the art of the fast bowler, and this afternoon he will practise his run-up and follow-through. The book tells him that no bowler needs more than 14 to 16 paces. At first Michael measures out the full sixteen paces, but it doesn't work. Neither does fourteen. But fifteen does. So Michael will bowl from fifteen paces.

The yard is not long enough for him to bowl the full distance of a cricket pitch, but he is not concerned by this. It is the run-up and the action that he wants to get right. Once that is second nature the ball will do what he wants. Throughout the remainder of the afternoon the ball will hit the back fence above the stumps, and the crack of the impact will reverberate around the neighbourhood like a rifle shot, telling everybody that that young Michael is at it again.

Still wearing his grey school shorts and an old shirt, he stands at the crease he has just painted onto the grass, faces back towards the white, weatherboard house, and slowly begins pacing out his run-up again. Even this must be practised so that the steps are even and the distance is not different every time he paces it out.

He has underlined in pencil the most important points in Lindwall's book, which he has read twice. At the top of the run, facing the back fence with an old cork ball in his hand, the boy's impulse is to run in now as fast as he can and bowl the ball with all the speed he can gather. But the book tells him to begin slowly, and so, against all instincts, he takes off slowly and doesn't over-stretch at the delivery stride because the great Lindwall doesn't. When the ball hits the fence it is with a dull thud, not the crack that he likes to hear. For the moment, he is content with the dull thud.

While he is slowly increasing his speed, he is vaguely aware of the sounds around him; the children in the yard of the adjacent house, a dog somewhere complaining each time the ball hits the fence and his next door neighbour hacking his lungs up into a bucket on his back porch. But these sounds are unimportant. He hears them but they don't concern him because they don't matter.

Then he hears the only sound that matters. The old cork ball has barely left his hand when he hears the snap of the impact against the fence, sees the ball ricochet off the edge of a paling, fly onto the side fence and bounce onto the lawn in front of him. He slows at the end of his follow-through, pleased with the sound and vaguely aware that the neighbourhood will be listening. He is aware of the raised eyebrows all around him and the muttered comments that the kid will destroy the fence before he's finished.

But for the next hour the boy lives in a world of rhythm and action. He aims in turn for each of the painted stumps: the leg, the middle and the off. And he is not content until he hits each of the nominated stumps like the great Lindwall, who impresses the crowds at exhibitions by calling the stump that he hits before bowling the ball.

Occasionally, the yelling next door disturbs his concentration. His neighbour has finished coughing and his wife has started yelling at him. She is famous for it. And it is always the same. The house is wrong. The street is ghastly. The suburb is stuck out on the edge of the world. She is ashamed of the address. Ashamed of him. Does he see where he's brought her? She will be yelling all of this while the ball hits the back fence again and again. Then she will cry like she always does, and everything will go quiet once more.

Throughout the episode Michael's eyes are focused on the three stumps painted onto the fence. And as he runs in he keeps his shoulders level, making sure his body doesn't sway from side to side, keeps his pacing steady so that when he reaches his delivery stride it is as smooth, as effortless and rhythmic as the great Lindwall.

Every ball is different. Every one has its faults, to be corrected by the next. But there are times when he feels almost nothing, not the weight of his being or the strain on his legs and back. Times when he is completely oblivious of the instructions flowing from his mind to his body, when he is almost a spectator to his own bowling. And the

LINDWALL, Raymond Russell

Born: 3 October 1921, Mascot (NSW)
Died: 22 June 1996, Greenslopes (QLD)

Bats: Right-handed
Bowls: Right-arm fast

First-Class Career

Debut: 1941–42 New South Wales v Queensland, Brisbane

M	Inn	NO	Runs	50	100	Ave	Ct	St	Runs	Wkts	Ave	5	10
228	270	39	5042	19	5	21.82	123	–	16956	794	21.35	34	2

Highest Score: 134* New South Wales v Queensland, Sydney, 1945–46
Best Bowling: 7/20 Australians v Minor Counties, Stoke, 1953

Test Career

Debut: 1945–46 Australia v New Zealand, Wellington

M	Inn	NO	Runs	50	100	Ave	Ct	St	Runs	Wkts	Ave	5	10
61	84	13	1502	5	2	21.15	26	–	5251	228	23.03	12	–

Highest Score: 118 Australia v West Indies, Bridgetown, 1954–55
Best Bowling: 7/38 Australia v India, Adelaide, 1947–48

picture that he sees, from the curve of the back, to the grace of the bowling arm describing its delivery arc and the velvet follow-through, is an exact replica of the great Lindwall in frozen action. And what he sees is made all the more powerful by the certain knowledge that, at the end of such a perfect delivery, there will be damage.

At times like these he is sure he has the gift of speed. And if he does he must nurture it, for in his bones he knows that true speed is a gift. Not something to be squandered and lost. Knows that when a gift is given it must be received with care. And knows that, if he nurtures it properly, it will be speed that will one day carry him along his street, out of the suburb and into the world of the great Lindwall. This is the importance of being fast, for the kind of speed that turns heads can do all that.

But for the time being he will practise every afternoon in his yard until the fence is shattered and another three white stumps will need to be painted on the remaining palings next to the damaged section. He will follow the instructions of the great Lindwall until action becomes second nature, and the instruments of bowling – his legs, arms, eyes, heart and head – are all one.

When this happens, he will bowl the perfect ball and it will become known as the ball that Michael bowled. The red train will stay just that moment longer in the platform before departing, the mill kittens will cease to gambol, the milk bar owner will look up, suddenly distracted from his lime spider and dream will meet reality. And even those who don't care much for the game will pause on the footpaths and streets of the suburb in a general acknowledgement that this is an event.

SHANE WARNE

The Long-Running Soapie

by Roland Perry

A midst the worst image crisis in Shane Warne's career, he declared his life had 'become a soap opera'. It was late 1998. He had just been exposed for taking money from an Indian bookie in exchange for match day information – weather and pitch reports – in 1994. Warne loved TV soapies – Melrose Place was his favourite.

Another who saw the dramatic possibilities in Warne was film star Russell Crowe. In the 22 March 1999 edition of *Woman's Day* magazine columnist Peter Ford wrote that the actor was interested in a movie based on the biography of Warne: *Bold Warnie*. Crowe, a cricket fan, would have been excited by Warne's parallel lives on-field and off-field, like a contemporary version of the successful TV drama 'Bodyline'. Except that Crowe saw much more potential in Warne. Don Bradman (played by Gary Sweet), the 'star' of 'Bodyline', was seen as a 'good guy'. A cleanskin. 'Warnie' had the image of a larrikin innocently drawn into a demimonde of evil. For an actor like Crowe trying to improve his range, Warne would offer potential. He had to shelve taking the film idea further when he received two big offers; one where he would fatten up and blond his hair to play the cigarette industry whistleblower in *The Insider*; the other in which he had to muscle up to play a gladiator. These two roles were perfect training in several ways for an intriguing, filmed version of Warne's life.

Warne's symbiosis with matters celluloid was evident when he was an unknown 19-year-old semi-professional playing League cricket in England in 1989. He was then taking lots of wickets and developing the kind of deliveries that would later bring him world fame. He was fat

---

Roland Perry is the author of Bold Warnie: Shane Warne and Australia's Rise to Cricket Dominance. *His other cricket books include* The Don, Waugh's Way, *and* Captain Australia.

and getting fatter on junk food and plenty of Aussie beer. Shane was a hit with the local girls. He seemed like a chubby version of an actor in 'Neighbours' starring Kylie Minogue and Jason Donovan, the Australian soapie that had been a long-running hit in England. Most of Britain's viewing public would watch the early-evening show as it soared to new heights of banality, and with it the all-important ratings.

The sanitised series, with its emphasis on sun and hints of sin, had captured the popular imagination. Everywhere Warne went he was asked about Kylie and Jason as if he had stepped out of the show himself. He seemed like a surfie, although the boy from bayside Melbourne had never been near a board. Yet it was more than just the look that attracted. He had a fun-loving Aussie manner, idealised in 'Neighbours', that was the antithesis of young men in England, who appeared cautious and withdrawn by comparison. England seemed, by contrast to the world in the soap, boring and grey. Its economy was running into recession; there was unprecedented unemployment. A hectoring Prime Minister was out of touch with ordinary people. The young were finding it hard to imagine any kind of future.

And in the middle of it all there was Shane. He was naive and carefree. This was a possible beginning of Warne's tele-script, even before there was anything world shattering to write about. He even 'starred' in his own video version of 'Neighbours' at a party. It was so risqué it had to be destroyed.

Warne came back to Australia thinking he would make the St Kilda Cricket Club firsts, but was shocked to find he had been dumped to the thirds. The Club took one look at his ballooned figure and didn't take him seriously. His weight topped 100 kilograms, which would have challenged Russell Crowe in the *Insider*.

This was a devastating moment for Warne. He had flown off to England after failing in a gut-wrenching effort to make the St Kilda Football Club's list early in 1989. His dream to play footy for the 'Sainters' was over. A hurt Warne overcame the misery by eating and drinking to excess and 'losing' himself in League cricket. This second rejection, by the cricket club, pushed him to a low ebb.

Yet he clung on to a fading dream. He wanted more than anything else to be a sporting hero. Warne knew in his heart that he could spin a cricket ball like nobody else. It had been seen here and there before his summer in England. But it consolidated when he got as much bowling as he wished playing on all those village greens. All through the seminal summer, Warne had one eye on Allan Border's Australians winning the

Ashes. The team had one leg-break bowler, Trevor Hohns, who was useful, but not a matchwinner. Warne kept comparing his own efforts and felt he could do better. He hoped to achieve Club firsts selection and then push for the state side. That scenario seemed now to have been hit for six, even before the home 1989–90 season began. In this 'down' moment he contemplated chucking it all in and playing social cricket with his old schoolmates. Then he could drink and eat all he liked and enjoy a game. Yet, even in the nets, no batsman at St Kilda could handle his ripping deliveries. He decided on one more season. If he didn't progress he would 'retire' from serious competition and become a 'could-a-been' champion – someone with unrefined skills having a whack in park cricket.

Underneath those layers of self-indulgence brought on by the hurt of rejection, Warne had a strong character. St Kilda, like all club cricket teams, moved into the 1990s more conscious of physical fitness. He responded to demands for running and exercise outside games and shed just enough kilograms to show the Club he was at least conscientious. Injuries to other players allowed him to slip into the firsts by Christmas 1989. His third game was against Waverley-Dandenong, captained by Test fast bowler Rodney Hogg. After facing a few deliveries from Warne he remarked: 'This bloke should be in the Test side, turning 'em like that!'

If it had come from anyone else but a Test player, it would have been a throwaway line. But Hogg meant it. In 20 years of cricket he had never seen or faced any spinner as gifted as Warne. In any other era, these words would have drifted into the ether and be lost. But at that moment, Australia's powerful cricket captain, Allan Border, had just dragged the Test team from the oblivion of the mid-1980s. He was looking to beat the West Indies and take the world cricket crown. Border couldn't match the Caribbean champions with speed. It had to be spin.

Word about Warne spread fast. Border heard about him. Victoria was urged to fast-track him into the state squad. Its manager Bill Lawry obliged. Warne had taken only a handful of wickets at club level but by the end of the 1989–90 season he was chosen for the Australian Institute of Sport's Cricket Academy for the 1990 winter. It was too quick for Warne. He responded poorly to the advanced fitness training, pinch tests, diets, restricted nightclub hours and discipline. Warne walked out before he was thrown out. The main black mark against the 20-year-old was that while on tour in Darwin, he insulted three women by a hotel pool when a prank backfired. The fast-tracking had been too fast for a 'Jack the lad'.

In other decades this incident may have seen Warne stamped as too hot to handle, and seen him ostracised. But Border wanted a top leggie in his armoury. He knew they matured 'late' and were better bowlers at 30 than 20. But the Australian skipper and the selectors would not wait. If Warne could produce anything like that elusive 'potential' there would be a place for him in the Test side. He made the State team by default towards the end of the 1990–91 season.

Rather than take jobs delivering pizzas and working in retail stores as before, Warne spent another season – 1991 – in professional cricket, this time in the Lancashire League. This was followed by a tour to Zimbabwe in an Australian second XI captained by Mark Taylor. Warne

was under scrutiny, and in competition with another leggie, Peter McIntyre. Both performed well, Warne taking a career best 7/49 in a first-class game. He had proved he could be a destroyer, and in front of Taylor and a national selector, John Benaud.

India was touring Australia in 1991–92. Border and Co. dearly wanted to groom a spinner in the Test series, with one eye on the following season against the West Indies. The Australian prime minister, Bob Hawke, colluded with national selectors and Border by selecting Warne in his XI to play a one-day game against the West Indies. The alacrity of Warne's rise without a trace of sustained wicket-taking ability was too much for the Victorian state selectors, who reckoned that he had not justified a place on merit. The frustrated national selectors bypassed the State and put Warne in a team to play the West Indies at Hobart late in 1991. He acquitted himself well against the West Indian stars, taking 7/56 over the two innings. He troubled the big names such as Lara and Richardson. It was enough. A tubby 95-kilogram Warne, at 22, was selected to play against India in the third Test at the SCG.

Warne threw a party at his parents' home and celebrated hard. The next morning he was driven, hungover, by his father to the ACB for a baggy green cap fitting. The media wanted to interview him. Warne asked the ACB to stall them while he threw up in the toilet. He flew to Sydney on New Year's Eve and was looked after by David Boon and Geoff Marsh. The clowning Merv Hughes relaxed him. Warne's nerves were eased by having to bat first. He ran the edginess out of himself making 20 runs in an invaluable 72 minutes at the wicket. No amount of counselling, if there had been any, cajoling or boosting could have been as useful as this effort with the bat. He was in a good frame of mind when he had to bowl. The weather dragged India's innings over three days. It got on top and Warne ran into a rampant Ravi Shastri (205) and a teenage Sachin Tendulkar (148 not out). Warne ended with the figures of 1/150. But he didn't sulk or make excuses. He remained cheerful. Border admired his pluck. He was persevered with.

At the end of the 1991–92 season, team coach Bob Simpson told Warne to lose at least 10 kilograms or he would be discarded. He was sent back to the Cricket Academy under Rod Marsh and put through a gruelling routine straight out of Sylvester Stallone's *Rocky*. Warne responded, shed the weight and emerged looking like a rock-hard gladiator. His Teutonic good looks (his mother, Brigitte, was an immigrant from postwar Germany) emerged.

The new Warne played Tests in Sri Lanka and dismissed three tail-enders for a few runs to win a Test. It wasn't enough to convince selectors that he had 'the goods'. He missed out on the first Test of the all-important series versus the West Indies in the home 1992–93 season. Border asked publicly for his return to the national XI. He was selected to play in the Boxing Day Test at the MCG. On the last day he provided great sporting drama by delivering one of the best balls in years – a magnificent flipper that bowled an in-form Richie Richardson. Warne then went on to take 7/52 and Australia won. He was a match-winner at 23 and had justified the faith Border and others had shown in him.

Border plotted his next big use of Warne – in the 1993 Ashes in England – with more thought, style and intrigue than a John Le Carré espionage novel. The skipper hid Warne for the lead-up to the Tests, and when he did play, he only bowled his stock leg-break. When Border unleashed him in the Tests, Warne's first ball was one of the greatest deliveries ever seen. At a brief point in its trajectory it was above the eye level of the batsman, England's chief clubber of spinners, Mike Gatting. When the ball landed well outside leg stump, he lunged at something not really there. This was because of the ball's exceptional drift. Gatting played where he thought the ball would land, but gravity and the curve had dragged it down and away into a blind zone. Gatting was mesmerised as the ball jagged past him and hit his off stump. He was left dumbfounded, not ready to believe he was bowled. An umpire's curt nod of confirmation sent the batsman on his way.

That ball, as it became known, was replayed so often that England was demoralised from the series' beginning. Warne went on to dominate the Ashes with 34 wickets at 25.79 runs a wicket. Australia won it 4–1. Off-field, the British media decided that Warne was its pin-up for the summer. The papers and magazines chased, photographed and wrote about him ad nauseam. Warne was dubbed a single, eligible Adonis in the glossies. The grubbier papers found old girlfriends willing to talk about even older affairs and beat-up stories of romance. Warne's Melbourne girlfriend, Simone Callahan, turned up in England to ward off the competition, real or imagined. Warne asked her to marry him and they became engaged. The media, unfazed, changed step, took him off the stud list and beat up different angles, such as 'How Simone Tamed Her Man'.

Warne continued to perform on the field, but by his own admission he began a period in 1994 as a 'bighead'. His success caused an on-field arrogance that culminated in him abusing South African bat Andrew Hudson as he left the Wanderers field after being dismissed. Warne was fined and reprimanded. Later in the year he was gambling at a casino in Colombo when approached by an Indian bookie named 'John'. By this time Warne, earning more than $400 000 with his ACB contract, plus triple that for ads and endorsements, had developed a big betting habit. Wherever he was, he headed for the garish, glittering casinos with mates such as Mark Waugh, another big punter.

This may have been the part of Warne's story that gripped Russell Crowe. Warne, the-big spending gambler and sports star, was set up for a sting by an illegal bookmaking ring controlled by the main Indian 'Mafia'. Warne and Mark Waugh seemed like perfect targets. Both were match-winners, who could swing games by individual efforts. If they could be controlled to fix matches, huge money could be wagered and won. First, there would be the hook. Warne was introduced to an Indian bookie – 'John' – in a dimly lit casino behind the Oberoi Hotel. Peter Sellers would have played him brilliantly, as he grovelled to, fawned on and flattered Warne with lines such as 'Oh, Mr Warne, you are my very favourite cricketer, the best. I love the way you play.'

The Indian looked on as Warne dropped US$5000 at a roulette table. The next day he invited Warne to his hotel room and continued the feigned sycophancy, telling him he was 'his biggest fan'. Then he shoved an envelope into his hand: 'Here is a token of my appreciation.'

Warne gave the money back. 'John' returned it. 'Please take it,' the Indian insisted. After a moment of too-ing and fro-ing, Warne took the money. The bait had been taken. Warne would now feel some obligation to 'John'. And the $5000? Warne blew it at roulette that night.

Here the 'Neighbours'/'Melrose Place' soapie turned into film noir, or a thriller with wide ramifications in real life. Soon after, Australia played Pakistan in a Test at Karachi, beginning 28 September 1994.

Enter, 'the Rat' – Salim Malik – the 'baddie' in the story. He had been so nicknamed because, as Warne later told a Pakistani court, some of the Australians thought he looked like the said rodent.

Malik was Pakistan's best bat and the link to the Indian underworld in fixing cricket matches. Aware that Warne was 'hooked', he rang him at the Pearl Continental Hotel where they were both staying and invited him to his room. It was 10.30 at night before the vital last day of the Test, which was poised on a knife edge.

At that meeting, Malik suggested that Warne and Tim May, Warne's room-mate, should bowl badly and thus deliver the game to Pakistan – for US$200 000. Warne returned to his room and discussed it with May. They both agreed to reject the proposal. Warne rang Malik and told him that he and May rejected the offer. Malik told him he was making a 'mistake'. Warne told him to go and receive fornication.

The next day, Pakistan needed 157 to win with three wickets in hand. The game swung this way and that and was won by Pakistan by one wicket. Warne gave it everything, taking 5/89 and winning the man of the match award.

That night at the hotel, Salim ran into Warne and told him: 'You were stupid [not taking the money]. You lost.' Warne reminded the Pakistani that his team had been very lucky. Malik again chided him over the money.

In a Hollywood script, the Rat would make a duck in the next Test at Rawalpindi, Australia would go on to win the three-Test series, and justice would be done. But this was real life. Malik made a brilliant 237 in the second Test, which was drawn, as was the third.

Malik's in-your-face bribery attempts continued. Having failed with Warne, he now went after Mark Waugh, the other player 'hooked'. Waugh also gave Malik short shrift when he offered him, his brother

Steve, Warne and May US$50 000 each to throw the next day's limited-over match. During the summer of Ashes Tests in Australia (won 3–1 by the home team, Warne taking a hat-trick at Melbourne), Warne and Waugh were rung by John who wanted weather and pitch reports. Clearly, the bookies felt they could still manipulate them, despite their rejections of Malik's bribery overtures. But early in 1995, the story of the attempted bribery broke. Salim was, for the first time, named as the 'bad boy' of international cricket – and accused by the Australians. In secret, Warne and Waugh confessed to the ACB that they had taken money from 'John'. They were fined the equivalent of the money they had been given. The issue was covered up. It was now a ticking time bomb. So many people knew of the incident that it was bound to be public, some day.

Meanwhile, back on the field, this time in the Caribbean, Warne was an important part of the team that beat the West Indies for the first time in 29 Test series and 15 years. He had been vital to Australia's revival following the dark days of the mid-1980s.

Warne married Simone a few days short of his 26th birthday in September 1995, and then prepared for another round with Malik and the Pakistanis, who arrived in Australia in late 1995. Malik made no effort to confront his accusers. During the games, the Australians snubbed him on the field, even refusing to 'sledge' him. This 'cold shoulder' treatment caused Malik to say to an umpire, 'Nice to have someone to talk to.'

In 1996, Warne had to make up his mind which went under the knife first: his spinning finger or his shoulder. He chose the finger and he was a late starter in the 1996–97 season against the West Indies.

It was a worrying time for Warne. If his finger didn't stand up, his career would be over. He did everything right in rehabilitation, overcame the operation and was back starring in Australia's 3–2 second successive series win over the West Indies. That season spilled into another in South Africa in early 1997, then a further Ashes tour of England. Warne, the pin-up boy of 1993, was now turned on by the fickle English media. They were sick of his grip over England and tried everything they could to lower his morale by writing down his skills and ignoring any of his good form. Sections of crowds turned nasty. Warne was abused. Mark Taylor, the skipper, was ridiculed for his poor form.

The Australians began poorly, losing the one-day series 3–0 and then the first Test. Warne and the rest of the team were struggling. They drew at Lord's. He was distracted by the birth of his daughter,

Brooke, during June, but prepared well for the third Test at Old Trafford, Manchester. Australia began its fightback with Steve Waugh scoring a gutsy century in each innings and Warne ran into form. All his histrionics, that would challenge Russell Crowe's abilities to mimic, returned. There was the confident body language; the querying looks down the wicket; the stroking of the chin as he considered that batsman's efforts against him; the grins; the frowns and grimaces; the charges down the wicket to appeal; the chitchat with 'keeper Ian Healy ('you were right about that Heals'); and the chirpy remarks for the ears of the batsman at the other end ('bit of a turner now').

He returned 6/38 from 30 overs, and with Waugh, won the match. Warne suffered fearful abuse at Taunton versus Somerset, with references to his weight and sexuality, from a group of profane, unfunny morons. Acting skipper Steve Waugh threatened to take his team from the field if it continued. The offenders were evicted.

Australia went on to win the next two Tests at Leeds and Trent Bridge, and took the series and the Ashes. Warne celebrated by doing the 'dance of the derriere' on the balcony in response to the continued abuse from spectators. It was twisted by the English media into a dance of derision for the vanquished foe languishing in the dressing room below. The vision and photos went out across the cricket world. Warne's image was of an arrogant gloater. It was wrong on both counts – Warne was never arrogant in victory – but the impression that would stay in the public mind.

Undaunted, Warne returned to Australia for the 1997–98 season to take on the Kiwis and South Africa, where he reached the heights, taking 39 wickets in six Tests, and raced through 300 wickets for his career. He lifted particularly for the Proteas, who, for the Australians, were the most competitive team next to the West Indies. Warne kept his 'bunny' Darryl Cullinan in his hutch, contained and beat Hansie Cronje and demoralised the South Africans.

When the selectors decided to pick 'horses for courses' in its one-day side, Steve Waugh became captain and Warne his deputy. Steve was injured and Warne showed his prowess as a leader. The style was pure Aussie Rules, as he exhorted his players to 'put in' and led with infectious enthusiasm. Australia rocked the Proteas by beating them 2–1 in the finals. Warne, as usual, came on to take telling wickets at vital moments. Had he reached his zenith on the cricket field? It was difficult to imagine him, or any spinner, ever doing better.

If Warne thought he had been through some character tests in the past, they were nothing compared to the next year. It began in April 1998 with thumpings from Sachin Tendulkar in India in Tests and one-dayers, and then the decision he had been dreading and putting off for years: surgery for his shoulder. No one in big sport, from javelin throwers to footballers, had ever recovered to perform as well as before the operation. Most had faded away. Warne had the operation in June and weeks later began the long, demanding rehabilitation. He put off his return to cricket until he could truly make it. In early games he was tentative about letting his re-made shoulder 'rip'.

If that were not enough tension for one mind, he had another pressure to contend with in December 1998, when it was learned that he and Mark Waugh had taken money from bookies for match-day information on the weather and pitches back in 1994. The media came down heavily on Warne in particular. He was in line to captain the country in Tests. He was already filling in often for Steve Waugh in the one-day team. Critics demanded that he never be made captain of Australia's Test team.

In the middle of all this his second child, a son, was born. A day later he was selected to make his comeback for Australia in the fifth Test of the 1998–99 Ashes at Sydney. It was at this moment that Warne made the remark, 'My life has become a soap opera in recent times.'

In one sense it was good for him that he saw events this way. Life was episodic. There would always be up and down days. For the moment he ignored the media and focused on his comeback.

A packed crowd on day one at the SCG was thrilled to see Mark Taylor bring him on before lunch. There was tension all round as he waddled in for his flat-footed three-step walk up. Then followed the little quick step to his delivery stride and finally the mighty shoulder heave and hip rotation accompanied by that familiar grunt of strained effort as the ball whirred on its way.

Warne did make the first breakthrough in each England innings at Sydney. But a cruel fact was clear. He was a shadow of his former self. It had little to do with the off-field furore swirling around him. Either his shoulder had not come up the way everyone hoped, or he had lost 'it'. For Warne, this was the amazing power to turn a cricket ball, or deliver a different ball, if needed, for every delivery in an over. His deliveries were not spinning. His famed 'drift' in the air was not there. To make his appearance worse, Stuart MacGill was turning the ball square and taking wickets the way Warne used to. The champion was feeling redundant and the media was reminding him of it every day.

What struck Russell Crowe was the pure drama surrounding Warne at this time, when he was down and almost out. He was still news even when he was sidelined or not taking wickets. And just to make sure he was on the back and front pages, and the lead item on the nightly TV news, Mark Taylor stood down as skipper, leaving the way open for a new leader. Steve Waugh looked certain to take over. But, Warne, on the canvas for the count in December, was up and challenging through January 1999. By chance Waugh was injured, leaving Warne to lead the one-day side in several matches. He performed well, not losing a game and leading with aplomb.

Off the field, the bribery and corruption scandal was hotting up. Pakistan was investigating its own players and needed testimony from Warne, Mark Waugh and Tim May, who had been approached by Malik. This led to a Pakistani courtroom being set up in downtown Melbourne, complete with a picture of Mohammad Ali Jinnah, the founder of Pakistan, and prayers to 'Almighty Allah'. Now the long running soap-cum-thriller had another dimension – the ever-useful dramatic counterpoint of a court. It was more colourful and combative than anything contrived on 'Law & Order'.

Pakistani lawyers grilled the players. They seemed more intent on proving the Australians were corrupt than enlightening the investigation into the criminal activities of Malik and Co. Under pressure, Warne was pure Warne – direct, ingenuous and confident. He was neither disrespectful nor genuflecting towards the aggressive interrogation. He came out of it well and more indignant about his own position. He had been forced by his employer, the ACB, to say he was 'naive and stupid' when he would rather have defended his actions. Warne was not thrilled about the way he and Mark Waugh had been portrayed. After all, he pointed out, he had never been involved in match-fixing. He should have been painted as heroic for exposing Malik's nefarious activities.

This kept Warne on the front pages. If you missed him there, he could be seen in TV ads for Nike, 'just doing it'. If you only read papers, he was also there in advertisements for a company making patches to prevent smoking. Warne's on-field efforts, courtroom appearances, battle for the captaincy and constant media attention assured advertisers of maximum exposure. During all this, Warne vowed to give up smoking for the sake of his family – for a tidy sum of

$250 000. No one bothered to ask him why he needed to be 'bribed' into giving up his little vice if he was concerned for his family's health.

To his credit, Warne lobbied openly for the captaincy. He did not utter any of the usual hypocrisy and false modesty about how he felt about the job and his capacity to do it. He wanted it. But in the end, Steve Waugh was appointed and Warne became his deputy. Their first assignment together was a tough one in the Caribbean.

Warne's form deteriorated during the Tests, and Waugh was forced to drop his deputy for the last game at Antigua, making the hurtful remark that the vice-captaincy was 'just a title'. Healy was the player whose advice he valued most. The resultant stress from his first dumping since 1992 drove Warne back to cigarettes. He was caught in photographs at a nightclub like a naughty boy behind a shelter-shed. Warne was ropable about his dismissal. Yet he faced the fact that the only way back was to find form. He did this to a degree in the one-day series that followed the tied 2–all Test series. He was the player of the competition, despite the official award going to Sherwin Campbell.

The Australian team flew on to England for the 1999 World Cup and performed poorly early. Warne took fearful hammerings in some games, soon after the *News of the World* ran a story: 'Cricket Ace Warne's Games With Wicket Maiden'. The tabloids were at it again, trying to unsettle Warne with a beat-up about his alleged affair with 'porn star Kelly Handley'.

It was the last formula ingredient, except for religion, missing from the Warne scenario. This time the media caused Warne serious concern. His confidence on the field, up in the one-dayers in the Caribbean, had been shredded. Now this unwanted attention off the field put pressure of a more personal kind on him. Warne wanted to throw in the towel. It was too much. Then skipper Steve Waugh took him for a long walk in Kensington Gardens near the team's London hotel. You could imagine how a director would handle this scene if ever it was reproduced in a film: *Long-shot of the two men walking a path near Kensington Palace; medium-shot of them passing skateboarders and other strollers; inter-cut close ups as key lines are uttered.*

The captain cajoled his star spinner into playing on in the World Cup. After the rejection in the West Indies and Waugh's insensitivity, this was the correct approach. Warne believed he was wanted. He came back late in the tournament to be a star and earning man of the match awards as Australia streaked to a win. Despite all the epitaphs written by a hopeful British media, he returned with all the vengeance of

Clint Eastwood in one of his stereotypical Westerns. His form allowed him to nose in front of the unlucky MacGill for a Test spot in Sri Lanka and Zimbabwe in August and September 1999. His form held and he retained his place for the mighty summer of 1999–2000. Warne lifted for the big contests, especially in the greatest of all in pure cricket terms – versus his old nemesis, Sachin Tendulkar. Warne used every minute cell of experience and ability to dismiss the world champion bat in the Second Test against India in Melbourne. The spinner regained some measure of revenge against the only outstanding bat to have his measure in nearly a decade as the world's finest spin bowler. In New Zealand, he broke Dennis Lillee's Australian wicket-taking record of 355 victims and looked set for a hundred more.

Right at the end of the long run of games from September to April, the match-fixing scandal blew up. South African captain Hansie Cronje was accused by the Indian police of corruption. Further stories of murder and bribery emerged. The Pakistan Government was prompted in late May 2000 to allow the release of the investigation by the brave justice Malik Mohammad Qayyum. In it, Salim Malik was found guilty and banned from playing cricket for life.

Salim Malik is the main culprit, the Qayyum report noted. 'There is clear evidence of match-fixing against him. He has brought the Pakistani national team into disrepute.' At last, the courage shown by Warne, Waugh and Tim May, (there have been two murders in this saga) had brought justice to the game, or perhaps the business of cricket. It would be a fitting end for any soap, drama or thriller concerning Warne.

But wait, there is more, perhaps the sequel. Any thespian's range would be tested by his behaviour as claimed by yet another British tabloid expose during the 2000 cricket season in England. This time the *Mirror* bought a story by a nurse, Donna Wright, who met Warne at a Leicester nightclub. She claimed that he left her lewd phone messages after she rejected his overtures for a dalliance. Who flirted with whom first was in contention. The issue was clouded by the fact that Ms Wright went to the newspapers with the story and not the police. This discounted the possibility of harassment by Warne and threw the story into the realms of sleazy beat-up. This complexity tarnishes the heroic image of Warne, but it may well appeal to Crowe, who might think that it stretched his on-camera talents.

But if Russell Crowe wants to make a movie or mini-series they should forget it for the time being. The story of Shane Warne, master spinner and media personality, has plenty of episodes to come.

WARNE, Shane Keith

Born: 13 September 1969, Ferntree Gully (VIC)

Bats: Right-handed
Bowls: Right-arm leg spin

First-Class Career

Debut: 1990–91 Victoria v Western Australia, St Kilda

M	Inn	NO	Runs	50	100	Ave	Ct	St	Runs	Wkts	Ave	5	10
160	213	30	2933	7	–	16.03	113	–	17308	653	26.51	29	4

Highest Score: 86* Australia v NZ, Brisbane, 1993–94, 86 Australia v India, Adelaide, 1999–2000
Best Bowling: 8/71 Australia v England, Brisbane, 1994–95

Test Career

Debut: 1991–92 Australia v India, Sydney

M	Inn	NO	Runs	50	100	Ave	Ct	St	Runs	Wkts	Ave	5	10
84	117	12	1613	4	–	15.36	64	–	9505	366	25 96	16	4

Highest Score: 86* Australia v NZ, Brisbane, 1993–94, 86 Australia v India, Adelaide, 1999–2000
Best Bowling: 8/71 Australia v England, Brisbane, 1994–95

International Limited-Overs Career

Debut: 1992–93 Australia v New Zealand, Wellington

M	Inn	NO	Runs	50	100	Ave	Ct	St	Runs	Wkts	Ave	5
146	84	24	753	1	–	12.55	52	–	5609	228	24.60	1

Highest Score: 55 Australia v South Africa, Port Elizabeth, 1993–94
Best Bowling: 5/33 Australia v West Indies, Sydney, 1996–97

DENNIS LILLEE

Another Interview with Mr Lillee

by Peter FitzSimons

Dennis Lillee on the blower, calling from somewhere in Perth from his car phone, with a basic question:

'Why, mate?'

Like, why would anyone want to do another interview with him, was there anything left to say? Surely the story has been done to death?

Yes, well Mr Lillee, without being too mealy-mouthed about it, perhaps because you're pretty much the most famous Australian sportsman of your generation, and seeing as I'm going to be in Perth anyway for the end-of-season cricket dinner, it seems the obvious thing to look you up.

'Oh. Well perhaps we could … hold on … I've just seen this dickhead who I don't want to see me. Just a sec while I duck down …

'It's okay, he's gone. Now, all right, let's see how we go, let's have a chat at the din … hang on, he's back, pain that he is … No, it's alright, he's gone … Alright. Let's just have a chat at the dinner and see how we go.'

Sure enough, a slap on the back reveals Lillee standing behind me, resplendent in his black tie and hand outstretched as he helps himself to a seat at the table.

Surely it must be like this for Lillee with just about every adult Australian he meets for the first time. He's mouthing the usual 'gidday-how'd-ya-be?s', while his interlocutor is on momentary autopilot – 'yeh, bewdy, how're you?' – all the while trying to make a connection between the hundred memories they have of the cricketer, with the man before them. For myself, for what it's worth, visions come of

Peter FitzSimons is a well-known journalist for the Sydney Morning Herald *and the author of a number of books including a biography of* Nick Farr-Jones *and* The Rugby War.

standing on the Hill as a 10 year old, shyly joining in the chant of 'Lilleeee … Lilleeee … Lilleeee' as the man charged in. And in the long hot summer of '75–76, my father's head continually popping up from somewhere in the tomato patch, holding the tranny and yelling to us kids the great news: 'Lillee's got another one!'

Yes, he looks good, does Lillee. Of course, he's older, a tad heavier, a lot balder. But then aren't we all? Within those parameters he looks very fit and friendly. Not only does he not mind a bit covering for you until your faraway look has gone, but he even helps you pick up the pieces of the conversation as if he's barely noticed a thing.

So what's he up to these days?

'Plenty. Plenty. An awful lot … just a sec …' We have been interrupted by a silver-haired lawyerly-looking type who has timidly approached our table for a genuine Lillee autograph. No problem at all, Dennis signs with the instant flourish of one who has done the same thing tens of thousands of times before and seems to do it almost without thinking, though his innate friendliness to the bloke seems genuine enough.

'Where were we?' he asks.

What you're up to these days. Lillee is just about to respond when an old team-mate comes up, all hail-fellow-well-met and roaring laughter and it's another few minutes before the former fast bowler can extricate himself.

Another quick autograph for a middle-aged woman, a couple more handshakes and backslaps in passing, a big 'hello' from a passing waitress, and finally Lillee gets it out.

He's been busy, yes, very busy. He's living with his wife and two children in Perth, but sometimes gets so busy he spends a lot more time away from them than he'd like. Specifically, he runs a few cricket coaching clinics, is associated with the running of a Perth nursing home, plays the stock market, has a couple of small building developments he's getting up, has been doing some media work and most lately, he's been busy in this new business venture.

It's a venture, as it turns out, which seems made for him as it relies heavily on a level of sporting fame that few other than Lillee can bring to bear.

'Mate, it's called Field of Dreams,' he announces not without pride, and spins the tale from there.

The basics of the concept are selling signed sporting memorabilia in outlets throughout Australia. Boxing gloves signed by Muhammad Ali, baseball bats with the Micky Mantle moniker upon them, cricket balls with the signature of D. K. Lillee right there – that you, too, can hold and touch and have under your own hand, all for a lousy $80 or so. All replete with a guarantee of authenticity, which states the sports star both signed and handled the particular merchandise.

After a bit of a false start last year, Lillee and his associates hope to get the whole thing properly up and running in the next few months, with about 40 outlets around Australia.

They've already opened a few shops, with AFL footballer Gary Ablett, Allan Border and Lillee proving the three biggest home-grown sellers of sporting memorabilia.

Hmmmm. Does he not think it a very strange thing that there is a whole market out there for things that are made instantly more valuable simply by him putting his signature on them?

Well, a bit odd perhaps, but that was neither here nor there for him. The fact is there's a market for it, it makes a lot of people happy and who is he to argue?

In pure business terms, it's not a bad deal. Lillee has, after all, an all-but unlimited supply of signatures in him, and he'd also have to be close on being the Australian expert when it comes to the power of fame.

He first got a real idea of how weird it all was when with the Australian team on the Ashes tour of 1972. Mick Jagger hisself, Jumpin' Jack Flash in the flesh, had come down to watch the game and inevitably gravitated to the dressing rooms at the end of the day.

'You couldn't believe it,' recounts Lillee, 'what he was like in our dressing room. I mean, this was Jagger probably at the height of his fame, and we were pretty amazed to be around him, but he was incredibly shy around us. He just loved the cricket … said he thought it was like ballet.'

And so it went. Lillee and Jagger ended up as best buddies, with Jagger making a point of spending a lot of time with Lillee in the West Indies when the Stones and the Australians happened to be touring there at the same time at the end of the 70s.

'Great guy,' says Lillee. 'Terrific guy.'

LILLEE, Dennis Keith

Born: 18 July 1949, Subiaco (WA)

Bats: Right-handed
Bowls: Right-arm fast

First-Class Career

Debut: 1969–70 Western Australia v Queensland, Perth

M	Inn	NO	Runs	50	100	Ave	Ct	St	Runs	Wkts	Ave	5	10
198	241	70	2377	2	–	13.90	67	–	20695	882	23.46	50	13

Highest Score: 73* Australia v England, Lord's, 1975
Best Bowling: 8/29 Australians v World XI, Perth, 1971–72

Test Career

Debut: 1970–71 Australia v England, Adelaide

M	Inn	NO	Runs	50	100	Ave	Ct	St	Runs	Wkts	Ave	5	10
70	90	24	905	1	–	13.71	23	–	8493	355	23.92	23	7

Highest Score: 73* Australia v England, Lord's, 1975
Best Bowling: 7/83 Australia v West Indies, Melbourne, 1981–82

International Limited-Overs Career

Debut: 1972 Australia v England, Manchester

M	Inn	NO	Runs	50	100	Ave	Ct	St	Runs	Wkts	Ave	5
63	34	8	240	–	–	9.23	10	–	2145	103	20.83	1

Highest Score: 42* Australia v West Indies, Perth, 1981–82
Best Bowling: 5/34 Australia v Pakistan, Leeds, 1975

Oddly enough, Jagger reminds him a bit of Jack Nicholson, another guy he gets on well with. And, of course, there were many such enormous celebrities that the West Australian palled around with over the years. The only one to really knock back any friendliness on his part was the Queen, who once declined to give him an autograph.

But what the hey? All up, it hasn't been a bad sort of knock-about-the-world life for a man whose proud claim is that 'my mother was a shop assistant and my father was a truck driver'.

If Lillee is comfortable with his own fame, understands its nature, and is prepared to dole out infinitesimally small parts of it as part of a business, he nevertheless seems unimpressed with it on his own account.

'Mate, most of it is just a lot of crap,' he says. 'Most of that over-the-top stuff that was written about me. I mean what is there really to say? I'll tell you what would do me: "He was a good bowler who got stuck in and had a go." I wouldn't say I was any bowling genius, or was born with any fantastic talent, but I had a go and did my best. That's all there is to say really.'

He seems genuine in such off-hand dismissal of his own celebrity. When asked in passing, for example, as to exactly how many Tests he has played, he is not sure.

'Either 69 or 70 Tests, you'll have to look it up,' he says. And although he thinks he 'took about 355 wickets', again it quite genuinely doesn't seem to be a number that pops immediately into his mind.

Lillee returns to his table as the night is swept away with many dignitaries and one interloper going to the podium – everyone making mention of Lillee's august presence among them. At each glowing mention of his name, Lillee neither shifts uncomfortably in his seat nor smiles nor nods. Such reverential treatment seems to be neither here nor there for him – it's just there, the way it has been for the past 20 years or so.

By midnight the crowd is starting to thin, except for a cluster around the middle of the room. Sure enough, that is Lillee's table. Just a few more people wanting a bit of a chat, a bit of a slap on the back, maybe just a small autograph.

Catching my eye, Lillee winks and gives a cheerio wave as he signs someone's program, before helping himself to some more wine. Without anything you can put your finger on, he gives the impression of one for whom the night is still very, very young.

The short answer of what Lillee is up to these days? He's enjoying himself.

BILL O'REILLY

Tiger, Tiger, Burning Bright

by Greg Growden

I was a dopey, self-conscious kid from the bush. I got a lucky break. One minute I was driving a tractor around and around a paddock. The next, I was summoning the courage to front the most imposing of figures.

Everything had happened so quickly. After fair to middling marks in my final school exam, I knew I hadn't done enough to negotiate an easy escape route from the trappings of a small New South Wales country town. I was resigned to a life of frustration, watching the clouds, crops, cattle and feral cats. I felt like crap.

But an odd phone call, a frantic overnight trip to Sydney, the strangest of conversations with a man, too down-to-earth, surely, to be an editor, who only wanted to talk about Aussie Rules football in Mildura, and I was off the tractor, stuck behind a desk, and being convinced that, yes actually, you're a cadet journalist with the august publication, the *Sydney Morning Herald*.

A few months on, I was climbing the steps to the Sydney Cricket Ground press box on a sink-or-swim mission. The *Herald* didn't have a backup cricket writer, and someone had to be blooded. Why not that embarrassingly shy hayseed with the drip-dry wide-collared shirts who seemed so out of place in the office?

The final word of advice came from the last proper gentleman of Australian sporting journalism, the then *Herald* sports editor Les Wheeler, who said: 'Don't worry son. Just go up to Tiger when you get to the press box and introduce yourself. He won't bite.'

I was convinced Tiger would. A kid who lived for cricket, relying on Alan McGilvray on the radio waves, and Ray Robinson on the printed

---

Greg Growden is a sportswriter for the Sydney Morning Herald *for whom Bill O'Reilly was mentor and hero.*

page to overcome the boredom of the wide open spaces, I knew all about Tiger O'Reilly.

His Irish temper. His steely glare. His inability to suffer fools. The nickname which perfectly portrayed his character. His uncanny talent in spooking out batsmen with near standover tactics. His reputation as Australia's greatest bowler, and the best Bradman had ever faced. His bowling action which was so elongated and antagonistic.

And … and … and if he had intimidated the best during his glorious 27 Test career tallying 144 wickets at the admirable average of 22.59 – what would he do to an 18-year-old bumbling fool?

That day, it took me ages to climb the 93 concrete steps to the *Herald* position in the old concrete press box. There were several toilet stops, a couple of U-turns, one or two diversions, and eventually I was in my spot, perspiring, shaking with nervousness.

I couldn't see Tiger anywhere. Twenty minutes later he arrived, booming the words 'Greetings all' as he flung his hat onto the long bench that ran along the front of the press box, burrowing into his small briefcase to find his binoculars, and then for the next half-hour sat transfixed in his spot, eyes to the glasses, watching every movement out on the SCG wicket.

I tried at least six times to approach him. I couldn't. Eventually, I noticed a large figure by my left shoulder. A hand was outstretched. I took it.

'You the new man from the *Herald*? My name's Bill O'Reilly. Don't worry … I'll look after you.'

And look after me he did, from our first meeting in 1978 until his death in October 1992, he was basically my second father. He was my mate. My mentor.

We were linked straight away.

'I've been told you're like me. Rural stock. Where are you from?'

I replied that I had come from just down the road from where he was born in White Cliffs. A fairly long road, but still a connecting road.

'Coleambally, eh? Know it well,' Tiger said, as he patted me on the back, and pushed his seat next to mine. 'I was just down the road from Coleambally at Carrathool in the middle of a long drought a few years ago,' he explained. 'As soon as I started to speak at the cricket dinner, it began to pour, and all the cockies ran out the room in glee. They came back soaked and excited, all patting me on the back for breaking the drought.'

Tiger was obviously more impressed with that feat than any of his many mesmerising Test bowling spells. Over the next 15 cricket seasons, we talked often about the bush. The important perspectives learnt from living in the country, the courage of the farmer, the spirit of his wife. Henry Lawson, whom he had met as a young child, often bobbed up in the conversation. Tiger was always first and foremost a proud Australian bushie.

From this developed a rich friendship, in which he stressed to me bush basics like being your own man, always standing up for your convictions, and how crucial it was to be honest in life and on the written page. Even now, I still think at least once a day about Tiger's guidelines to a fulfilling life, to ensure I stay on the right path. I still compare people, good and bad, with him.

He remains my guiding light.

And I am most grateful that my real father met my second father. Indeed my father's most lingering memory of my wedding night was his gnarled farmer's hand shaking Tiger's gnarled spinning hand. Not surprisingly, the most poignant wedding shot is one of myself, my wife Elizabeth, Tiger, and his marvellous bride Molly, all holding hands, celebrating marriage, ours only a few minutes old, their's almost 60 years.

The second day of that Sheffield Shield match, I bounded up the stairs, hoping to glean as much information, advice and knowledge before the pair of us had to get serious and start thinking about what exactly we would write for the *Herald*. He, the distinctive, authoritative column. Me, the ball-by-ball babble.

That day, and countless others which followed, followed a basic, but always fascinating structure. In the first session, Tiger was the raconteur. He kept an eye on the on-field proceedings, but was in the mood to chat with anyone and everyone. A stream of visitors would pass by to talk to Tiger, and the conversations were always rivetting, especially as there was invariably a gathering of scribes, past players, cricketing identities around his seat, discussing every subject under the sun.

One day we may be gossiping around Bradman, or bringing up Jack Fingleton stories, or having bets on how many runs would be scored off that over, prompting the players to occasionally turn around and peer towards the top of the M. A. Noble Stand, wondering what all the cheering was about.

The next, we would be discussing Roman history, Australian politicians he had met, from Ming to Whitlam, discussing the merits of different Australian authors or musicians, the good and bad points of Catholicism or the ethics of his job as the *Herald*'s cricket columnist – which had earnt him the reputation of being not just Australia's premier cricketer, but also its best cricket writer.

He would point to the players gate in front of the Members' Stand, and bellow: 'Once they are through those gates, they're mine. I can write whatever I like about them. What they do the other side of that gate is no interest of mine.'

'But wouldn't you like to meet some of the current players?'

'Ha. I'd rather eat a hot meat pie.'

As Tiger could be so penetrative in his criticism, several players tried to approach him in the press box, in an attempt to get on his good side. It never worked. Tiger was civil, but the player soon got the idea he shouldn't cross that well-defined line, and left.

A well-known Test player was so upset with one of Tiger's columns that he wrote him a biting, anonymous letter. Tiger, with great mirth, sent it straight back to the Australian dressing room, circling all the spelling and grammatical mistakes – and giving it four marks out of ten.

Then the lunch break.

Often Tiger would be invited to a SCG Trust or a New South Wales Cricket Association lunch. More often than not he would brush them, and not go, explaining he did not want to attend a gathering of 'the wax works'.

Instead he preferred being with his journo mates, laughing his way through lunch, taking his time over a long schooner glass of beer.

The scribes loved him in their company, because Tiger was a man with absolutely no ego. Unlike so many sportsmen, who lose sight of where they have come from, Tiger always welcomed the common man. If Tiger was standing in the middle of a group of famous identities, which was often, he had no hesitation in inviting a lowly journalist over to join him in the round. The rest of the group would offer disparaging hand-over-the-mouth remarks, but never Tiger. He was a real man's man.

Often over lunch, we talked about alcohol. And Tiger would demand those at the table had a drink with him. It was important for cordial relationships, he explained. As told in his masterly autobiography, *Tiger*, he was once an abstainer, but through the advice of such luminaries as Stan McCabe and Vic Richardson he discovered that the only proper way to overcome loss of body moisture during a game was to 'shout ourselves a cold beer'.

We avidly followed his stringent advice.

Back to the press box for the second session, and Tiger would not be so animated. His stints peering through his binoculars would be longer. He would start mulling in his mind what exactly he would write.

But he could be distracted. Two of the most memorable moments involving Tiger in the press box occurred during this second session.

He was a close friend of McGilvray's, and, like a number of other close observers, had become disenchanted that the ABC broadcaster had turned into a notably grumpy figure in the years just before he had retired. McGilvray was a proud man, and not exactly complimentary about several of the younger commentators who were being groomed to take over his position.

So many of McGilvray's old colleagues were too scared to confront him about it, believing their head would be unnecessarily bitten off as well. Not Tiger.

One afternoon, he saw McGilvray walking across the back of the press box towards the ABC commentary area.

'McGilvray ... get here,' he yelled. 'I want a word with you.'

McGilvray sheepishly obeyed.

'Follow me.'

McGilvray followed O'Reilly to a far corner of the press box, and for the next 15 minutes was told how much of a 'silly old fool' he had been in being so acidic about all those around him. Every word said echoed around the box, especially Tiger's farewell of; 'Now pick up your act, McGilvray. You're better than that.'

'Yes Bill,' a timid McGilvray replied as he headed for safer climes.

As Tiger was as forthright in real life as he was on the written page, several notable Australian cricketing characters would sometimes sneak into the press box, to earwig.

One day, again in the second session, Tiger was off his long run around how he had no respect for several high-ranking cricketing identities. Unbeknown to Tiger, one of his prime targets was sitting above him, hiding himself in the second row.

Suddenly Tiger saw the identity's reflection in the glass in front of him.

'Bloody typical,' Tiger bellowed as he got to his feet, shooting a look at the burrowing official. 'Sitting there with your ears burning. Either show your face, or piss off.'

The official didn't just 'piss off' … he fled back towards the dressing rooms.

During the third session, Tiger went to work. Out of his briefcase would emerge a school exercise book, and for the next 40 minutes, he would be leaning over it, in the most beautiful handwriting giving his summation of the day's play, which usually had a plea somewhere about the importance of spin-bowling, that anyone who claimed to be a cricketing coach should be drowned at birth and limited-over cricket was a travesty of the game.

Then the book would be slammed shut. He would saunter across, with book in hand, to the *Herald* phone, and ring through his piece to an office copytaker.

This was always the highlight of the day, and people from all around would gather in the row behind Tiger to hear him describe his thoughts of the day as he slowly read his article to the copytaker, who was typing away back at the *Herald* office, before sending the article to the sports section.

Tiger had a marvellous relationship with the copytakers, who over the years had become scarred by being used and abused by flustered journalists, over-stressed by the demands of deadlines. But he would punctuate his recitation of the article, with jokes, enquiries about the copytaker's family and general observations of life.

But what made it so memorable was his rising inflexion, perfect grammar and Irish lilt as he read out his piece. He should have ventured onto the stage. It was cricket's version of Olivier reading

O'REILLY, William Joseph

Born: 20 December 1905, White Cliffs (NSW)
Died: 6 October 1992, Sutherland (NSW)

Bats: Right-handed
Bowls: Right-arm leg-break googly

First-Class Career

Debut: 1927–28 New South Wales v New Zealanders, Sydney

M	Inn	NO	Runs	50	100	Ave	Ct	St	Runs	Wkts	Ave	5	10
135	167	41	1655	1	–	13.13	65	–	12850	774	16.60	63	17

Highest Score: 56* Australia v South Africa, Johannesburg, 1935–36
Best Bowling: 9/38 Australia v Somerset, Taunton, 1934

Test Career

Debut: 1931–32 Australia v South Africa, Adelaide

M	Inn	NO	Runs	50	100	Ave	Ct	St	Runs	Wkts	Ave	5	10
27	39	7	410	1	–	12.81	7	–	3254	144	22.60	11	3

Highest Score: 56* Australia v South Africa, Johannesburg, 1935–36
Best Bowling: 7/54 Australia v England, Nottingham, 1934

Hamlet. It was so hypnotic, with all the journalists around simply wishing that they could write and speak like Tiger.

The story completed. He would whisper sweet-nothings to the copytaker, raise his right hand, and proclaim: 'Goodbye all. Enough is enough. I'm going home.'

And right until the end, he was so pugnacious, courageous, a young man in a crinkled body.

In 1987, Tiger eventually became a victim of those dreaded concrete steps – which he would always count as he made his way to his spot in the box.

90 … 91 … 92 … and then smash. Instead of looking down at the final step which led to his favourite seat that looked down the SCG wicket, he peered ahead to see who had won the toss.

Tiger crashed to the floor, causing great concern among the pressmen, particularly myself and colleague Phil Wilkins. After all, Tiger was in his prime at 81.

However, he immediately rose to his feet, dusted off his immaculate suit, and growled: 'Be buggered, that's not going to kill me. What's all the fuss? Damn it, be off with you all. I don't want the sympathy vote.'

Well, he will always get the sympathy vote from me. On the day Tiger died, Phil and I both cried long and hard for him, as did countless other scribes around Australia, when they heard that their great mate had left us. It jolted the system as we always thought he was immortal.

Well, he is immortal. We still think of him, talk to him, laugh with him, and love him. He made me.

ALLAN BORDER

AB & Me

by Graeme Blundell

In 1990, the film *Awakenings* was released to great fanfare and New York subways filled with the film's poster. There was Robin Williams standing on the shore while Robert De Niro, newly freed from the prison of his paralysis, stood on a rock in Long Island Sound, arms lifted above his head in triumph. In one subway, some wise guy drew a balloon coming out of De Niro's mouth, filled with the words: 'I sure am glad Harvey Keitel isn't in this movie with me.' And, in the 80s, Allan Border often reminded me of a shorter, Antipodean Keitel, that actor of piercing stare, earnest thoughtfulness and meaty physicality. But, while Harvey was, at that stage of his film career, seen as a dead weight, when it came to cricket, the Australian barracker emphatically wanted Allan Border first on any list.

Border's glamour was maybe less haloed – he was even more of an everyman kind of hero – but, like Keitel, it seemed he spent years in the desert, eking out his career in unsung roles before he cemented his place in our consciousness as a grumpy saviour, a grinder and grafter without parallel. From the start, he wore faint lines in his face, barely visible, like a 40 year old was wearing a 20 year old's skin.

The stocky wielder of the 2 lb 10 oz bat – when he started middling them, an onslaught was on the cards – was author of some of cricket's greatest escapes. In March 1984, against the West Indies at Port-of-Spain, he batted in two innings for 630 minutes and 198 in-your-face runs, defying waves of nausea, the surging Joel Garner, 535 hostile deliveries and a damp pitch, and did not lose his wicket. 'Border was simply Border, predictable, secure, unemotional, a battler from birth,'

Graeme Blundell is an actor, writer, director and biographer of Brett Whitely and Graham Kennedy whom the editor remembers bowling fizzing offies for Rest of the World against Kingower.

wrote columnist, and one-time player, Peter Roebuck. Every time he went out to bat you felt that his blood was stirring like an animal at the end of winter. He was on the move again, a win at the back of his mind, more often an action to stave off defeat, but heads would get kicked and he didn't care about leaving anybody puzzled afterwards about how he did it. Predictable, secure, unemotional. Like a soldier.

In the middle 80s to the 90s, he was also Australian cricket; it is hard, now, to even remember who else played in all those lost or drawn games in the middle 80s. There was the cavalier, neurotic Jones, the caricature Tasmanian Boon with the trademark moustache that seemed to engulf him like a casually tossed aside carpet off-cut had landed under his nose, Greg Ritchie with a bum like a panto dame and the lady's man Simon O'Donnell who seemed never able to step up.

For the barracker, it was a heart-breaking time during which, in my household at least, wine glasses were thrown at the television set, howls of dismay echoed through the deserted rooms and a wife grieved alone in her bed, evaluating grounds for divorce, every time we looked like losing. (The kids stayed with friends during the cricket season. It's no wonder I kept forgetting their names.) Often, I just watched the cricket in a kind of motionless vigil, knowing for certain that as soon as I moved a wicket would fall. Or if I coughed before the end of another antic-laden Merv Hughes over.

'You take it personally,' Susan, now my partner in these days of smug cricket success under the redoubtable Steve Waugh, and in happy marriage, says. 'When one of them fails it is as if he has personally let you down. He hasn't done it deliberately to upset *you*, you know.' But, in those dark days in the 80s, it *was* personal. The decade had begun in high spirits but, well before the curtain fell on its end, there was tragedy all around and the tumbrels began to gather in the moonlight. Many of us, who had started the decade full of hope, awaited the final cheque, the bailiff's knock. The film and television industries collapsed. The shop was closed, the fire sale prepared. Government auditors, fanatics of precision, went around closing theatres, singing their siren song of stability, salvation and solvency.

You couldn't even escape to the cricket. The game was too uncertain, too often disappointing. Too mediocre. And, goddamn it Susan, I *was* personally frustrated, discouraged and let down.

Cricketers lived out their dreams and I lived out mine with them. Any actor will tell you that all too often, our life is joyless, small-time heartbreaks and quiet desperation, rumour and grievance; much of it spent disguising depression. Time usually passes like a long ride in an underground tunnel. Words you once learned inscribed in some idiotic mental puzzle, run through your head to pass the time, and you wait, just ticking over, for a ray of sunshine. But cricket has always flowed in my blood, along with red wine, providing salvation and redemption. When it was on, the thermostat went up.

'Other men might inherit from their fathers a head for figures. A gold pocket watch all encrusted with the oxidised green of age, or an eternally astonished expression,' wrote Frederick Exley, in *A Fan's Notes*, the greatest book about the destiny of most of us – to sit on life's sidelines. From his father, Exley acquired 'this need to have my name whispered in reverential tones'. It was the same for me. I wanted to be spoken about the way people talked of my father when it came to cricket. And, when it came to life.

Jack Blundell was a great player, elegant and fluid like Ian Redpath, all loose wrists and naturally soft hands. He played district cricket before the war and then sub-district cricket for Port Melbourne, Balwyn and Ivanhoe with considerable success. He was not quite as good as his elder brother, Norm, who played district cricket for South Melbourne and for the Victorian State side. I was not as good as either, though, if I missed out on Norm's ability to miraculously spin the ball, I inherited, as he had, the same rather bulbous nose of their father. 'You used to say when you were little that you were going to be a great cricketer like your father,' my mother says. 'But, you never were.' Like Exley, it was my destiny to be part of the roar of the crowd, to sit in the stands with most men and acclaim others.

Cricket was the family's obsession. 'That's all the family ever talked about,' my mother says now. 'When we started to go out together before the war he talked about cricket and he talked about it for the rest of his life.' Jack died in 1963, when I was 16, of bowel cancer after years of chronic illness related to his war service in New Guinea, and for years had made regular medical visits to the Repatriation Hospital. They could do little for him apart from supplying, monthly, large glass jars of a thick white liquid. 'We all went to watch him play though, for years,' says my mother. 'You boys loved it but I used to moan about it every week. On the way home, every time, your father would say, "Well, it wasn't so bad was it?"'

My brother and I played with him in a church competition in the years before he died, for the Reservoir Baptist Church, where my one claim to fame was, one year, taking the most slips catches. My mother remembers him coming home on hot Saturday nights after the match and sitting outside our weatherboard house in working-class Reservoir, on a long wooden ramp that led up to the kitchen from the backyard. He was very sick. The cancer was killing him but no batsman in the Preston and Northcote Churches Competition would ever make as many runs again. 'Why do you do it?' she would ask him. 'Because I love it,' he always replied.

Allan Border obviously loved cricket too, but he lived with so much disappointment, was let down by his team-mates so often, that I wondered how on earth he could persevere emotionally. He attacked confrontation like a soldier. A lifetime in cricket was like rushing down a narrow corridor, eyes fixed to the front. He looked forwards, not backwards. He concentrated on what was ahead. That was how he did it.

What stays in the memory is a sense of an unsophisticated mind fumbling on the edge of simple and popular poetry. He made batting look as contagious and unsubtle as an old-time dance tune and, without apology, presented his performance as a genuinely vulgar art, like the acts of the great stage comedians. He had a gift for seeing an opening and going for it. They used to say in vaudeville, 'Get on, deliver and then, get off!' Though, there were times when they couldn't get Allan Robert Border off. He was first on the selector's list for a decade. 'Perhaps only a seam in the hands of Sarfraz Nawaz has been picked more often,' suggested Andrew Denton at a celebratory dinner in the 90s. 'Play until you need a runner with a walking frame.'

His approach was simple and direct. 'He is utterly practical,' wrote John Woodcock of the *Times*, 'not so much style as *modus operandi*.' Unsmilingly, he walked to the crease, always unshaven (as Ian Chappell was), often fully bearded, and usually in a crisis. Then, playing no percentages at all, he dropped ball after ball, dead-batted so that they fell at his small boots. His eye in (it was rarely out), he began to cut, straight drive with a punching, jolting shot of great power but no risk, and, cranking up a level, whip the ball to leg. This last shot he played according to one admirer 'with the sureness of touch of a chef tossing a pizza'.

He could hit the ball two hundred yards in four seconds. Playwright Tom Stoppard wrote that the cricket bat, while it looks like a wooden club, 'is actually several pieces of particular wood cunningly put together in a certain way so that the whole thing is sprung, like a dance floor.' Hit a cricket ball with this dance floor, whack, it travels. And, according to the playwright, 'all you've done is give it a knock like knocking the top off a bottle of stout, and it makes a noise like a trout taking a fly …' Or, it does when hit with the sense of travel Allan Border imparted to the red pill. The bat, no cudgel in his fine hands but an instrument of rhythm and grace and sweet sounds.

The 'Little General', as some called him when he, grudgingly, became captain in 1984 and the enigmatic Kim Hughes (a character surely written by Tom Stoppard) wept his way into the wings. He was curt and characteristically modest about what he did. 'I just play a couple of shots reasonably well and then become harder to get out.' Cricket was a war of attrition, he said, no point in fighting fire with fire; he just waited for them and scored off the bad balls. It seemed easy but he was thinking on several wavelengths at the same time. The way a great comedian plays a crowd, holding them, pausing, listening, waiting for the right moment, and then letting rip usually with the devastating effect of a stray spark in a box of fireworks. And, like great actors, he always had something in reserve. Laurence Olivier used to say: 'Never show your last 10 per cent' believing that the imagination of the audience would supply the rest.

Border engaged our sympathies so precisely because he never invited them. He was a god to actors, I think, because of his control and discipline and the way that, while he reflected – even personified – the average bloke, when overwhelmed he was never cut down to size the way we actors were, so heartlessly we felt, in our lives.

I loved watching him: the tense fuck-you look around the field, that evaluative Border deadpan stare, before he firmly ground his bat; the simplest of defensive prods with almost no back-lift, sometimes with the energy of a short left-hand jab; the left-hander's down-on-one-knee sweep for six; the way he chased in the field, single-mindedly running after the ball, no natural runner but his whiplash left arm a baseball pitcher's weapon. I have a sense of nostalgia for the way the television close-ups caught on the grizzled sunburnt face looking up for a moment at his audience, slightly puzzled, a hankering for the commonplace and the time when cricket was a simpler game for captains. As a bowler, he favoured underrated off-breaks, his limpid delivery laying five out of six balls on a nagging length, the ball more often than not rising less than the flight would suggest probable.

And he was humble, if grouchy. Like an actor who aspires to the weaknesses of a character rather than the strengths. Journalist Terry Smith, chatting with him at the SCG in 1991, found 'he gave a fairly convincing impression of being a prisoner in a privileged world'. You saw him interviewed and he was always guarded, edgy, bridling at the suggestion of any controversy. His tone was always melancholy and subdued, as if he was meditating on why destiny had brought him to this or that place, always phlegmatically trying to identify and vanquish demons. The self-deprecatory smile removed any need to be taken too seriously but you could see he was thinking hard. (Again, at these moments, he reminded me of Harvey Keitel. Stardom was a mystery to him. On a film set, a young girl diffidently asked Keitel who he was. Harvey pointed at the canvas chair that bore his name. 'That's you?' she asked, nonplussed. 'No, I'm here,' he said. 'That's my chair.')

Great artists make us feel proprietary about them. They invade us so strongly they become part of the way we look inwards and outwards; we can't approach new works without a sense that we are intimately involved. With Border, we shared his struggles, though we knew little of his life outside cricket, and an aura of distinction and achievement accompanied every pigeon-toed walk to the crease. His inheritance at the beginning was a bad team, which he carried for three scowling years. He knew about wallopings, and low clouds coming in on the wind that sent ominous spits with them, ironic intervals of sunshine when all he prayed for was rain, of empty honour in loss, but he stepped across the magic white-chalked line into legend.

When he came out, usually at five for twenty, no matter what the state of your life, sitting in front of the goggle box, beer in hand, you felt yourself becoming a part of popular response, an experience not just the sum of private excitements but mass feelings, mass enjoyment, the MCG roar, the SCG scorn and the WACA's glee as the Doctor came in. He had the ability to take us out of ourselves the way great actors can; he made us an excited audience. He got our hopes up and then was able to put over what he wanted of suffering and truth. For there were big themes as he carried a team on his bricklayer-like back.

BORDER, Allan Robert

Born: 27 July 1955, Cremorne (NSW)

Bats: Left-handed
Bowls: Slow left-arm orthodox

First-Class Career

Debut: 1976–77 New South Wales v Queensland, Sydney

M	Inn	NO	Runs	50	100	Ave	Ct	St	Runs	Wkts	Ave	5	10
385	625	97	27131	142	70	51.38	379	–	4161	106	39.25	3	1

Highest Score: 205 Australia v New Zealand, Adelaide, 1987–88
Best Bowling: 7/46 Australia v West Indies, Sydney, 1988–89

Test Career

Debut: 1978–79 Australia v England, Melbourne

M	Inn	NO	Runs	50	100	Ave	Ct	St	Runs	Wkts	Ave	5	10
156	265	44	11174	63	27	50.56	156	–	1525	39	39.10	2	1

Highest Score: 205 Australia v New Zealand, Adelaide, 1987–88
Best Bowling: 7/46 Australia v West Indies, Sydney, 1988–89

International Limited-Overs Career

Debut: 1978–79 Australia v England, Sydney

M	Inn	NO	Runs	50	100	Ave	Ct	St	Runs	Wkts	Ave	5
273	252	39	6524	39	3	30.63	127	–	2071	73	28.37	–

Highest Score: 127* Australia v West Indies, Sydney, 1984–85
Best Bowling: 3/20 Australia v West Indies, Madras, 1989–90

Graham Greene once complained – it was in the 30s – that there had never been a school of popular English 'bloods', the thriller. (Crime writing is another common actor's obsession.) 'We have been damned from the start by middle-class virtues, by gentlemen cracksmen and stolen plans and Mr Wu's,' Greene wrote. 'We have to go back farther than this, dive below the polite level, to something nearer to the common life.' And that is what Allan Border provided as his subject and spectacle, 'life nasty, brutish and short'. In the theatre of 80s cricket, he saved us from the sermon and the tract, the drawing-room comedy, the dolled-up classics and superannuated musicals. His performance was like blood on a garage floor, the scream of cars in pursuit, all the old excitements at their simplest and surefire level, and the power of physical excitement. There was an inherent poetic value in what he gave us, like there is in the best thrillers, last charges and fights to the death, heroic sacrifices and narrow escapes. And among the gunshots, the last stands and the flag waving there was a gentle and melancholy kind of poetry. There is redemption in failure, you learn from mistakes, there is strength in loss. There was always a catechism-like feeling to the cricket of the man his team-mates called 'AB'. For years, we watched him with weary, sometimes angry obstinacy try to breathe life into Australian cricket, like a paramedic, administering decade after decade of CPR to a patient he refuses to admit he has lost. He represented human values beneath the heroism and patriotism.

But by his testimonial season in 1993–94, he was like a pop star. Performing at Brisbane's ANZ Stadium, U2's legendary lead singer Bono spoke to him in Sydney on a comically oversized telephone. He asked the great batsman whether the British were responsible for inventing cricket as well as pub rock. 'Yeah, it was the Poms who invented the game but they've come a gutser since,' Border said, thinking he was talking to a 'Mr MacPhisto,' the pop star's comic alter ego, the crowd roaring with good-humoured laughter. 'What?' yelled Border. 'You're in a bar somewhere …' The crowd bayed for more and Bono ordered them to sing with him to congratulate the great batsman on his life in cricket. A crowd big enough to fill the SCG, many with tears in their eyes, sang, 'I Just Called to Say I Love You'.

I don't know if my Dad would have approved of the pop star accolade, as he was a purist of the old school. 'I always played the game the right way,' he used to say. Just like Allan Border. And my biggest regret when I think about my father is that Jack never saw Allan play.

EDITOR'S XII

S. Barnes, Petersham coll., who, bat-
... difficulties last Saturday...

SID BARNES

The Great Upsetter

by Rick Smith

Sid Barnes was a controversial character. He terrorised administrators, upset some colleagues and inspired others. His schemes and pranks made headlines, while his many acts of generosity were done in secrecy. In the end the administrators removed him from the Test team on the grounds that he was not a fit and proper person to represent his country. He neither forgot nor forgave their actions. Consumed by bitterness, the remainder of his life never provided fulfilment or satisfaction. It ended in depression and death by his own hand.

In this controversial life one thing is beyond doubt. Sid Barnes was a magnificent batsman, and with the elegant left-handed Arthur Morris he formed a partnership at the top of the Australian order which was a major factor in the success of Don Bradman's 'invincible' 1948 side. Sid had started his career as a dasher in the middle order, but became a rock-solid opener, one of the hardest in the game to dismiss. According to fellow Test player, Bill Brown, 'He was a very good opening batsman with his strength mainly on the back foot in the cut and hook. He had strong shoulders and wrists. All in all, he was very sound, with not a weakness that I could spot. He would drive more when he was younger and became less aggressive and more circumspect as he got older.'

Off-spinner Ian Johnson was a fellow 1948 tourist who played both with and against Sid, and he made the following assessment of his technique, 'He lifted the bat back towards third slip, but it was a very quick movement and swung almost in a circle until by the time the bowler was at the crease it was perfectly straight so he was able to come forward directly at the ball. He was an extremely hard batsman

Rick Smith was an A Grade cricketer in Tasmania, and is the author of Cricket's Enigma: the Sid Barnes Story.

to dismiss and when bowling to him you realised it. He was a very good player.'

Sadly, Sid's talent has never been given the recognition it deserves. First, it was interrupted by the Second World War, then cut short by the administrators. In addition, Sid removed himself from two series following the triumphant 1948 tour because of what he considered poor payments. So, in a first-class career, which lasted from 1936–37 to 1952–53, he played just 13 Tests, but in them he scored 1072 runs at 63.05. It is an average bettered only by Bradman of all Australians who have played a similar number of times.

Sid Barnes was born in the Sydney suburb of Annandale on 5 June 1916, where his mother had come following the death of her husband four months earlier. He had contracted typhoid on their Queensland property and had died an agonising death at the age of 26. Sid's mother was an extraordinary woman. She turned herself from a farmer's wife into a businesswoman, renting properties and operating a taxi service. Sid learned many things from his mother, principally the value of money. He revered her and would defer to her judgment throughout his life. But he was no mummy's boy. Jane Barnes would have no pampered brat. She brought him up to be tough and independent, to help those in need and to understand that money was the sign of success. His tailored suits and big American cars were visible proof of this.

In fact, money was the reason for Sid's introduction to cricket. Horrie Barnes was a good batsman and he offered to pay his little brother sixpence a time to bowl at him. Although he initially agreed because of the money, he found he enjoyed the game and it became a consuming passion. He developed into a free-scoring batsman, a capable wicketkeeper, a bowler of straightish leg-breaks and topspinners and a brave close to the wicket fieldsman.

As Sid's cricket career blossomed his confidence increased, and was to become legendary. Early in 1936–37 he was invited to the SCG nets to bowl at the England team. Angry at the amount of work he was asked to do he complained to New South Wales coach George Garnsey who told him to be grateful for the experience. 'Don't worry about that,' Sid shot back, 'I'll be playing against these fellows soon and I'm not showing them all my tricks.' Perhaps Garnsey's laughter died away later that season when Sid was chosen in the twelve for the tourists' return match against New South Wales. He carried the drinks, but made his debut in the next match, scoring 31 and 44, and was on his way.

As the youngest player on the 1938 England tour, Sid's plan was to match himself against Bradman. It might seem incredible arrogance, but he believed that only by matching it with the best would you get the most out of yourself. Confidence would never be in short supply at any stage in Sid's career.

What should have been a triumphant tour began in disaster when Sid injured his wrist during a solo early morning training session. Throughout his career he was obsessive about practice. As he was leaping up to catch a steel cable, his hand slipped and he fell. In England he was told that he would be out of action for the first half of the tour.

When he did finally begin to play he was quickly into form and was selected for the final Test. It was a rough introduction. Wally Hammond won the toss and England batted and batted, finally declaring at 7/903. With Bradman and Fingleton unable to bat, Australia crashed to defeat. Sid made 41 and 33 and could have been forgiven for thinking that Test cricket was a ruthless contest. If he played it tough in the future perhaps it was because he'd been set a perfect first example.

Either side of the war he was in astonishing form. Eight games in 1940–41 produced 1050 runs at 75 with six centuries scored in successive matches, and when cricket resumed in 1945 he picked up where he had left off with five hundreds in five games, followed by a successful end-of-season visit to New Zealand. In this form he could be seriously considered Australia's best batsman, Bradman included.

When the first postwar Ashes series took place in 1946–47 Bradman made the suggestion to Sid that he consider opening the batting, seeing a benefit in pairing him with Morris. Anything Bradman said was good enough for Sid and he moved to the top of the order. Realising the need for a good start he eliminated shots he considered risky, concentrated on playing predominantly off the back foot and making the most of his trademark square cut. He rarely ventured forward and his scoring rate slowed, but he became even harder to dismiss. They were a rare pairing: the poised, polished, elegant Morris and the gritty, pugnacious Barnes. Arthur Morris still believes Sid to be the best player of the new ball he's ever seen, while England's opening bowler Alec Bedser, who had the heartbreaking task of opposing the pair in two series, felt Sid was 'one of the best opening batsmen I ever faced and one of the most difficult to get out'.

The new opener was revealed in the second Test in Sydney. Batting in difficult conditions after the early loss of Morris, Sid made repeated appeals against the light, much to the disgust of the England team. When captain Wally Hammond complained to Sid, he was told, 'Shut up! You'll be out here for hours yet.' The appeal was granted and over the next two days Sid kept his word, adding 405 for the fifth wicket with Bradman before the Don was out for 234. Shortly afterwards Sid, on the same score, hit a tame catch to mid-on. When he reached the dressing room after 642 minutes at the crease he told George Tribe that the pair were now linked, 'Alphabetically it will be Barnes and Bradman. Me up there, number one.'

Controversy occurred in the next Test in Melbourne when Sid jumped a turnstile because he did not have his ticket and was refused entry by a gatekeeper. As he was the not out batsman it was vital he get into the ground. The official knew who he was, but refused to budge, so Sid felt he had no alternative. Stories spread that he had sold his ticket, but team-mate Ernie Toshack was with him and said he gave it to an old lady who wanted to see the Australians but couldn't get into the ground. When he refused to apologise for his actions Sid put another wedge between himself and administrators. He made 45 and 32, missed the fourth Test with fibrositis, then ended the series with 71 and 30.

That winter he went to England ostensibly for business, but he also managed to play quite a lot of cricket. In addition he made plenty of contacts who he would make full use of during the 1948 tour. There was one snub when he was refused a net at Lord's, a discourtesy to such a prominent Test cricketer. Sid was so incensed he vowed to return and make a century there.

Before that he had to make the team. He was late getting back to Australia and missed the first two Tests against the Indians. He regained his place for the third game, then scored 112 in the next in Adelaide. He and Bradman (201) added 236 for the second wicket, recreating visions of their partnership against England the year before.

After 33 in the final Test there was one further obstacle to overcome. Sid's wife Alison, whom he had married during the War, was staying in

Scotland with relatives. The Board of Control had strict rules prohibiting wives on tour and only the intervention of Bradman swayed the issue.

The 1948 tour was a triumphant progress. Early on the captain had planned an undefeated campaign. It almost never happened. Yorkshire nearly beat the Australians in a low-scoring match. Neither Barnes or Bradman played in that game, and from that moment the captain decided that either himself or Sid or both would play in every game. No batsman could earn a finer compliment, especially when one considers that Arthur Morris, Lindsay Hassett, Keith Miller, Bill Brown and Neil Harvey were some of the others available. Apart from a couple of minor games against non-first-class opposition and the universities, Bradman kept to his plan.

Sid played in four of the five Tests, making major contributions in three of them. In the first game at Trent Bridge he made 62 and 64 not out. The second innings was important as Australia needed 98 to win, but the weather was threatening and Sid went on the attack to get the runs as quickly as possible.

So he came to Lord's eager to pay back the slight of the previous year. So keen was he that he bet £8 on himself at 15–1 to score a century. He was out for a duck in the first innings and looked a long way from collecting. However, he made sure of his money and his revenge with 141 in the second innings. On scoring the hundredth run he ran down the pitch eyes blazing with triumph.

During the tour Sid had been fielding very close on the leg side. The position attracted criticism as being unfair and intimidatory. It was certainly successful. England captain Norman Yardley admitted his batsmen were unsettled. It was also dangerous without the protection of helmets and shin guards. But Sid had courage. When he was struck by a pull shot from Cyril Washbrook the crowd cheered. Sid calmly moved one step closer. He would never be intimidated.

However, his luck ran out in the third Test at Old Trafford when he failed to notice that Ian Johnson's slow, flighty off breaks had replaced the accurate left armers of Ernie Toshack. Sid was struck in the ribs by a huge blow from Dick Pollard and collapsed in agony. He was carried off by four policemen as no stretcher could be found, and when he reached the dressing room he emerged from his suffering long enough to see whether Bill Brown, who was operating the movie camera, had got the pictures. When these were later screened to packed houses, Sid would comment to the audience that the blow would have killed a lesser man.

After spending the night in hospital he made a brave effort to bat, but collapsed after 20 minutes at the crease. He took no further part in that drawn game, or the next Test at Headingley when Australia produced an astonishing and successful run-chase.

Sid returned for the fifth Test at The Oval. After England was dismissed for just 52, he and Morris added 117 for the first wicket before Sid was dismissed for 61. With any chance of an opposition comeback squashed, he grabbed his camera and rushed onto the balcony to film Bradman's final Test innings. When his skipper was bowled second ball for nought Sid joined him in the rooms. As they were both taking off their pads he informed Bradman that he had his entire innings on film. Who else would have taken such a liberty? The irony was that it was Sid's last Test innings, too.

Cricket was not the only item on the agenda in England. Sid's various business deals amused and astonished his team-mates. So much was happening that his room-mate asked to change rooms to get some sleep. Although the items were many and varied, English cloth formed the greater part as Sid could see a market for it in postwar Australia.

In addition to the trading he developed the infamous autograph stamp to save time signing, and when a calendar was produced of the team Sid's picture was missing. He rejected the offer of £5, saying that £50 would be more like it.

When the team returned to Australia he left the boat in Melbourne because he heard rumours that customs officials were waiting for him in Sydney. The movies he made played to packed houses, earning money for charities and no doubt a quid or two for Sid. However, some of his comments about administrators during the screenings offended those gentlemen, further colouring their opinion of him.

Cricket then took a back seat to family and business. He made himself unavailable for the 1949–50 tour of South Africa, citing 'peanut payments' and then covered the 1950–51 Ashes series as a journalist. The retirement of Bradman, whom he idolised, and the failure to find a satisfactory partner for Morris left Australia with a weak top order, so Sid decided to make a comeback in 1951–52. After scoring 107 against Victoria he appeared a certainty for the Adelaide Test against the West Indies. The selectors picked him, but the Board refused to have him, citing non-cricketing reasons. Rumours abounded, and under intense pressure Sid went out and scored another century for New South Wales. Considering the circumstances, this might have been his finest innings.

No reasons for the Board's actions were forthcoming, but a letter appearing in the *Sydney Morning Herald* supporting the Board gave Sid the chance to launch a defamation action against the writer and call Board members as witnesses. What emerged was a series of petty, almost vindictive reasons for his exclusion. The turnstile incident was mentioned, as was filming the King at Lord's in 1948 (Sid had the monarch's permission to do this) and he apparently took Ernie Toshack 20 metres away to play tennis while he was twelfth man. Sid won the case and decided to have one last attempt to win back his Test place in 1952–53. With the South Africans touring and a series in England to follow, there was plenty to play for.

The form was good enough as he made 43 and 79 not out against the tourists, playing their best bowler, off-spinner Hugh Tayfield, with ease. When he followed this with 152 against Victoria, it seemed he must be picked. He wasn't and Sid discovered you could win a battle and lose a war. Realising his Test career was over he gave up.

He volunteered to be twelfth man in Adelaide for New South Wales against South Australia and staged a famous stunt by delivering the drinks in a double-breasted suit, carrying a radio and other objects. He passed out cigars, sprayed the players with scent and tried to comb Keith Miller's hair. Unfortunately, the joke went on too long and Sid walked off to an embarrassed silence. His first-class career ended soon afterwards.

Sid spent the remainder of his life pursuing various business and property ventures and working as a journalist. His column, 'Like it or Lump it', then 'Take it or Leave it', was popular with readers who couldn't get enough of his acid-tipped views. As in his playing days, respect had to be earned and those who did could be assured of support, but he was merciless to others. Administrators were particular targets, but players were often on the receiving end. When skipper Ian Johnson had a run of poor form in England in 1956 Sid took to calling him 'Australia's non-playing captain'.

The last five years of his life were blighted by depression which put enormous strain on his family and other relationships. His life ended from an overdose of pills on 16 December 1973. Whether this was deliberate or not has never been determined. He was 57.

Some sportsmen retire in comfort to mull over past glories, some are consumed by bitterness at the treatment they received. When Sid Barnes is discussed the talk goes along the lines of 'Great player, but …' Let's lose the 'but'. Sid Barnes was a great player. End of story.

BARNES, Sidney George
Born: 5 June 1916, Annandale (NSW)
Died: 16 December 1973, Collaroy (NSW)

Bats: Right-handed
Bowls: Right-arm leg-break googly

First-Class Career
Debut: 1936–37 New South Wales v South Australia, Sydney

M	Inn	NO	Runs	50	100	Ave	Ct	St	Runs	Wkts	Ave	5	10
110	164	10	8333	37	26	54.11	80	4	1836	57	32.21	–	–

Highest Score: 234 Australia v England, Sydney, 1946–47
Best Bowling: 3/0 Australians v Canterbury, Christchurch, 1945–46

Test Career
Debut: 1938 Australia v England, The Oval

M	Inn	NO	Runs	50	100	Ave	Ct	St	Runs	Wkts	Ave	5	10
13	19	2	1072	5	3	63.06	14	–	218	4	54.50	–	–

Highest Score: 234 Australia v England, Sydney, 1946–47
Best Bowling: 2/25 Australia v India, Melbourne, 1947–48

VICTOR TRUMPER

The National Treasure

by Ross McMullin

Victor Trumper! The legendary name brings to mind the stirring Beldam photograph, that memorable image of Trumper in full flight executing a glorious straight drive. Uninhibited stride towards the ball, bat poised at the top of a high backlift, the undersized cap they used to wear (that looked so peculiar when donned by present-day successors for a commemorative session recently) perched above the handsome face, eyes focused intently on the ball – which is, you sense, about to be dispatched afar with rare power as well as enchanting grace. Surely the most famous cricket photograph of all, it not only provides a graphic glimpse of what was so special about Trumper, it's also the classic evocation of an era, cricket's 'golden age', which Trumper embodied more than anyone else.

Trumper's legendary status derives not only from his run-making. Just as important was the way he made them. He played all the shots with stylish flair and invented new ones of his own, most notably the 'dog-shot', his remarkable way of dealing with spearing yorkers by lifting his right (back) foot and whipping the ball away behind square on the on-side. With exceptional hand-eye coordination, nimble footwork and a computer-like capacity to discern line and length rapidly, he could reduce bowlers to hapless despair with his unique ability to transform the delivery on its way towards him into a length that suited the shot he wanted to play. No batsman was more dangerous in adverse batting conditions. And these dashing strokes were played with a full, fluent swing of the bat, with elevated backlift and flowing follow-through. Attempting to gauge the quality of

---

Ross McMullin is a historian and author of a forthcoming biography of World War I hero, 'Pompey' Elliott. He is a stylish bat and measly medium pacer for Melbourne annual social teams.

Trumper's batsmanship via mere averages and statistics, Neville Cardus concluded, would be like trying to judge 'the essential quality of a composition by Mozart by adding up the notes'. Trumper remains, as historian Bede Nairn has written, 'cricket's supreme batting stylist, timeless and unassailable in his symmetry of artistry and elegance'.

His temperament also shaped the legend. Modest, unassuming and generous, he frequently threw his wicket away after making a century to give team-mates a turn at the crease. During the 1902 tour of England he made 11 centuries, yet his highest score was only 128. Team-mates raved about his kind, selfless nature. Frank Iredale was one:

To be near him seemed to me to be an honour … His loving nature made many friends. I never knew anybody who practised self-effacement as much as he did … No work was too hard for him and if he did more than his share no word passed his lips. If there was a bad seat on a train, he was in it. If the sleeping compartment happened to be over the wheels, one could always be sure that Victor would change his place to take it. On the steamer going to England he was always helping somebody.

Trumper was cavalier with money and possessions – cricket gear in particular. Unlike other batsmen, he wasn't fussy about bats, giving plenty away, and he tended to shun such flash accoutrements as rubber grips on the bat handle and batting gloves. His obliging, amiable nature did not preclude a firm stand on matters of principle; he displayed steely solidarity in the 1912 dispute with the Board of Control, refusing with five senior colleagues to tour England. Trumper's personality was as attractive as his enthralling batsmanship.

Born in Sydney in 1877, Trumper grew up in Surry Hills and Paddington. An older schoolmate, M. A. Noble, was to become his Australian captain. They came to cricketing prominence together with impressive innings for a New South Wales 'juniors' team against Stoddart's English tourists in December 1894. Trumper was promoted into the senior New South Wales side the following month, but cheap dismissals in his first two matches seemed to confirm the stern appraisals of some observers that the young newcomer was too flashy. Trumper did not represent New South Wales again for two years.

It was not until 1898–99 that he really made his mark at intercolonial level. A double century against New Zealand and an astonishing 292 not out – including a century before lunch – against Tasmania brought him into calculations for the 1899 tour of England. Noble, by now a Test regular, advocated Trumper's inclusion, but the majority view on the selection committee was that Trumper had been too inconsistent and other emerging players had better credentials. The team was announced without him. Before it sailed, however, an influential Victorian watched Trumper score 260 not out in a Sydney grade match and returned to Melbourne in raptures about the prodigious batting genius he had seen; then, in a practice match for the departing tourists, Trumper made a brilliant 75 for the Rest of Australia in such compelling style that he was hastily added to the touring party.

Selected for the first Test at Trent Bridge, Trumper missed out with a duck and 11 (oddly, he had scored 11 and 0 in his initial first-class match), but was retained for the second Test at Lord's. The faith his senior colleagues displayed in his undoubted promise was vindicated. Australia was 4/189 when 21-year-old Trumper strode to the wicket past his old friend Noble (just dismissed for a solid 54) and joined Clem Hill. Both batsmen ended up with 135, Trumper remaining not out. After Hill's dismissal Trumper and the tail put on 150 runs; Trumper made two-thirds of them in a superb chanceless innings, paving the way for a notable victory in that Test and  series (each of the other four matches in this era of three-day Tests was drawn). Later in the tour, Trumper plundered the Sussex attack on his way to the first triple century by any Australian in England.

His international career launched, Trumper was only moderately successful in Australia's 4–1 triumph over the visiting Englishmen in 1901–02, but drained everyone of superlatives during his wonderful return to England in 1902. It was a notoriously wet 'summer', pitches were uncovered and English cricket had never been stronger. For batsmen, the home side could choose from such hallowed names as McLaren, C. B. Fry, Ranjitsinhji, F. S. Jackson, Abel, J. T. Tyldesley, Hayward, Palairet and the legendary hitter Jessop; Lilley was a distinguished 'keeper-batsman and the outstanding attack Trumper had to contend with covered every contingency with Lockwood, Hirst, Braund and Rhodes (all capable batsmen as well).

Still, Trumper dominated that sodden season with batsmanship of incomparable brilliance and artistry. 'On every sort of wicket, against every type of bowling, Trumper entranced the eye, inspired his side, demoralised his enemies and made run-getting appear the easiest thing in the world,' raved renowned cricket historian Harry Altham. Even Wisden, normally a model of sober restraint, went into rhapsodies about batting 'so brilliant and so consistent' – and 'just as dazzling' after a night's rain as on hard dry pitches – that it reduced England's finest bowlers 'to the level of the village green … The way in which he took good-length balls off the middle stump and sent them to the boundary had to be seen to be believed'.

Trumper's most memorable 1902 innings came in the Fourth Test at Old Trafford, one of the most exciting Ashes encounters ever. Australia batted first on yet another wet wicket; the outfield was heavy and very slow, even muddy in places. McLaren told his bowlers to keep things tight early on so that when the pitch dried out later and batting became formidable, England would have their opponents on toast. Trumper confounded these plans with a breathtaking counter-attack. He unleashed an extraordinary array of captivating strokes. No bowler could restrain him, not even the miserly Rhodes; Trumper danced forward and lofted him over the sight-screen. Despite the wet pitch, slow outfield and well-credentialled attack, he was playing the most wonderful innings that had ever been seen in Test cricket. At lunch Australia was 1/173 – so much for keeping things tight – and Trumper's chanceless 103 not out was the first century before lunch in a Test. Perhaps unsettled by the stirring reaction from crowd and colleagues during the lunch break, Trumper was dismissed by Rhodes soon afterwards. His team-mates struggled on the difficult pitch and Australia did not reach 300, but at stumps England was 5/70. Plenty of twists and turns lay ahead, but the thrilling win Australia eventually achieved (which decided the series) had been set up by Trumper's sublime wizardry.

In the next Ashes series (Australia 1903–04), no batsman in either team had a better aggregate or average than Trumper. When Australia was caught on a lethal sticky wicket in Melbourne and dismissed for 122 (Rhodes, unchanged, 7/56), Trumper – first in and last out, caught at long off – contributed more than half with an exhilarating 74; no one else managed more than 18. His 185 not out at Sydney was a masterpiece. Absorbed in his sporting goods shop in the morning, he suddenly realised he was running late. Hastily grabbing a new bat from the rack, he caught a taxi to the SCG just in time to produce another classic. Len Braund tried to tie him down, to no avail: 'It didn't matter where I pitched the ball, Trumper could hit it into three different places in the field.' His 'footwork was perfection', affirmed Lilley, who described this innings as the most brilliant he ever saw from his wicketkeeping vantage point. Afterwards a Trumper admirer visited the shop and asked whether he could buy a bat his hero had used; Trumper obligingly observed that the one he made the 185 with was available. Thrilled, the inquirer nervously asked how much it would cost. It had been worth two pounds five shillings, Trumper replied, but now it was second-hand he could have it for a pound. This encounter typified the generous, unworldly approach that ensured Trumper would struggle in small business; he didn't have an avaricious bone in his body. It was also in 1903 that he made 335 in only three hours in a grade fixture, a virtuoso display that enraptured all who saw it (including a future premier whose bowls match on a nearby green was abandoned after being frequently interrupted by the bombardment Trumper created as he regularly cleared the boundary).

Trumper in his prime had no peer. Contemporaries, whether team-mates or opponents, said so repeatedly. Yorkshire all-rounder George Hirst, asked by his England captain where he wanted the fielders placed, was fatalistic: 'It doesn't much matter … Victor will still do as 'e likes'. When Victorian wicketkeeper Elliott Monfries first scrutinised Trumper's free-flowing style from behind the stumps, he thought 'If you do that again and the ball does anything you'll get yourself out. But when the ball did do anything it seemed to make no difference whatever, as it found itself plumb in the centre of the bat and sailing out into the field.' Noble's veneration for Trumper's genius never wavered. 'You had to be in with him to realise his ability to the full,' Noble wrote. 'The most difficult and dangerous strokes were made with consummate ease.' Australian 'keeper Hanson Carter was among many admirers who would not tolerate anyone being compared to Trumper. 'If you want to try and classify the great batsmen,' he said, 'put Victor Trumper way up there – on his own – and then you can begin to talk about the rest.' Another team-mate who wouldn't hear of anyone being in the same street as his revered hero was Charlie Macartney, who emulated Trumper's attacking approach and duplicated the rare accomplishment of an Ashes Test century before lunch.

Present at Headingley when Macartney became the second batsman to achieve that feat was Arthur Mailey, another Trumper devotee. Late in Trumper's career Mailey, then an up-and-coming wrist-spinner, had played against his hero in a Sydney grade match. His account of their encounter remains one of the finest cricket stories ever written. Mailey vividly describes how the 'unbelievable, fantastic' prospect of playing on the same cricket pitch as the 'ethereal and godlike' idol in the photo on his bedroom wall sent Mailey into such a state that he 'behaved like a half-wit'. 'In my wildest dreams I never thought I would even speak to Trumper – let alone play against him,' and 'I think I was partly out of my mind.'

All he wanted was the chance to bowl to his hero. Mailey's father, captain and the spinner himself all expected that if this happened he would be carted, but Mailey didn't care. His main worry was that something untoward – illness, war, an earthquake – might intervene to prevent Trumper from playing. When Mailey bowled to Trumper his first ball was a nervous blur, but he was pleased with its successor. As it curved through the air prior to spinning sharply away Mailey felt convinced it was the most perfect leg-break he could deliver. Trumper, 'poised like a panther', propelled it to the boundary with a classical cover-drive – 'the most beautiful shot I have ever seen', Mailey declared. A few balls later Mailey tried a wrong-un, which also came out satisfyingly. Trumper was deceived in flight, and stumped. 'Too good for me,' he said smilingly to the bowler as he departed. An emotional swirl swamped Mailey: 'There was no triumph in me as I watched the receding figure. I felt like a boy who had killed a dove.'

Trumper's health was never robust. Increasingly and insidiously troubled by illness, his brilliance became spasmodic. There were glory days still. Against the visiting South Africans in 1910–11 he blazed in successive Tests 159 in under three hours and, a week later, 214 not out at Adelaide; early in 1914, touring New Zealand with an Australian side, he conjured one last epic, an extraordinary 293 in only three hours after going in third last! By then, however, he was in the grim grip of Bright's disease. As the great madness in Europe erupted that was to blight a generation and shatter so much of what was special about the pre-1914 era, cricket's golden age very much included, it was poignantly symbolic that the dashing romantic paragon of that era was fatally stricken. By April 1915, when his countrymen landed at Gallipoli and the casualty toll began to surge, Trumper was confined to his sick-bed. Two months later, with many Australians painfully sensing that things could never be the same again, news of the death of Victor Trumper at the age of 37 was distressing confirmation. The

TRUMPER, Victor Thomas
Born: 2 November 1877, Sydney (NSW)
Died: 28 June 1915, Darlinghurst (NSW)

Bats: Right-handed
Bowls: Right-arm medium

First-Class Career
Debut: 1898–89 New South Wales v South Australia, Adelaide

M	Inn	NO	Runs	50	100	Ave	Ct	St	Runs	Wkts	Ave	5	10
255	401	21	16939	87	42	44.57	171	–	2031	64	31.73	2	–

Highest Score: 300* Australians v Sussex, Hove, 1899
Best Bowling: 5/19 Australians v Cambridge University, Cambridge, 1902

Test Career
Debut: 1899 Australia v England, Nottingham

M	Inn	NO	Runs	50	100	Ave	Ct	St	Runs	Wkts	Ave	5	10
48	89	8	3163	13	8	39.05	31	–	317	8	39.63	–	–

Highest Score: 214* Australia v South Africa, Adelaide, 1910–11
Best Bowling: 3/60 Australia v South Africa, Johannesburg, 1902–03

funeral, at this especially emotional time, was a memorable event; huge crowds blocked Sydney streets for hours.

The adoration Trumper inspired was tenaciously maintained. Not even Bradman's amazing record-breaking feats could disturb it; if anything, they reinforced it. Aficionados would insist that Bradman was a mere technician, an automaton, whereas Victor Trumper was an artist. Three years after Trumper's death, with the terrible Great War still raging in Europe, Charles Bean, Australia's official war correspondent and a fervent nationalist of admirable idealism, was devastated to learn that his hero Brudenell White, the senior staff officer he regarded as the brilliant, charming, self-effacing and irreplaceable architect of Australia's military force, had been promoted out of the Australian army. To Bean, this departure was a calamity. He expressed his sense of desolation very simply. 'We have lost our Trumper,' he lamented. Even decades after Trumper's death grizzled, hard-boiled old-timers would wax lyrical with shining eyes as they reminisced wistfully about him.

Although Trumper's legendary status derives from the way he batted (and lived his life) as much as the runs he scored – quality as well as quantity – it is nevertheless true that the quantity was most impressive. Batting on uncovered pitches, troubled by ill-health for much of his career, his record uninflated by pedestrian compilations on featherbed pitches against limited attacks of emerging Test nations – of all the great batsmen in the history of the game, none was less motivated or affected by statistics than Victor Trumper – his career Test average of 39 is, compared to other golden age luminaries, first-rate. He should surely have been included in the ACB Australian team of the twentieth century. In this notional national team Trumper would have been superbly suited to a middle-order Doug Walters-type role, though he could open or bat anywhere when quick runs or a counter-attack were required; if any of his contemporaries could have been participants in selecting it he would certainly have been among the first chosen. When an international panel of 100 experts voted to select Wisden's five cricketers of the century – that is, from all countries – only six Australians were awarded more votes than Trumper.

Victor Trumper was a marvel, a genuine national treasure who should never be forgotten.

STAN McCABE

An Excitement to the Eye

by Phillip Derriman

It is almost 60 years since Stan McCabe last appeared in a first-class match, which means that, as a batsman, he is now at the outer limit of first-hand recollection. There aren't many old cricketers left who played with or against him at the top level and are able to talk about what they saw, but there are a few, and for that we can be thankful, because above all McCabe was a cricketers' cricketer. More than any other player you can think of (with the possible exception of Arthur Morris), McCabe's reputation is based primarily on the regard which fellow players had for his ability. When you speak to old cricketers about him, and I have spoken to many over the years, you find that, almost universally, they consider him very special: an individual who was both enormously gifted as a cricketer and appealing as a personality. These two qualities are not often found in one person, but clearly they were both present in McCabe.

Bill O'Reilly said this about him in an unreported speech that he made at a dinner in Sydney in 1986, six years before his own death and 18 years after McCabe's: 'Stan McCabe played his cricket exactly the way I would have liked to have played mine. If there was a buccaneering shot to play that would last in your memory forever, the man to play it was McCabe. Don Bradman did everything absolutely dead right. He was aggressive, he would smash the opposition to smithereens, but never at any stage while he was doing it to you would you feel beholden to him. But if Stan McCabe hit you through the covers for four, you'd almost feel like going up and saying, "Thanks, Stan. That was very nice of you".'

Phillip Derriman is a Sydney journalist and cricket writer, and is the author of The Grand Old Ground, Bodyline, True to the Blue *and co-editor of the anthology* Bat & Pad.

O'Reilly was unashamedly a McCabe admirer (he loved him, it seemed, almost as a brother), yet the kind of view he expressed about McCabe here was often expressed by others. McCabe was affable, easy-going and unpretentious. The worst anyone said about him was that he drank too much, especially in later years. Somehow, his endearing personality seemed to fuse with his batting, a fact which makes it difficult to assess him purely as a player. How do you separate the man from the batsman, when the two were always seen as one? Was he as great a player as they said he was? Or was he really just a nice guy with a nice batting style?

His statistics alone show he was more than that. McCabe averaged 49.38 in all first-class matches and 48.21 in Tests, a record which probably entitles him to be rated ahead of all other Australian batsmen in the 1930s other than Bradman. Bill Ponsford finished with a Test average fractionally higher than McCabe's, 48.22, but Ponsford certainly did not make the impact in the Australian batting line-up that McCabe made, and it must also be remembered that Ponsford was dropped in the most famous of all 1930s Test series, the Bodyline Tests of 1932–33. What the records do not show (the figures are probably available, but they have yet to be extracted) is how rapidly McCabe scored. This is a pity, because the speed of McCabe's runmaking was a feature of his batting. We do know that he scored faster than Bradman in England in 1930, without, of course, making nearly as many runs. In the 1930 Tests, Bradman scored at the rate of 3.7 runs per six balls faced and McCabe at 4.1. The fact that 20-year-old McCabe scored as fast as this in his first Test series says something about his approach to the game.

Like most other great cricketers from the country, McCabe was a town boy, not a farmer's son. His father was the barber at Grenfell, the central-west New South Wales town where Stan was born on 16 July 1910. Stan was one of four cricket-playing brothers, one of whom, Les, showed a special flair for the game, too, although we need not take too seriously the suggestion that Les was actually the more talented of the two. In 1924, aged 13, Stan was awarded a scholarship at St Joseph's College at Hunters Hill in Sydney, the celebrated GPS boarding school known to all as Joeys. He made the school's first XI early the following year, an unusual feat for a 14-year-old, and went on to become the school's batting star before he left at the end of 1926.

Ordinarily, McCabe's presence at a GPS school might have set his cricket back, for, in Sydney at least, GPS schools have had a very poor record at producing top players, the likely explanation being that boys at these schools play most of their cricket with other boys until the age of 18. But McCabe left school at 16, so he was too young to be disadvantaged. In any case, Bradman seemed to think McCabe's time at Joeys had actually helped his game. 'He, like myself, was a country lad but his cricket was all polish and grace,' Bradman wrote, 'for he came to the city early and gained experience on turf before his style was set.'

Talent-scouted by E. A. 'Chappie' Dwyer, who took teams to Grenfell in 1926–27 and again in 1927–28, McCabe was brought to Sydney and progressed so rapidly in colts and grade cricket that before 1928 was over he had made his first-class debut for New South Wales. He was just 18 at the time, and, clearly, his talent stood out like a flashing light. Then, just over a year later, another astonishing promotion: he was included in the Australian team that toured England in 1930. Again, McCabe did not *earn* his selection, for at that time he had not scored a single first-class century. The selectors could see his class and obviously considered him too bright a prospect to resist. McCabe played in the first Test, beginning inauspiciously with scores of four and 49. From then until he retired, he was not once omitted from an Australian team.

McCabe was a shortish man, 173 cm tall, who looked even shorter as he grew older and put on weight. At the time of the Bodyline Tests in 1932–33, he was a slim and lithe 65 kg, but by the time he retired he had become plumpish and moon-faced.

In the absence of good newsreel footage which might explain to us now why he was so admired, his batting style is not easy to categorise. By all accounts, he was not an *elegant* batsman in the old sense of that word. As Arthur Morris observes: 'He was no Kippax.' Yet he obviously batted with an ease and a fluency that excited the eye. Jack Fingleton wrote that McCabe played his shots with less effort than any batsman he ever saw.

I asked Arthur Morris to name a present-day batsman who reminded him of McCabe. For instance, might Mark Waugh be a rough approximation of him, albeit one who is taller and more sedate? Morris replied that no current batsman reminded him of McCabe, because no current batsman played predominantly off the back foot as McCabe did. 'He was completely a back-foot player,' Morris says. 'I don't think I ever saw him go up [the pitch]. Some present-day batsmen can play back and forward like Steve Waugh, but, no, there's no powerful hitter off the back foot like McCabe. I suppose the last of them was Norm O'Neill, and he ended up on the front foot because everybody kept giving him advice.

'McCabe was probably one of the fastest-scoring batsmen in the world, which makes it sound so silly when people say someone's been forced onto the back foot, as if that was defensive. Most of the really quick-scoring batsmen I've seen have been back-foot players. He was off the back foot and, boy, could he crunch them! I fielded when he got a hundred against O'Reilly, St George versus Mosman, and, God, he hit that ball like a cracker. I fielded at gully and the balls kept going past me, faster and faster. A tremendously powerful player. He played close to the body, over the top of the ball all the time. As I say, powerful, very powerful.'

McCabe scored only six centuries in his 62 Test innings, not a particularly high conversion rate for a batsman of his standing. Ponsford, by comparison, scored seven in 48. McCabe did get to 50 in just over 30 per cent of his innings (a higher rate than Ponsford), from which we may deduce that he lacked either the appetite for making big scores or the mental application needed to make them. Jack Fingleton once noted: 'I never met a batsman who cared less about centuries.' On the other hand, it happens that three of McCabe's six centuries were momentous innings, which in his own day came to be regarded as classics. One was his 187 not out against England in the first Bodyline Test of 1932–33; the second was his 189 not out against South Africa at Johannesburg in 1935–36; and the third was his 232 at Nottingham in the first Ashes Test of 1938. They are the three great landmarks of his career.

Fingleton, who played in all three matches, rated the Bodyline innings the best of the three, given the odds that were loaded against him. It must be appreciated that McCabe then was by no means the big-name player he later became. He was just 22 years old, and although this was his fourth Test series he was still a junior member of the team who was probably lucky to have held his place in the side as long as he had. This was his 20th Test innings, and he had yet to make a Test century. His parents had come from Grenfell for the match, and he sat with them, probably in front of the Members' Pavilion, until it was his turn to pad up. Before leaving, he said to his father, 'If I happen to get hit out there, keep Mum from jumping the fence.'

By now, the Englishmen's bowling tactics were well known, and McCabe had obviously worked out his own way to deal with them. He would attack the fast, short-pitched bowling with his favourite shot, the hook, and take a chance on not getting caught in the bodyline leg-side trap. McCabe was a fierce hooker, but he did not have Bradman's gift of keeping the ball down. Indeed, A. G. Moyes cited McCabe's tendency to hook in the air as one of the flaws in his technique. The odds were certainly against him, but luck was on his side. McCabe played hooks and pulls with abandon, but somehow none went to hand. The scorer's diagram showed that 15 of his 25 fours were hit between square leg and midwicket.

McCabe freely admitted he had been lucky with what he called his 'Sydney-or-the-bush' approach. 'I had a charmed life,' he said. 'I was lucky. I could have been out any time.' He was not blessed by luck again that series: in his other nine Test innings he scored only 198 runs. For the time being, though, he was a national hero, although McCabe certainly did not revel in that. He later told Chappie Dwyer, now a Test selector, that he had deliberately avoided reading the newspaper accounts of his innings. 'I took a book to read on the ferry,' he said. 'I thought there might be a lot of exaggerated praise in them [the newspapers] that it wouldn't do me any good to read.'

Bradman did not play in that first Bodyline Test, and he was not in the touring party in 1935–36 when McCabe played his great innings at Johannesburg. This may be significant, because some of his contemporaries, including Gubby Allen of England, believed Bradman's presence higher up the batting order had the effect of stifling McCabe's own run-making. He scored his 189 in 197 minutes and hit 29 fours. On that same tour he and other Australians played a South African team at baseball, and McCabe made several good hits. McCabe's biographer Jack McHarg has recorded that when McCabe was complimented on this, he replied with typical modesty, 'How can you miss? They're all bloody full tosses.'

The story has often been told of how Bradman called other team members out to the dressing room balcony while McCabe was playing his great innings at Nottingham in 1938, saying, 'Come and see this. Don't miss a moment of it. You will never see the like of it again.' McCabe scored the 232 in 235 minutes, hitting 34 fours and a six. With

McCABE, Stanley Joseph

Born: 16 July 1910, Grenfell (NSW)
Died: 25 August 1968, Beauty Point (NSW)

Bats: Right-handed
Bowls: Right-arm medium

First-Class Career

Debut: 1928–29 New South Wales v Queensland, Sydney

M	Inn	NO	Runs	50	100	Ave	Ct	St	Runs	Wkts	Ave	5	10
182	262	20	11951	68	29	49.38	139	–	5362	159	33.72	1	–

Highest Score: 240 Australians v Surrey, The Oval, 1934
Best Bowling: 5/36 New South Wales v Queensland, Sydney, 1929–30

Test Career

Debut: 1930 Australia v England, Nottingham

M	Inn	NO	Runs	50	100	Ave	Ct	St	Runs	Wkts	Ave	5	10
39	62	5	2748	13	6	48.21	41	–	1543	36	42.86	–	–

Highest Score: 232 Australia v England, Nottingham, 1938
Best Bowling: 4/13 Australia v South Africa, Sydney, 1931–32

uncharacteristic emotion, Bradman wrote in his autobiography: 'Towards the end I could scarcely watch the play. My eyes were filled as I drank in the glory of his shots.'

The six McCabe hit that day was only his third in 55 Test innings. Bill O'Reilly happened to be batting with him at the time, and he told this story about it. 'Ken Farnes came on to bowl with the new ball after McCabe had passed his century,' O'Reilly said. 'The third ball he bowled, Stan just pivoted on his feet and hit him clear over the square leg fence for six. As the ball was thrown back to Farnes, he walked back along the wicket towards me and he said, "Bill, what can you possibly do with a man like that?" I said, "Go down and get his autograph".'

The war determined that McCabe would be barely 28 when he played his last Test. It is interesting to speculate how long he might have gone on if there hadn't been a war. He opened a sports store in Sydney a few months before the war began, and it may have been to his advantage, business-wise, to keep playing at the top level for as long as possible. On the other hand, his health had always been fragile, and his oddly shaped feet (they had abnormally high arches) were a growing problem, so his playing life may not have been a long one. His last first-class match – for New South Wales against Queensland at the 'Gabba in November–December 1941 – was also the last played in Australia before the wartime recess. In his final innings he made a modest 41.

McCabe died in 1968 when he fell down a cliff, fracturing his skull, near his home in Mosman, apparently having slipped while throwing away a dead possum. McCabe had been ill at the time, and a rumour spread that he had jumped to his death. People close to him have always dismissed this as absurd, and the coroner apparently agreed.

Jack Fingleton once expressed the view that McCabe had no great liking for Test cricket. He thought McCabe did not easily bear the nervous strain of it and, moreover, could not bring himself to play the cautious, canny type of game which Test cricket often demanded. One-day cricket might have suited him, for as well as being able to score rapidly he was a competent medium-pace bowler (he took 36 wickets in Tests) and a good fieldsman. Neville Cardus wrote that McCabe was in the Victor Trumper line and that 'no other batsman today but McCabe has inherited Trumper's sword and cloak'. Bill O'Reilly, in the speech previously mentioned, said, 'If I had Aladdin's lamp and could use it, said my prayers every night for a month assiduously, I would ask for this: if I was given reincarnation I'd come back as a cricketer and I would be Stan McCabe. Take the rest, it doesn't matter.'

WARWICK ARMSTRONG

The Big Ship

by Ray Robinson

We are still waiting for the rise of another Test captain as overpoweringly successful as Warwick Armstrong. Neither before nor since has a victorious international cricket skipper come through his campaigns with the proud record of never having lost a Test match.

The leviathan of Australian cricket in the first quarter of the twentieth century was a man to be looked up to and a man used to being looked up to. Unless they were as tall as Jack Gregory, all men had to raise their eyes to look at him, a commanding 190 cm (6 ft 3 in). His teams called him 'The Big Ship'.

In youth Armstrong was tall and slender, like the mast of *Gipsy Moth IV*, but in maturity his shape made you think of a hull rather than a mast, a hull as capacious as one of those tankers too enormous to pass through the Suez Canal. A simple substitution of initials could have transformed W. W. Armstrong into the S. S. *Armstrong*, a vessel more noted for tonnage than tact, and one not above a little gunboat diplomacy at times. In displacement, 125 kg gradually built up to 133 kg (21 st). His bills of lading showed more than 16 000 runs, 45 hundreds and some 830 wickets in 269 first-class matches. His career from 1899 to 1921 yielded him averages of 46 runs an innings and 19 runs a wicket.

Warwick Windridge Armstrong was born on 22 May 1879, at Kyneton, 80 kilometres north-west of Melbourne. He was educated at Cumloden School, Alma Road, and the University College, Armadale. In the Victorian XI at 20 he made 118 in his first match. New Year's Day 1902 brought his first Test at 22 – on a Melbourne gluepot. Sent in ninth, Armstrong made a few without losing his wicket in either innings.

Ray Robinson (1905–82) was the doyen of Australian cricket writing, from whom we learned all the best yarns. 'The Big Ship' is from On Top Down Under *and reproduced with the permission of Brian Robinson.*

In the Melbourne pavilion Armstrong's shirt and boots dwarf other relics. The tent-like shirt, unstitched, would make a headsail for Jim Hardy. Before the first of his four Test tours of Britain he was being presented with a travelling case when jockey Percy Kennedy called out, 'Will he be able to get his boots into it?'

Legends fastened on to him, as barnacles have a way of doing to big ships. In confidence, dominance, willpower and ability to get his own way, Armstrong is the nearest down-under approach to W. G. Grace.

June was at its sunniest when the Australians played Hampshire in 1921 and a Southampton newspaper reported that Armstrong, strolling around the ground while Bardsley and Macartney made centuries, became aware of a little boy dogging his heels. He thought it a manifestation of hero worship, but the boy's persistency at last made him say, 'Here, give me your autograph book and I'll sign it.' The boy: 'I ain't got one.' Armstrong: 'Then what do you want?' The boy: 'Please, sir, you are the only bit of decent shade in the place.' Warwick's shade was not only long and wide but cool, real cool.

On his first tour, 1902, *Wisden* predicted a great future for the 23-year-old Australian, playing two matches a week for the first time in his life. On his second visit, 1905, he headed the bowling with 122 wickets and made 303 not out against Somerset, his tallest score. Only three Australian visitors have exceeded it – Macartney 345 against Notts, Bradman 334 and 304 in Leeds Tests and Simpson 311 in the Manchester Test, 1964. On Armstrong's third tour, 1909, his 6/35 in England's second innings at Lord's brought his captain, Noble, the first win in Anglo–Australian Tests by a skipper who put the other side in.

No ball that Armstrong drove, and no deckchair he sat on, was ever the same again. Edmund Blunden said he made the bat look like a teaspoon and bowling like weak tea. His 248 not out at Lord's in 1905 was a 4¼-hour ordeal for the Gentlemen. Four men posted in a long-field cordon were unable to prevent many drives reaching the boundary. Armstrong knew how to plant his big boots wide apart to magnify the arc of the bat's swing. The massive Victorian's square-cut had stunning force. Pace bowling suited him best. One of his six Test centuries, 132 at Melbourne, was against South Africa's puzzling googly bowlers, a year after they had perfected Bosanquet's invention to take a rubber from England. As Armstrong grew bulkier, his difficulties with spin increased and arch-flighter Mailey tormented him in a way that bordered on bear-baiting.

Troubled by malaria after a wartime visit to New Guinea, he was 88 in one Test in the last over before tea and doubted whether he could continue after the interval. Three fours off Fender in that over took him to 100. Being so gross did not prevent his stealing runs, or rather the first run, aided by a flying start. When he got under way it behoved his partner to give 'The Big Ship' a wide berth. If he fell in the field he looked like a beached white whale.

Despite his weight he seemed tireless as a slow bowler who could land the ball almost as he liked for hours on end. His twisting hand imparted as much overspin as leg spin, causing batsmen trouble in detecting which were his 'straight breaks'. As England moved into a winning position at Trent Bridge in 1905, Darling used Armstrong to put a brake on scoring. The hefty all-rounder wheeled along 35 overs wide of the leg stump for 50 runs. In all, his 52 overs (24 maidens) yielded only 67 runs for one wicket. Such negative tactics must have been hard on Nottingham people who paid to see cricket.

On an average Armstrong had to bowl 92 balls for each Test wicket, compared with Benaud's 79 balls. No other Australian has totalled 10 wickets and 100 runs in a match in England, as Armstrong did with 11/70 and scores of 55 and 50 not out against Middlesex in 1905. No taker of 100 wickets on a tour has got as close to 2000 runs on the same trip, 98 short.

Through the second half of his career he had to ride out storms. He was one of six leading players England missed seeing in 1912 because of the stormiest row Australian sport has endured.

In addition to making runs Armstrong made enemies in positions where they could do him harm. Three times Victoria's selectors tried to push him off his pedestal. Armstrong treated them with utter disdain. The First World War raged while he was ageing from 35 to 40, well beyond the age at which leading Australians now quit cricket for business.

In 1920 he scored his best batting double, 157 not out and 245 for Victoria against South Australia, first man to total 400 with two century innings in a match. Coming just before the selection for the first postwar Test against England, it clinched the claim of Australia's senior player to the captaincy, but the fact that he was the last of the disobedient six was not forgotten.

He was the star of the first Test in Sydney. Nobody knows why he gave medium-pacer Kelleway the first over instead of fast bowler Gregory. It was a surprise, as Hobbs had been expecting first ball at the other end. The sight of Russell's bails flying first ball satisfied most people that a tactical genius was in command. In the second innings Armstrong, padded up, had whisky with his mates at the members' bar. He went out to make the highest score of the match, 158, with the most terrific driving most of the watchers ever saw. It forced even that master cover, Hobbs, back almost into the outfield and left several fieldsmen with sore hands. Most of his 17 fours were drives, enabling him to score 45 runs an hour and leave the Englishmen 659 to get. To make sure they didn't, he dismissed Hobbs lbw for 59. His main contribution to the second Test victory was to take six wickets. In the Adelaide Test England led by 447 to 354 but Armstrong hit hard for 121. By regaining the Ashes with three wins straight, he established himself as a national hero but his leg had been severely bruised.

He went to Sydney to captain Victoria against New South Wales but did not practise and, minutes before the game, withdrew from the team. One day he was reported to have been seen a mile or two beyond Sydney Cricket Ground at Randwick Racecourse – and with a man of his dimensions the odds were against mistaken identity. Back in Melbourne the state selectors wasted no time asking questions. They dropped him from the Victorian XI to play the English XI on the following Friday.

Besieged for an explanation, administrator Ernest Bean refused to give any reasons. He was mistaken if he fancied such a big ship could be sunk without trace. To a protest meeting convenor H. D. Westley said the most dastardly outrage in the history of cricket was the culmination of a series of oppressive acts against players. He moved, 'This meeting of lovers of sport expresses condemnation of the treatment meted out to Australia's greatest cricketer Mr W Armstrong, who has been omitted from the Victorian XI without even an opportunity to make an explanation.'

The lovers of sport decided on a monster indignation meeting at 3 p.m. on Saturday outside the Melbourne Cricket Ground, inside which the bereft Victorian XI would be playing the Englishmen. By refusing to issue the usual pass-out checks, the VCA required all protesters who left the match to pay again to re-enter. Despite a partial boycott, 17 000 watched play until 3 p.m., when about 8000 dragged themselves away from Patsy Hendren's batting. Those who could not make such a sacrifice heard the outside crowd cheer the speakers. Those outside, in turn, heard the insiders cheer Hendren's approach to 200. Before the protesters carried the same resolution, Westley said:

I desire to apologise to the English cricketers for the indignity placed on them by the holding of an indignation meeting outside the ground where they are playing. But the Englishmen are true sports and I am sure they are in sympathy with the objects of the meeting.

Inside, barrackers bawled, 'Put Armstrong on!' and, 'Why don't you give Ernie Bean a bowl?' As the day closed with Hendren 262 not out and Marylebone Cricket Club 445 for five wickets, a disconsolate wail crossed the field, 'Oh, where's Warwick?'

On the third night of the match, a full meeting of the VCA heard facts which the uncomfortable selectors failed to ascertain. Falling back on the old stand-by of beleaguered officialdom, suppression, the VCA issued a limited statement but it came to be known that vice-captain Mayne and Dr R. L. Park (player-physician) had agreed that Armstrong's bruised leg had been unfit for play.

His appearance in the fourth Test set off a unique demonstration. First, the thousands in one stand gave him a standing ovation. As that subsided the crowd in the next stand took it up, in the manner of a choral round. Because of a recurrence of malaria he lowered himself in the order, hoping for a weekend's rest before batting, and sent for a couple of stiff whiskies. But loss of five wickets for 153 obliged him to go in. As a youngster who had no right to be listening, I heard later that, as Warwick walked in to bat, he saw among the sea of faces the countenance of Bean, wearing an expression that seemed to say 'I've got him now!' The sight of the teetotaller, seemingly gloating, sobered Armstrong if he needed sobering. He pulled the innings round to give Australia a lead of 105 and after 3½ hours walked off amid the plaudits of the crowd for his 123 not out.

In the second Test the guileful giant had trapped Hobbs lbw by following a number of leg-breaks with a topspinner delivered with seemingly the same action. As the great opening batsman walked out, he said good-naturedly, 'Never again, Warwick!' In the fourth Test, googly bowler Arthur Mailey took his wicket the same way. As Hobbs walked past, Armstrong remarked, 'Got you again, Jack!' He had instructed Mailey to try the same ruse.

Though they backed him against official injustice and were subscribing a fund for him, Melbourne barrackers were not always respectful. If he failed to reach an edged ball, they would yell, 'You big jellyfish' and coarser terms of endearment.

A clean sweep of five Test victories might have been expected to assure the triumphant general of the captaincy for the first postwar tour of Britain. The selectors' choice was announced as unanimous, yet A. G. Moyes, who was a state office-bearer close to inner circles, probably had good reasons for saying that in the Board vote Armstrong scraped in by the narrowest possible margin.

If a captain can be no better than the side he has to handle, as every losing skipper knows, Armstrong had a long start. The Australian Imperial Forces' successful 1919 tour of England bequeathed him the nucleus of a powerful side, imbued with fine team-spirit. Possession of Gregory and McDonald enabled him to show England his new method of opening a Test attack with express bowlers at both ends – the most far-reaching strategical change of his period. In a cartoon Tom Webster said things looked bright for England until play began at 11.30 a.m. and Armstrong handed the ball to Gregory. In addition to the two fastest bowlers, Australia had the two most effective slow bowlers. Bowlers went into action happy in the knowledge that they had the two finest slipsmen, Gregory and Hendry, the two best outfielders, Bardsley and Taylor, two of the best covers, Andrews and Pellew and wicketkeepers as good as any, Carter or Oldfield. Hardly an error was made in the field. Armstrong could write down his batting order from men who were to make 37 hundreds on the tour while only eight centuries could be raised against them. It would be superficial to say he had it easy – no Test tour is ever that – but no captain ever had it so good, unless it was Sir Donald Bradman after the next world war.

As 11 of Armstrong's 15 players had captained their district teams, their knowledge of strategy and general tactics enabled them to take their places in the field for different opponents with a minimum of direction. Armstrong's captaincy came through this expert surveillance well, although from what I have heard his players did not rank him as a tactician with Noble, Trott or Collins. Unlike vice-captain Collins, Armstrong seldom bothered to take part in discussion groups in the team's hotel to cook up plans to dismiss leading opponents. Mailey regarded him as a tenacious and relentless fighter, full of courage and determination, who bluffed rather than cajoled the opposition out.

Other members of his team looked to him as a strong character who would not allow an opposing skipper to score a point at his or his team's expense. He was an indomitable fighter in his team's interest. All-rounder Hunter Hendry told me that many rights and privileges of players today derived from stands made by Armstrong.

After difficulties about hours and travel, Armstrong called a meeting of his players and proposed a stand to alter arrangements that would affect their play. The program which the Australian Board had allowed no rest days before Tests. The captain said it was intolerable they should be expected to finish late against a strong county, travel overnight to a Test city and, if he lost the toss, find themselves in the field with a hard day ahead and tired fast bowlers. Three opponents consented to dropping the third day to save the Australians overnight journeys to the Nottingham, Lord's and Leeds Tests and a fourth compromised by finishing at 4, enabling the Australians to reach Manchester by 7 p.m.

Suggesting that Test umpires be not appointed until the day, Armstrong said, 'The umpires are paid little for their services and, as there is a lot of betting on Tests, it would be wise to remove them from temptation.' Next day Lord Harris said, 'people don't bet on cricket' and Armstrong replied, 'If you'd like £500 on the next Test, My Lord, I can get it on for you.'

His team won the first Test in two days, the second Test by 1.35 p.m. on the third day and had the Ashes settled by 5 p.m. on the third day at Leeds.

Armstrong called total abstainers in his side 'the lemonade crowd'. Though he might have looked condescendingly on their way of life, he did not underestimate their cricketing ability. They formed two-thirds of his touring side. The batting depended chiefly on the clear eyes of Macartney, Bardsley, Andrews, Taylor, Ryder and Mayne, the wicketkeeping on Carter and Oldfield, and at that time googly bowler Mailey was a total abstainer too. If there was drinking to be done for sociability's sake, the duty was carried through – and carried through well – by the minority, Armstrong, McDonald, Gregory, Hendry and Pellew.

Providence was on the side of big ships, as well as big battalions. The dry 1921 summer reproduced almost Australian conditions. After

ARMSTRONG, Warwick Windridge

Born: 22 May 1879, Kyneton (VIC)
Died: 13 July 1947, Darling Point (NSW)

Bats: Right-handed
Bowls: Right-arm leg-spin

First-Class Career

Debut: 1898–99 Victoria v Tasmania, Hobart

M	Inn	NO	Runs	50	100	Ave	Ct	St	Runs	Wkts	Ave	5	10
269	406	61	16158	57	45	46.83	274	–	16406	832	19.71	50	5

Highest Score: 303* Australians v Somerset, Bath, 1905
Best Bowling: 8/47 Australians v Nottinghamshire, Nottingham, 1902

Test Career

Debut: 1901–02 Australia v England, Melbourne

M	Inn	NO	Runs	50	100	Ave	Ct	St	Runs	Wkts	Ave	5	10
50	84	10	2863	8	6	38.69	44	–	2923	87	33.60	3	–

Highest Score: 159* Australia v South Africa, Johannesburg, 1902–03
Best Bowling: 6/35 Australia v England, Lord's, 1909

34 matches without loss, they went down to MacLaren's all-amateur side at Eastbourne by 28 runs. At Hastings four days later, as Arthur Gilligan was about to throw the ball to the wicketkeeper to run out Andrews, his arm was struck by Armstrong's bat as the captain bustled in at the bowler's end. Warwick said, 'You don't think I did that on purpose, do you?' Gilligan's next ball to Armstrong knocked his cap off. In their last match the Australians lost and had to be content with equalling the 1902 team's record of only two defeats.

In addition to heading the bowling averages with 100 wickets on his last tour at the age of 42 he was one of the four fastest scorers, 43 an hour, in totalling 1213 runs. On 26 tours from 1878 to 1972 only four Australians have taken 100 wickets as well as scoring 1000 runs – Giffen and Armstrong each three times, Trumble in 1899 and Gregory in 1921. Because of many blows on the leg in England Armstrong was unable to play in South Africa. On his four visits to England he took 409 wickets in 125 matches at close to 17 runs a wicket and totalled 5650 runs at 40 an innings.

Armstrong was the first Australian all-rounder to play 50 Tests, on the heels of England's Wilfred Rhodes. He made six Test centuries (top score 159 not out) and eight 80s in 84 innings for 2863 runs (average 38) and bowled 8000 balls for 87 Test wickets (average 33). Forty-four catches sank into his fleshy hands.

Always unequivocal and sometimes gruff, Armstrong to some people typified not so much the kangaroo as the wombat. Respect for their outsize captain's ability enabled his players to put up with such incidents as the night he ordered them to be in bed by 11 p.m., yet did not get back to the hotel until 1 a.m. himself.

Armstrong's salary as Melbourne pavilion clerk (it was £228 in 1911) sounds meagre today. To the fund begun by the 1921 protest meetings, sympathisers subscribed £2500.

On appointment as general manager for James Buchanan's whisky in 1935 'The Big Ship' changed register to Sydney. At 34 he had married Aileen O'Donnell, 21, a grazier's daughter. Armstrong was a widower when he died at 68 on 13 July 1947, leaving £90 000, the richest Test captain Australia has had, except one.

STEVE WAUGH

A Decade of Waugh

by Mike Coward

Steve Waugh, Pragmatic Professional, 1990.

Possibly he does resemble an elite player of the 1930s, but Stephen Waugh has been the prototype of the preferred Australian cricketer of the 1990s from the moment he was thrown to the lions in the colosseum that is the Melbourne Cricket Ground in December 1985.

That he enters the final decade of the twentieth century as one of the world's foremost cricketers is testimony to his pride and determination as much as it is to his prodigious talent. A lesser man and a lesser cricketer would have been crushed by the expectations of a nation unused to dismal failure in international cricket.

Waugh was hurried to the front line five months before his 21st birthday at a time when Australian cricket was bankrupt of inspiration; comatose after being kicked in the teeth by Kim Hughes and company, who were more intent on counting Krugerrands than the cost of their actions of playing in South Africa. For the first 22 months of his international career Australian cricket was at its nadir and captain Allan Border was, more than once, close to resignation and nervous breakdown.

He was a boy alone and unprotected on an errand that would have daunted many a seasoned and hard-nosed professional. But he did not flinch nor complain. As careers folded about him he prospered because he took nothing for granted. He revealed himself to be a laconic soul of warmth and intelligence who was prepared to observe and to listen. Not even the negativism which pervaded Australian cricket at the time could mask the fact that Stephen Rodger Waugh was exceptional.

Mike Coward writes illuminating cricket prose for the Australian, *among other publications, and is the author of* Cricket Beyond the Bazaar *and* Caribbean Odyssey.

As the southern and northern summers have come and gone and a boy's wonder and naivety has been replaced by a man's awareness and maturity, there has been growing speculation that Waugh may well possess the innate qualities of a leader and therefore will be a strong candidate to succeed Border.

Certainly it has been interesting and pleasurable to watch close at hand his development both as a cricket person and as a distinguished and versatile cricketer. The signs suggest he is the most accomplished of the 'New Age' cricketers. Essentially quiet and self-effacing, he is as adept at the one-day game as he is at its traditional form. Furthermore, while he has a strong sense of cricket history and an affection for cricketers of the distant past, he is one of very few internationals who will speak in defence of the limited-overs game. He is very much the pragmatic professional of the 1990s. Perhaps that is hardly surprising given that in his first 26 months as an international he played in 19 Test matches and 58 limited-overs internationals.

The eldest of four boys, he has an active and inquiring mind and unlike many of his contemporaries is unafraid to look back if the knowledge acquired will help him look ahead. At the time of the Bicentennial Test match in Sydney in 1988 Waugh became friendly with Hunter 'Stork' Hendry who was feted at the match as the world's oldest surviving Test and Sheffield Shield cricketer. Subsequently Waugh visited Hendry and learned much about Australian cricket in the 1920s and 1930s and heard colourful tales of Stan McCabe, a cricketer he much admired. Sadly their relationship was brief as Hendry died in December 1988 at the age of 93. Now Waugh quietly visits 'Stork's' widow, Vida, at a nursing home in Sydney's Double Bay.

Photographs taken immediately after the tied Test match at Madras in 1986 and the World Cup final at Calcutta the following year reflect his interest in cricket history and the game's memorabilia. On each occasion he can be seen proudly holding a stump, a trophy of his part in history. While he fell victim to the paranoia which beset the Australian team in Pakistan in 1988 – as it always does – Waugh has been among the most inquisitive and open-minded cricket tourists to the Indian subcontinent in recent years. Invariably he is at the forefront of any excursion and in 1989 was one of a small group who inspected the work being undertaken by the international aid agency, Foster Parents Plan, in a slum in Madras.

From Sydney's sprawling and unfashionable western suburbs, Waugh has quickly developed into one of Australia's most versatile and influential players. Even that may be a gross understatement according to the English journalist, Robin Marlar. Writing in the London *Sunday Times* at the height of Australia's Ashes campaign Marlar said: 'Waugh is, whether the Australians yet recognise it, their finest player.'

There is no doubt that Australia's long-awaited rise in stocks is largely due to Waugh's exploits. The new spirit of Australian cricket so evident in England in 1989 had its genesis in India in 1987 where, as 16–1 outsiders, Australia won the World Cup for the first time. Waugh's achievements throughout that campaign were remarkable and earned him, along with rave notices from critics around the world, the sobriquet of 'Iceman' for his calm in the most stressful of situations.

In the opening match against India, the defending champions, he bowled Maninder Singh to engineer victory by one run with one ball remaining. At Indore, in an abbreviated qualifying match against New Zealand, he took three wickets in five balls to secure a three-run win and in the semi-final at Lahore, tore 18 runs from the last over, from Saleem Jaffer – exactly Australia's winning margin. And he administered the *coup de grâce* at Eden Gardens by running out Bill Athey and claiming Allan Lamb and Phillip DeFreitas.

Such a succession of wonderful solos reflected his unconditional commitment to the one-day game. At the time he said: 'I know a lot of people don't like playing it, but I think it is a part of cricket today. It presents a different set of skills and as it's going to be a part of cricket there is no point in whingeing about it. You have to learn to adapt to play it. It's probably not as good a game as Test cricket, but I still think it is a good game and a challenge. I think people put it down too much. I know old-fashioned people never really played a lot of one-day cricket and so, as with anything new, they don't want to have much to do with it.'

It was during the World Cup campaign that Border said so prophetically of Waugh: 'By the time we get to England in 1989 he could be a great player.'

Waugh arrived in England in 1989 without a Test century and with a Test average of 30.62. Five months later he returned to Australia with substantial, successive and undefeated Test centuries to his credit and a Test average of 40.13 – a statistic more in keeping with his special abilities. He was at a loss to explain why he had been unable to score a hundred in any of his previous Tests in Australia, New Zealand, India and Pakistan, where he had failed so dismally that he was very nearly omitted from the team.

He had long been concerned at his failure to convert a number of substantial innings to three figures – a fact which caused Rod Marsh to publicly question whether Waugh had the temperament for the Test match arena. When he reached his hundred (of 177 not out) at Headingley he felt as though a massive weight had been lifted from him and he thanked Lawrie Sawle, the team manager and chairman of selectors, for showing such faith in him. In celebration he scored 152 not out at Lord's and 92 at Old Trafford and for the series accumulated

a colossal 506 runs at 126.50 from just eight innings. Waugh scored at the rate of 3.76 off every six balls faced compared with Sir Donald's 3.70 when he stunned the international cricket community by scoring 979 runs at 139.19 with four centuries in 1930.

Reflecting on Headingley Waugh said: 'There was a bit of pressure because I hadn't scored a century before and I'd blown it twice in the 90s. I wasn't thinking about it before the game but when I got to 90 I thought I had better do it this time. At 99 I was chewing hard on the gum but there wasn't much saliva there. I thought I'd better get it this ball or I'm gone.'

While Marlar and Denis Compton and other eminent English judges pronounced Waugh a revelation, his heady achievements came as no surprise to the buffs of the West Country. In 1987 and 1988 Waugh consistently performed outstanding deeds for the generally immature and impressionable Somerset and both Peter Roebuck and Vic Marks spoke in glowing terms about his contribution to the club in the wake of the revolution. With the greatest respect they talked about his mental toughness and competitive instincts as much as his splendid technique and wonderful temperament.

'I knew he was good but I don't think I knew just how good,' said Roebuck, who remembers with excitement – and gratitude – Waugh's exceptional hundreds against Sylvester Clarke and Surrey and Courtney

Walsh and Gloucestershire in 1987. Marks observed that Steve relishes responsibility in a way which an Englishman of his age wouldn't.

Highly self-disciplined although certainly not averse to the celebratory binge, he has willingly accepted responsibility since he made an unconditional commitment to cricket ahead of a teaching career. 'I lasted about three hours in college and just walked out. I don't think teaching was really my go. I've just been lucky cricket has turned into a job,' he said.

But, in a sense, he is still teaching: by his demeanour and deeds in the middle he is educating a whole generation of Australian cricketers. And that augurs well for the game, whatever its form.

Steve Waugh in the Village of Hope, 1998.

India! A land of incomparable beauty and variety, and of hideous prospects like the slums of Bombay and Calcutta. A land where the sublime often stood side by side with the very worst this world can offer, but where both elements were always more vibrant, more human and ultimately more alluring than anywhere else.   – Dominique Lapierre

Bangalore: Steve Waugh takes guard and waits to face the first of 250 boys, aged from seven to 17, who are fighting for the privilege to bowl to Australia's most admired cricketer in India. Waugh is opening the innings of an imaginary Test match and opening his heart to the boys at the Udayan village on the outskirts of Barrackpore, 35km north of Calcutta.

While they may share an interest in cricket, this is not the reason these boys are together and wanting to touch and be photographed with the semi-divine in shorts and an Australian Cricket Board cap. All are children of leprosy sufferers who, from the moment they are born into a squalid world, are so cruelly stigmatised.

Although the educated classes have a greater understanding of the disease, the illiterate underclasses continue to shun the entire family of a leprosy sufferer. As a consequence the children become outcasts and are not permitted to mix with 'normal' children and are not admitted to 'normal' schools

So, for at least a year, the boys can escape hell by staying at Udayan, founded in 1970 by the Reverend James Stevens. A few of the boys have touches of the disease. But not many. And in this safe and loving environment they will receive appropriate treatment and, in all probability, be cured. Indeed, among the primary aims of Udayan is to remove the children from constant exposure to leprosy, free them of the crushing stigma and 'educate and train them for a normal, dignified existence as self-sufficient, contributing and proud citizens of India'.

The administrative officer of Udayan for the past 14 years, Ghanashyam Das, says the whole world must learn that leprosy is not hereditary, cannot be contacted by mere touch and is curable at every stage. Nor is the disease the curse of God.

God, or in this context, the thousands of gods in the Hindu pantheon, indeed moves in mysterious ways.

In normal circumstances, Waugh would not have had the time to lend his support to an appeal aimed at extending Udayan to accommodate female children of leprosy sufferers. But so comprehensively beaten were the Australians in the second Test match in Calcutta, Waugh had a free day.

A man with an inquiring and open mind who has become a successful diarist in recent years, Waugh received a letter when he returned to his hotel after the humiliation at Eden Gardens. It began:

I am glad that you are fighting it out for Australia, despite a problem with your leg. And, I am sorry that the match is not going as all of you may have liked yet to go. But, this means that you may have SUNDAY to spare.

Cricket is not the biggest love in my life. So, there must be a purpose in God's will that I sat through three days of the current match from the bedside of a patient I was tending to. And, I noticed you, when there were a few close-ups of your face … the dashing man with compassion writ large on his face.

This morning I wake to read your interview in the Telegraph! I find that my impression of compassion in your heart is not unfounded. It raised a hope in my heart. Perhaps, your charitable heart can help some very deprived children of Calcutta.

And so Waugh met Shamlu Dudeja, a noted worker and benefactor for the destitute, dispossessed and disadvantaged in Rudyard Kipling's *City of Dreadful Night* which in recent years has reinvented itself as the *City of Joy*.

As it happens, the author of *City of Joy*, noted journalist Dominique Lapierre, is another luminary from the West who has taken a keen interest in Udayan and has used his celebrity status to focus attention on the plight of the children.

Indeed, Lapierre has made both an emotional and financial investment to the village and endeavours to visit every year. As you drive into the spacious, well-tended, tranquil grounds well away from the iniquitous slums where the boys were born, there are signs which shout proudly: 'Udayan is supported by royalties of Lapierre's *City of Joy*'.

Scarcely able to believe Waugh does not live all his life in a television set and is actually among them, the boys follow their god as he inspects the dining hall and classrooms which double as bedrooms. At the end of the day the boys roll out mats kept in the corner of the classroom and sleep on the stone floor.

As part of the latest campaign to raise awareness and desperately needed funds, supporters in India and abroad are encouraged to donate a bunk bed for two at the cost of US$80. Alternatively, US$50 will build a patch of wall in a building for girls.

Waugh, toting a camera that has served him well on his frequent visits to India over the past 12 years, happily posed for a 'team' photograph.

For a moment, the father of one daughter, Rosie, aged 20 months, was surrogate father to 250 boys. And, it must be said, his parenting skills were impressive as he herded his charges into position for photographs that he hopes will draw attention to the cause. In India an autograph or photograph with a celebrity of Waugh's standing is powerful currency.

After leaving the mass of smiling, laughing, waving children, he asked to be taken deep into the slums to meet their parents. Here, he saw men and women shockingly disfigured by the disease and compelled to live in conditions unfit for habitation. Living in shame and rejected by the rest of society, the leprosy sufferers beg in the street to stay alive. Yet for the pain of their lives they greeted Waugh smilingly.

Waugh, who often talks of the profound experience of once having met Mother Teresa, clearly was moved by his Holy Day in the City of Joy. So much so that when he reached Bangalore for the Test match and his body would not let him play, he sought the help of India's exciting young and socially aware cricketers, Rahul Dravid and Saurav Ganguly, to draw attention to the village of Udayan and the children.

It is said there are eight million leprosy sufferers in India. 'That means there are at least 16 million children of those sufferers,' Shamlu Dudeja said. May the gods look kindly on them in this shamefully ignorant world.

WAUGH, Stephen Rodger
Born: 2 June 1965, Canterbury (NSW)

Bats: Right-handed
Bowls: Right-arm medium

First-Class Career
Debut: 1984–85 New South Wales v Queensland, Brisbane

M	Inn	NO	Runs	50	100	Ave	Ct	St	Runs	Wkts	Ave	5	10
285	441	74	19220	86	58	52.37	231	–	7772	243	31.98	5	–

Highest Score: 216* New South Wales v Western Australia, Perth, 1990–91
Best Bowling: 6/51 New South Wales v Queensland, Sydney, 1988–89

Test Career
Debut: 1985–86 Australia v India, Melbourne

M	Inn	NO	Runs	50	100	Ave	Ct	St	Runs	Wkts	Ave	5	10
128	204	38	8373	42	22	50.43	92	–	3181	89	35.74	3	–

Highest Score: 200 Australia v West Indies, Kingston, 1994–95
Best Bowling: 5/28 Australia v South Africa, Cape Town, 1993–94

International Limited-Overs Career
Debut: 1985–86 Australia v New Zealand, Melbourne

M	Inn	NO	Runs	50	100	Ave	Ct	St	Runs	Wkts	Ave	5
295	264	53	6713	40	2	31.83	71		6648	191	34.81	–

Highest Score: 102* Australia v Sri Lanka, Melbourne, 1995–96
Best Bowling: 4/33 Australia v Sri Lanka, Sydney, 1987–88

DOUG WALTERS

The Last Boy from the Bush

by Damien Murphy

In the summer of 1970–71, the Boxing Day Test at Melbourne had been rained out. In consolation, Melbourne had the first taste of cricket's future when Australia played England in a one-day match at the MCG on 5 January. On 21 January, the teams were back at the MCG. An hour before the Test started, a BBC sports producer was on the phone from London talking to the outside broadcast director in the control room of Studio 31 at ABC-TV's Melbourne headquarters in the suburb of Ripponlea. 'Give us plenty K. D. Walters. There's a lot of interest here after the West Indies thing [at the SCG in 1969 Doug became the first Test cricketer to score a double century and a century in the same match].'

Only the ABC bothered with cricket then. Before satellite television, it was not unlike cricket's radio days when Australian commentators got the scores by telegram and provided their own sound effects in the studio. In 1971 British viewers got 30 minutes of highlights cobbled together in Studio 31 from the day's play, the videotape spool put on a 6.30 p.m. flight to England for broadcast two days later.

I was working as a vision mixer at Ripponlea. It is like a film editor but instead of splicing film together, the mixer sits next to the director in the control room console, pushing buttons that choose various sources for the television picture being broadcast or recorded – cameras at the MCG, telecine (film) and the newfangled videotape. Back then, a videotape machine was as big as a Falcon sedan and the newest toy was 'instant replay'.

Damien Murphy was the Big Ship of Melbourne journalist who moved to the Sydney Morning Herald, *possibly because the surf is warmer up north.*

In the glacially slow draw the Test became, Doug's dashing first innings was the only thing worth televising. Until he walked onto the MCG with his trademark dapper little no-nonsense step and made for the centre, the only time the director had called for an instant replay was when a wicket fell. For a few brief hours Doug dragged the game out of the paralysis that Test matches were becoming afflicted with.

Doug sort of mucked around at the first balls. The English quick John Snow roared in and sent down a thunderbolt. Doug sort of missed. Next one he got an edge and was lucky not to get caught. He missed Snow's third but by then his eye was in and he cut across the line and sent the Englishman's fourth to the fence. Nobody had hit a four for hours. 'Right, videotape,' the director said into the microphone. 'We'll have that shot of Walters for replay please.' There were, I think, another six fours until Doug was out for 55. He didn't bat in the second innings. Time ran out. The spectators had got the message the day before and hardly bothered turning up from lunch on day four.

Doug played his cricket when the people stopped coming and he played cricket when they came back with World Series, one of the few to straddle the two eras of modern cricket. His unique achievement was to somehow effortlessly personify both. In some ways he was the last of the boys from the bush, one of those blokes whose shy, sly, laconic no-nonsense nonchalance was quintessentially part of the Anzac spirit yet he seemed equally at home among the moustaches, beer, bullshit and bodyshirts of World Series. He had the sort of swagger that is Sydney, a larrikin confidence that borders on exhibitionism and he remained King of the Hill at the SCG for all of his 16-year first-class career, the mascot of the Baby Boomers who wanted to hang around with mates long after marriages and mortgages and jobs stole away their youth.

The young Doug Walters was widely touted as the next Don Bradman. Both were country boys with alliterative links to their home towns: Bradman came from Bowral, Doug from Dungog, poetic talisman of the old and fading pastoral Australia.

The young Doug learned his cricket on an ant-bed wicket at his parents' dairy farm outside Dungog in the foothills of the Great Divide north west of Newcastle. First he played with his mum and dad and his brother and sister, then the Dungog school team. It was during this period he developed the swashbuckling right-hand batting style that was to thrill cricket for three decades. It was pure bush and pure delight, distilled in the great Australian exultation, 'have a go'.

In 1962, that style caught the eye of a New South Wales selector, Jack Chegwyn, who took a team of name players to Maitland and watched the dairy farmer's son score 51 and take four wickets. Chegwyn knew the makings when he saw it and he took the boy down to Sydney in 1963–64. Doug made his debut in the New South Wales Sheffield Shield side a few months later at the 'Gabba. He was out for one, but recouped with a second-innings 50. Then came the big hits: the first century on the MCG and a 235 against the Crow Eaters in Adelaide. He had started the journey from K. D. Walters to Dougie, the trip from institutional patronage to national hero. But on the field, his team-mates called him Freddie, for reasons that have been obscured by time.

The next year, 1964, at 19 he was sitting in his car outside a Darlinghurst hotel, puffing on a fag and listening to the radio news when he heard he had been selected for the Test against England in Brisbane. A few days later he joined the few who opened their Test career with a century, scoring 155 and followed with 115 in the next Test in Melbourne. In the fifth Test he scored 60 and took 5/53 with his medium pacers.

In September 1965 Doug's marble came up in the Vietnam conscription ballot. While tertiary students could defer their call-up until they completed studies, country boys had no such chance. In those early days of the Vietnam conflict, the Second World War was still a burning memory in the minds of Australian fathers, most of whom had fought and the general feeling was that when a boy was called, especially a boy from the bush, he did his duty. Doug did the right thing.

Conscription barely took the shine off Doug's game. But many said he was never the same again. He played a few Tests during his Army service. But only on accumulated leave, the Army too dumb to realise the public relations possibilities in having a serving Test player in their ranks. Doug became swallowed by the relative obscurity of Army life but returned to civilian life in March 1968 and was playing in England by mid-year. Two years in the Army had affected his game and he couldn't crack the ton in that damp northern hemisphere summer. But back home five months later, he was back on whack, shattering Bradman's record with a 242-knock first innings on the SCG against the Windies. He followed up with 103 in the second innings just to make sure the Hill knew he was back in town. Ever the tight-lipped warrior, Doug managed the record despite a probable hairline fracture at the base of his spine or a cracked rib, the result of slipping down the steps outside his Parramatta flat a couple of nights before while putting out the garbage – another addition to the tales of the ordinary life of Doug that made him so much one of the crowd.

He slammed 669 runs against the Windies but faltered the following year in South Africa, finishing with only 258 runs for an average 32.25. The rot was slowly spreading again when he played England in 1970–71, when his batting average climbed to only 37.3.

In England the following year, he crashed. Snow, the man he easily fended off on the MCG in January 1971, had Doug's measure. By the fifth Test he was dropped after 36 successive appearances for Australia. Doug was never really good in England. They said the ball moved around too much and proved too evasive for the hitting across the line technique Doug had perfected as a kid in Dungog. Back home, he missed the Tests against Pakistan but was back in the Windies where the dam burst and he belted an average 71 runs an innings, including a blazing 112 between lunch and tea at Port-of-Spain.

That was the thing about Doug: his unpredictability. He could be bowled out by a parish league plodder but when a wicket was falling apart and taking its toll of the classical batsmen, Doug would often save the day with flash and dash.

A friend, the journalist Peter Bowers, can remember working on the defunct Sydney tabloid the *Sun* in 1969 when he got the idea of getting Australia's sports stars to explain the finer points of their game to young readers. 'We had swimmers, golfers and tennis players and, as captain of New South Wales, Dougie was the natural choice for cricket,' Bowers recalled. 'The trouble was Dougie was so unconventional, there was nothing classical about his technique … we had to get someone else to interpret his grip, and his stance, etc. in a classical context so the kids reading the stuff wouldn't end up tanglefooted and flat on their backs.'

Doug's best remembered knock must have been Perth in 1974 when his career was sauntering between the doldrums and disaster. Just before Christmas, with Cyclone Tracy about to hit, Doug walked onto the WACA before tea and hit a quick three runs. At stumps he was 103. The century in a session was all the more memorable because

WALTERS, Kevin Douglas

Born: 21 December 1945, Dungog (NSW)

Bats: Right-handed
Bowls: Right-arm medium

First-Class Career

Debut: 1962–63 New South Wales v Queensland, Sydney

M	Inn	NO	Runs	50	100	Ave	Ct	St	Runs	Wkts	Ave	5	10
258	426	57	16180	81	45	43.84	149	–	6782	190	35.69	6	–

Highest Score: 253 New South Wales v South Australia, Adelaide, 1964–65
Best Bowling: 7/63 New South Wales v South Australia, Adelaide, 1963–64

Test Career

Debut: 1965–66 Australia v England, Brisbane

M	Inn	NO	Runs	50	100	Ave	Ct	St	Runs	Wkts	Ave	5	10
75	125	14	5357	33	15	48.26	43	–	1425	49	29.08	1	–

Highest Score: 250 Australia v New Zealand, Christchurch, 1976–77
Best Bowling: 5/66 Australia v West Indies, Georgetown, 1972–73

International Limited-Overs Career

Debut: 1970–71 Australia v England, Melbourne

M	Inn	NO	Runs	50	100	Ave	Ct	St	Runs	Wkts	Ave	5
28	24	6	513	2	–	28.50	10	–	273	4	68.25	–

Highest Score: 59 Australia v Sri Lanka, The Oval, 1975
Best Bowling: 2/24 Australia v England, Birmingham, 1972

most of east coast Australia saw it, three hours behind, on black and white television. Next day he was out quick smart but the memory of the evening knock remains unsullied. I remember mates saying he wanted to get back to the stands for a quick smoke.

In fact, fags were integral to the Doug legend. A chain-smoker at the height of his career, Doug got his taste for cigarettes early in life at Dungog, and when he came to town to work in Sydney they got him one of the traditional sportsman's jobs of the time – cigarette company representative. To young Doug, being paid to smoke must have been beyond his wildest dreams.

At his peak, sports writers always described how Doug would sit beneath the stands in the locker room awaiting his turn to bat, but hardly ever watching what was happening out in the field. Instead he'd play cards, five hundred or bridge, and puff cigarettes until he got the call. Legend has it sometimes Doug would finish the hand before ducking onto the oval. Others wrote how he would ask someone handy to hang onto his fag while he popped out for a quick slash. Still others said he trained for a game by chucking a dart at a board before returning to his hand of cards. Call it country cousin cool in the face of fire.

And then there were the practical jokes and of course, the grog. His beer consumption on flights to and from England became the stuff of urban legends and he finally confirmed the tally in the appropriately titled 1988 book *One for the Road*: 44 cans went down on a flight to England in 1977. His mate Rodney Marsh beat him by one in 1983. Doug admitted a swimmer beat them both in recent years.

All that stuff came out in the World Series days when the outcast professionals were struggling to inject a bit of personality into the business of the game. Doug and 22 other Australians joined Kerry Packer's World Series Cricket in 1978. He went for the money. The crowds came for the excitement. And Doug was one of the better entertainers. Still, the cricket in him made him take one last go at England and he nearly got the elusive century but Tony Greig, the spoilsport, caught him at Old Trafford on 88.

In 1981, Doug was still at it, topping the Australian batting averages, but the selectors knew that he and England were never meant to be, so he was dropped from the Ashes tour. Doug took the hint and retired, a long forlorn way from the thrill of hearing his name outside the Darlinghurst pub in 1965. Now he earns his money talking about his glory days as the game amateur and the grim professional.

RICHIE BENAUD

The Man Himself

by A. G. (Johnnie) Moyes

Richie Benaud's rise from mediocrity to stardom was extremely slow and tortuous. He certainly didn't burst into the limelight overnight as some have done. For four or five years he hung onto his place by the skin of his teeth, chiefly because the selectors had enough vision to recognise a talent which needed time to develop.

Many who looked on figures as the only guide wondered just how long he would cling to his position among the elect. They expected at any moment that he would lose his grip and slip into obscurity, but, sustained by his own ambition to make good and supported by the faith others had in him, he finally climbed the long hill to cricketing immortality. On the way up he must have stopped often enough to ponder his moderate list of achievements and his lack of opportunity as one of the lesser lights of the team, but always his advance continued and ultimately he scaled the heights.

What were the reasons for this rise from mediocrity to fame, from near-famine to plenty? Earlier in his career Benaud more often than not came into the attack when others failed, and he was not even the first string among the spinners. It is not a simple matter for a young bowler, particularly one of the type which develops late, to produce the performances that merit headlines. He is asked to do what men of greater skill and experience have failed to achieve. That happened to Benaud – and to Davidson.

At the same time his knowledge and his skill were developing. He was learning the hard way, and by the time the others left the scene he was ready to take over. This happened in South Africa. Benaud became

---

A. G. (Johnnie) Moyes (1893–1963) was a SA batsman picked for a Test tour cancelled due to World War I. 'The Man Himself' is from his book Benaud *(1962) reproduced by permission of* HarperCollins*Publishers.*

the No. 1 spinner. The other in the side was Kline, a bowler of a very different type. Benaud knew that his chance had come. He realised that the team now looked to him as the chief menace, and he showed by his deeds that the years spent almost in drudgery had not been wasted. With Davidson it was exactly the same. Both rose to the occasion, as the gifted will do when the opportunity offers.

In a moment the clouds of depression rolled away. Like the student who has been trying to solve a problem without much help from others, and who suddenly discovers the answer, Benaud found that all the pieces were now fitting into place to create a perfect machine. Good length, admirable control and Benaud became inseparable companions. He brought his bowling under the control of his mind. He could not only see the weaknesses in the batsmen but could also lay them bare, and he had the equipment to experiment until he got results. He developed a variety which gave the batsmen no peace of mind. He could change his method of attack without faltering in length and direction. He introduced more and more tricks as he developed his art. It was fascinating to watch him grow to bowling maturity.

Of course, that ointment obtained in New Zealand was of tremendous assistance. No man can go on bowling when his finger is red-raw and bleeding – especially a bowler who is expected to work as hard as Benaud has done. The hardening of the skin brought with it the hardening of purpose and of endurance which have helped Australian cricket so materially.

Benaud is of the Grimmett rather than the Mailey type; not that he will not use flight to suck the batsman forward and beat him in the air as Mailey did, but he persistently maintains the pressure in the Grimmett tradition. Benaud has never believed in giving the batsman any rest. He is attacking all the time, and using much variety in that attack. His topspinner and his bosie are surprises, not props. He is never so mechanical that the batsman will know what to expect. He has been helped also by his ability to make the ball bounce a little higher. Perhaps his height has been an advantage here, but many batsmen have told me that they were confused and defeated more by the ball's bound than by its flight, length and break. Maybe it has been a combination of all these virtues which has so often confounded them.

Benaud has always been a thinker. No slow bowler can reach the top of the hill – it is a difficult upward climb – without much planning, perseverance, and hard work. There is no proper pathway to success except through blood, sweat and tears, for the spinner must learn to take a hiding without giving ground. Purposefulness, endurance and brains are prime necessities. Benaud has these qualities, and that is why he finally emerged from the clouds into the sunshine of rich and continuous success. He is without doubt one of the most gifted slow bowlers in cricket's long history.

When walking out to bat, and when awaiting the ball, Benaud has always looked the aristocrat. That illusion fades somewhat when he begins the sweep of the bat, because his technique differs rather acutely

from that laid down in the best textbooks. He has never been a perfectionist in style. He has never worried unduly about the position of his front foot. His bat is often at an angle when the purists demand straightness, and sometimes, as he would readily agree, he has played curious strokes. In spite of all this, he has always been rugged and dangerous. He has often cut good bowling to pieces, and he has done it at a critical time. What more can we ask of a man than that he shall succeed in the crisis? After all, 19 centuries in first-class cricket tell their own story.

During his distinguished career Benaud has displayed certain outstanding characteristics – tremendous physical courage, a wonderful eye, a will to challenge the bowlers, and the ability to get away with it. No thunder or lightning could make him flinch. We have never seen him crouching near the pitch, peering anxiously from under the peak of his cap – when he wears one – like a frightened mouse in the pantry. Rather has he stood strong and reliant, like a giant oak resisting the full force of a gale. Hall, Statham and Trueman at their fastest and in their most venomous moods have never caused him to give ground. He has ever been ready to explode into a hook shot which is both thrilling and productive when played off the right ball. Sometimes he played it off the wrong ball – that is not peculiar to Benaud – but very often it has brought him runs and satisfaction. His keen eye has allowed him to overcome certain deficiencies in technique because his bat, even when far from straight, has often been in the right place at the right time in attack or defence – often enough to frustrate the ambitious bowler. His obdurate defence has on occasions been as valuable as his most violent attack, though he has always preferred aggression. No sprinter willingly competes in a 5000-metre race.

Benaud has always had the will to challenge the bowler. In fact, he has both as batsman and captain waged unceasing war against stodge. He has enjoyed taking a risk both to get runs and to see that matches are finished, and maybe this is why at times his strokes have looked ungainly and plebeian when he has missed and been bowled. He has always been at his best when flogging the attack with a heavy bat and ceaseless zest, and when on the rampage has played many innings which will be recalled long after the result of the game has been forgotten. That, surely, is how a batsman would want to be remembered.

The first Australian captain I can remember was M. A. Noble. Unfortunately I have no vivid memories of him or of his leadership qualities in Tests. Those who played with him have told me often enough what an exceptional tactician and strategist he was. Later I knew him in club cricket, listened to his broadcasts, read his writings and could always appreciate his deep knowledge of the game. Only once did I play against him in a first-class cricket match – it was in Victor Trumper's Testimonial – but Noble did not captain New South Wales against the Rest of Australia on that occasion. The evidence I have is therefore pure hearsay, but it adds up to one conclusion – that he was definitely a superb captain and very much of a disciplinarian.

Clem Hill I knew well, and I played under him often enough. Here was a captain who could get the best out of his team-mates, but he was not, I think, out of the ordinary as a planner. Though he was a grand batsman, and a man to rely on, his captaincy ran on rather conventional lines.

Next came Warwick Armstrong, whose bulk gave him an appearance of domination. He led a well-equipped side with two fast men of rich quality in Gregory and McDonald, a magnificent spinner in Arthur Mailey, and others who could and did provide adequate support. He had Collins and Bardsley to open the innings and Macartney to follow – altogether a team which ranks among the best ever. Any one of several could have captained it with assurance. It wasn't a tough job. Nor in 1920 and 1921 was England strong. She had lost a generation in the First World War and had not recovered. I doubt if Armstrong was in any way exceptional as a captain, though he was good and was a magnificent cricketer.

H. L. Collins was a fine leader, a shrewd thinker, entirely unostentatious, and able to command the loyalty of his associates. He was said to be lucky. Perhaps so, but he succeeded to the leadership when some of the stars were beginning to go down the other side of the hill, and he lost the Ashes. Bert Collins nevertheless ranks very high on my list.

Jack Ryder never had a chance to show what he could do with a good team. He was given one consisting of some who were past their best and others who had not yet been fully blooded. By the end of the season 1928–29 the team had improved out of recognition, but Ryder was discarded when the 1930 side was chosen for England and didn't get the opportunity to show what he could do with a reasonably well-equipped line-up.

That chance went to Bill Woodfull, who had a unique record in that he twice recovered the Ashes, both times in England. He led his side to victory in 1930, was beaten in Australia in 1932–3, and won again in England in 1934. No captain within memory was so thoroughly respected and admired by his mates for moral and physical courage. He gave the side a start against all types of bowling. Nothing could daunt him. In the bodyline controversy he bore himself with a dignity that is still remembered by those who knew cricket in those distressing years. Woodfull won, and deserved to win, the affection of all. I know that he had mine. Yet Woodfull never raised the crowd to any pitch of excitement, despite their admiration of him. He made very few mistakes, but he worked along conventional lines rather than by infusing some gingering element into his team. All the same, cricket owes him a big debt.

Vic Richardson often had a touch of recklessness. In olden times he might well have been found riding into action with Prince Rupert and his Cavaliers. Vic had courage and the urge always to take a chance, but he never had the opportunity of leading a side against England. He would have made a good job of it.

Don Bradman, who followed Bill Woodfull, was a different type altogether. He had the most extraordinary prestige ever acquired by an Australian player. He was a team in himself, almost an insurance against defeat. As a captain he could assess possibilities and probabilities, and get results. One great bowler who played under him told me that Bradman could lay down a policy and forecast correctly just what would happen – and within what period of time – provided that policy was carried out.

After Bradman came Hassett with his impish humour. He had a natural inclination to brightness, and some of his batting was a delight. In Tests he held it in check and adopted much more prosaic methods. This meant that he didn't create much enthusiasm among the onlookers. Hassett had varying success as a leader and at his best was very good indeed.

Ian Johnson followed his fellow Victorian. Perhaps his best days were behind him when he was given the task of leading Australia. Perhaps also he did not always receive the support that should have been given him. This didn't help at a time when England was in the midst of a revival. Craig was next, the youngest of them all. Reference has been made to his fine work in South Africa. He would have led Australia against England as well had he not taken ill. When hepatitis bowled him out, Benaud reigned in his stead.

When Benaud was appointed captain of the Australian team in the 1958–59 season he didn't have any great amount of prestige to support him. He had headed the averages in the West Indies and had taken 31 wickets in what were to most people unexpected victories in South Africa. But both these series were played far from our shores. We had no really intimate contact with them. Against England Benaud's figures had not been even moderate, and these are the figures by which a cricketer is judged. Lacking experience in leadership as well, Benaud had to start from scratch. Why did he succeed, and where does he rank among Australian captains? No doubt there will be some disagreement on the latter point, but certainly none on the former. He most certainly did succeed. At the start he was overflowing with exuberance. If a wicket fell there was much rushing about, with players hugging one another as at a young people's picnic after the finish of the egg-and-spoon race. Sometimes it seemed rather like gloating at the downfall of an honourable foe, and it was too lacking in dignity for an Australian team. One could understand, if not endorse, this outward and visible sign of inward jubilation. The Australians had been badly thrashed in three series by England; the iron had entered the souls of those who had been on the receiving end. Now the wheel was turning full circle, so let joy be unconfined!

That boyish phase – that is all it was – soon disappeared. Gladness and dignity were admirably mixed, with every now and again an upsurge of excitement which soon subsided. The team settled down.

Additions were made to the building erected on that sound foundation laid in South Africa. It became a pleasing structure, stronger at all points, reinforced as it were with the steel of confidence until it became near-perfect and seemingly unshakable. Benaud himself developed a poise and an authority which enhanced his status as a leader.

It always seemed to me that after his first Test as leader Benaud declined to consider defeat even remotely possible – or, rather, that he would not admit the possibility. He had the air of confidence which uplifted his team-mates; they admired his cricket, his general outlook, his determination, his capacity to plan. They were infected by his urge for more attractive contests. If they got into a mess they were willing to try to hit their way out of it, as Davidson did at Manchester in 1961. They were prepared to stand with their leader in taking chances. The game was to them – as to him – a challenge, an entertainment, and most certainly not a form of hard labour.

Benaud has proved often enough that he will take a risk. If he was in doubt his team would urge him on, and he would be ready to listen to advice even if he did not always accept it. Once he had made up his mind he would expect loyal co-operation from everyone. He would brook no rival captains in his company – which is perfectly right and proper.

Benaud is the finest captain I have seen since Bradman. There are many points of similarity between them. Neither has lost a series. Both have tried to win instead of merely seeking not to lose. Both could estimate probabilities and plan ahead. Both could alter their tactics to meet changing circumstances. Both were positive. An American magistrate, asked why his decisions were accepted by both parties, replied: 'I'm always positive. I may be positively right or positively wrong, but I'm positive.' There is a lot in this. Men will follow one who knows how to make a firm decision.

Bradman had greater prestige than Benaud as a player, and he dominated the game by his fantastic scoring. He could make it so much easier for those who followed. His teams could win when the odds seemed against them – as in Australia in 1936–37, when they lost the first two Tests and then took the series, and again at Leeds in 1948, when they scored more than 400 runs in the last innings on a wearing pitch to win the match. In the 30s Bradman led Australia against an England side which included a magnificent technician in Hutton, a glorious strokemaker in Hammond, who had rare gifts and could knock the stuffing out of the best bowling (as he did at Lord's in 1938

BENAUD, Richie

Born: 6 October 1930, Penrith (NSW)

Bats: Right-handed
Bowls: Right-arm leg-break googly

First-Class Career

Debut: 1948–49 New South Wales v Queensland, Sydney

M	Inn	NO	Runs	50	100	Ave	Ct	St	Runs	Wkts	Ave	5	10
259	365	44	11719	61	23	36.50	254	–	23370	945	24.73	56	9

Highest Score: 187 Australians v Natal, Pietermaritzburg, 1957–58
Best Bowling: 7/18 New South Wales v MCC, 1962–63

Test Career

Debut: 1951–52 Australia v West Indies, Sydney

M	Inn	NO	Runs	50	100	Ave	Ct	St	Runs	Wkts	Ave	5	10
63	97	7	2201	9	3	24.46	65	–	6704	248	27.03	16	1

Highest Score: 122 Australia v South Africa, Johannesburg, 1957–58
Best Bowling: 7/72 Australia v India, Madras, 1956–57

in an innings of 240 against Australia, one of the choicest pieces of batsmanship I have ever seen), the unpredictable Compton, a tough fighter like Eddie Paynter, and others with them in those and later years. These men provided a more gifted and talented array of batsmen than England had in 1958, 1959 and 1961. Bradman certainly had O'Reilly, that master of the bowling art, as a counter in the thirties, and Lindwall, Miller, and Bill Johnston in 1948. But England had men who knew how and when to attack. Australia held the Ashes in spite of all they could do, though not always by a wide margin.

In 1958–59 and 1961, apart from an occasional inspired innings by May, Cowdrey or Dexter, and some obduracy by Subba Row, England had a much more defeatist attitude. An aggressive captain could keep on attacking them, and Benaud did this with an attack which seemed always rather less venomous and penetrative than the 1948 line-up. This does not suggest that Benaud would not have countered the more virile methods of the earlier England teams I have mentioned. I believe he would have, but there has been no chance to prove it. Perhaps the chance will come in 1962–63. Meanwhile, although I place him below Bradman, I include him in the same paragraph. That, surely, is fame for any man.

DON TALLON

Much in a Name

by Ray Robinson

Sherlock Holmes, who could tell a man's occupation from his dress and appearance, probably could have identified wicketkeepers in street clothes, even if their hands were in their pockets. Points for a detective to note would, I suppose, be unblinking gaze, non-creaking knees, round shoulders and wrinkles across the back of the neck. Sometimes names make it easy. Duckworth, Corrall, Rist, Fiddling, Tallon, Saggers – there is only one place in cricket for men with such names. And obviously there would be no future in the gloves for Sydney's National Gallery director, Hal Missingham.

Percy Corrall has carried no lariat for his Leicester round-up, but before he goes down he makes a motion often seen in the cattle country: he spreads his hands wide on each side of his hips, like a stockman heading off a horse escaping from a corral. In 1933 when he was 27, a blow on the left ear from Washbrook's bat put him in hospital on the danger list, but it has not deterred him from the closest stance of English 'keepers.

Frank Rist kept wickets throughout Essex's ordeal of fielding while the 1948 Australians scored their record 721 in a day, on a sunny Saturday at Southend. When it was over Wade's 34-year-old deputy said his knees felt like footballs. The ruddy, 5 ft 11 in (180 cm) keeper had to wait until 664 for a wicket – a snick by Loxton after the powerful Victorian had clouted up 120 in 88 minutes, third century of the day. Rist had the consolation that in the 721 he allowed only seven byes – four of them off one ball. Friends joked that the Australians let few balls pass. Little scope for wristplay behind the stumps.

Ray Robinson's Don Tallon piece is in From the Boundary *(1950) and reproduced with the permission of Brian Robinson.*

It is sound policy for a 'keeper to shape to take every ball. Fiddling and Tallon do. Even if the ball is hit for four or six Ken Fiddling goes through the motion of pushing a handful of air toward the bails. This short, fair Yorkshireman is not always as orthodox in other ways. He uses the right hand alone more often than anyone else I have noticed. In awaiting returns from the field he does not always circle to keep the stumps between the thrower and himself but gambles on intercepting the ball from side-on. He and Griffith are the only capless keepers I can recall in first-class cricket. His sandy head is thoroughly brushed, never a hair out of place. After one interruption by rain in a match against the Australians he forgot to slip an intimate piece of equipment into place before coming out; the twelfth man, E. Davis, smuggled it out to him with a sweater as a blind. Fiddling caught brilliantly for Yorkshire against Hassett's servicemen in 1945 but greater opportunity attracted him to Northants in 1947, before he turned 30. The only time he stops chewing on the field is to watch the bowler deliver and to follow the ball to the bat or his gloves.

Tallon! The very name brings to mind an eagle swooping on its prey. The lean, hard-bitten Queenslander's presence has made batsmen feel they are being attacked from two directions, that they are as much in danger of being torn down from behind as of being overcome by the visible foe at the bowling crease. No other man within my memory's span has kept wickets with such intensity and brilliance – the efficiency of an Oldfield or a Strudwick, heightened by a verve that was not in their make-up and extended by a taller man's reach. Don Tallon has been as ravenous for victims as Duckworth; less obviously only because he seemed actuated more by an implacable inner hatred for batsmen than the bouncing hostility of the Lancashire man. As with Bradman among batsmen, Tallon has combined the skills of more than one 'keeper. He alone exceeded 300 wickets before he played 100 first-class matches.

Paganini's wizardry on the violin caused superstitious folk to say the devil guided his fingers. Tallon is the Paganini of wicketkeepers. You see this first in the mystic passes his gloves make before the bowler begins: he gives occult signals by wriggling his fingers; with elbows close to his body he draws his hands sinuously down in front of his chest. He stands nearer the stumps than the others – stands guard over them, alert as a sentry, left foot behind the middle stump. As an outlet for nervous energy his feet smooth down the already-level ground. He puts his wrists against his hips, then wipes his forehead with the strip of bare forearm between gauntlet and shirtsleeve. Taking the peak in both hands he resettles his cap on his curly, brown head, tugging it nearer his eyes. He stretches his shoulders, hitches his trouser waistband, stoops halfway, then folds like a pocket knife until legs, thighs and body seem all one piece, balanced on level feet. Though rather tall, he squats nearer his heels than the others, with elbows outside his knees. He raps the earth with his fists, makes a final pass before his face with open gloves, and peers past his right forefinger before he poises his hands in front of his shins as the bowler runs up. He crouches there, motionless, until his eyes read the ball's secret.

Often scenting a wicket before the batsman becomes conscious of danger, he whips into position in readiness for the victim's mistake. His footwork is full of short, quick steps, his legs rarely straddle wide. He is a master of the sway and the lean to keep eyes and hands true to the ball's course – so much so that he looks as if most of his close-up keeping could be done with a book under each armpit. His glovework is full of wristy curves, convex for the knee-high ball, concave for the skidder. He is as fussy about his hands as a pianist. The wicketkeeper is the nerve-centre of the field; when Tallon is there it is a highly strung nerve. As the ball approaches he often jams his tongue into the right corner of his mouth. When the bat denies him the ball he goes through the taking action just the same, bringing his hands back like a chef drawing a tray from an oven. The ball that seems certain to bowl the batsman causes most 'keepers to stand upright to acclaim the happy sight; embarrassment and four byes usually result if it misses. If the stumps stop the ball from coming to Tallon, as like as not he will catch one of the flying bails.

In his leathery face, tanned by the Queensland sun, his hazel eyes almost disappear amid a network of wrinkles – the result of days staring along baking wickets in shimmering glare, enough to cause mirages to appear at the other end. A sardonic-looking smile occasionally creases his lean cheeks, accompanied now and again by a laugh that sounds hard and dry. Strangers don't find him easy to talk to. He walks to his position with an air of brooding concentration. Sparely built and lithe (5 ft 10½ in or 178 cm and 11 st 4 lb. or 71 kg), he could be a dismounted boundary rider, accustomed to hours of solitude on some vast cattle station in Western Queensland. Behind the stumps he is a man of two words: 'How's that?' (When Tallon came in to bat in Sir Donald Bradman's testimonial match and played nowhere near an off-the-wicket ball every fieldsman joined in a pre-arranged appeal.)

Tallon fits exactly the picture of the Australian cricketer – sun-dried, hard and efficient – formed by many English people who don't get to know the men personally.

In stumping or running out batsmen from balls taken wide he has sometimes ripped a stump out of the ground, as if his gloves really did have talons. When a batsman clumps down on a yorker he darts around as if to wrench the ball from under the bat. His clamant appeals have been bad for batsmen's nerves; they burst from him, demanding satisfaction; often he holds the ball on high as proof. Refusal is a wounding injustice.

Events made Tallon what he is, toughened the outer man. Of four brothers who learned the game on a back-lawn wicket prepared by their father, Les Tallon, Don was the most gifted, though Bill became an interstate player too. At 13, Don was chosen in the Queensland schoolboys' team, at 14 he was peeping over full-size pads as he kept in A Grade matches with the men in Bundaberg's Hinkler Park (named after the aviator, another famous son of the sugar-and-rum town, 217 miles north of Brisbane). At 16 the boy from Bundaberg played for Queensland Country against the Englishmen in 1933 and stumped Sutcliffe for 19. At 17 he was in the state XI. He became regular state 'keeper at Christmas, 1934, and went to work in a Brisbane motor-car company's store. His keenness laid him open to criticism for too-frequent and too-dramatic appealing, to convince Brisbane umpires (so southerners said).

In three more years his swiftness and safety had won him first place in the estimation of the cricketers whose opinions matter in these things: bowlers. Some bowlers in other state teams used to say they wished they had him out there in the middle with them. Secondarily, he could out-bat all other Australian 'keepers. The brilliance of his 193 against Victoria in 1936 set all Australia talking.

Omission from the 1938 tour of Britain put him in a ferment of bewilderment and frustration. It hurt him like a kick in the face. War was approaching – he might never achieve his lifelong ambition to play for Australia in England. He feared that his only chance had been wrongly denied him. Men's hands were against him.

After that, Tallon gritted his teeth and set out to show how wrong his omission had been. Between then and his disappearance into the Army I believe he reached the highest pitch ever attained by a 'keeper. He had the satisfaction, a bitter satisfaction, of setting up a series of records. In season 1938–39 he evicted 34 batsmen in Queensland's six first-class matches – figures no other 'keeper has approached in an all-Australian season; four times in 10 innings at least six men fell to his deft glovework. At Sydney he caught nine and stumped three New South Wales batsmen to equal Edward Pooley's world record of 12 in a match for Surrey, which had stood for 70 years. At Brisbane he dislodged seven Victorian batsmen in an innings to equal another world record by Smith, Farrimond and Price. He passed 100 wickets for Queensland in 32 matches – remarkable in a team lacking a regular leg-spin bowler, a wicketkeeper's best friend. His hands were so unsparing that batsmen became resigned to the fate awaiting a trailing toe or a touch with the bat. Before the Hitler–Hirohito war stopped first-class cricket he scored a hundred before lunch (in 90 minutes) against New South Wales, the only batsman to achieve the feat at Brisbane.

This superb 'keeper had to wait until he was 30 before he played in a Test match, in 1946 in New Zealand. By then, Queensland had gained the googly bowling of Colin McCool from New South Wales. Tallon welcomed him suitably with six catches and stumpings in their first match together. The pair became an outstanding combination. Their first united effort against Englishmen yielded four stumpings and two catches in the match and brought Tallon's total for Queensland to 170 wickets in 50 games in which he had worn the gloves. When he missed stumping Edrich off Cook, broadcaster Jack Fingleton broke the staggering news to listeners by saying: 'A most astonishing thing has just happened …'

Though Tallon was an automatic choice as Australian 'keeper he had a sleepless night before the team for the first Test against England was announced. This shadow of doubt had pursued him ever since his pre-war omission from the tour of England; his fellow players' reassurances could not banish the fear that he might be denied his rightful place, as in 1938.

Before he got to Britain at last, at the age of 32, Tallon underwent an operation on his tonsils, but he kept wickets so impressively that he was chosen one of *Wisden*'s Five Cricketers of the Year. Watching him, Duckworth told me: 'He gets smoothly to balls that would have had me scrambling. In fielding the ball with gloves on he is the cleanest I ever saw.' Yet England did not see him at his superlative best; he touched it several times but without the match-after-match consistency of his pre-war peak. The 1948 summer was too chilly for the Bundaberg sport-storekeeper. As the Australians were travelling through a village one asked: 'Where's the King's Arms?' Tallon grunted back: 'Around the Queen, in this weather – if he's got any sense.' Midway through the season he had to break from his lifetime habit of wetting his chamois inner gloves. On a misty May day at The Oval, the first time Lindwall let himself go in England, the fast bowler came galloping out of the fog like Dick Turpin's ghost. One ball whizzed over a batsman's shoulder; Tallon sighted it late, just had time to throw up one hand to save his face. He ripped off his gloves and shook his hand in the air to cool it. His right middle finger was bruised. In the second Test a dive for a leg ball from the fast bowler damaged his left little finger again and it was x-rayed.

Australia's dependence on fast and fastish bowlers in 1948 kept Tallon mostly in the backstop position and limited British crowds' opportunities to see his close-up mastery, his stumpings of camera-shutter speed and precision – often only one bail flicked off. In the third Test, still worried about his little finger, he and the fieldsmen at square-leg and point all were convinced that he stumped Compton (35) off Ian Johnson in England's first innings. Umpire Frank Chester's decision went against them. Disconsolate as a bear with a sore paw, Tallon squirmed down into position again: in such a moment he missed the absent McCool's calming 'Take it easy, Joe,' from first slip. Twice in the last three-quarter hour that evening and once next day he dropped Compton; two of them were little more than finger-end touches, low and wide, in dull light, but Tallon was savagely self-critical.

When the stumping of Compton was disallowed I looked through binoculars from Old Trafford's rooftop press box but could see no clear line on the pitch; the crease was a dark mass of roughened turf, cut up by players' boots. It would ease the umpires' task if the creases were repainted at every interval. Not that this would guarantee freedom from error. Keeping wickets for Brighton (Victoria) between the wars, Roy Hayball appealed for a stumping but was refused. Chatting after the match he said to the umpire: 'That must have been a very close thing,' and received the reply, 'It was. His toe was on the line.'

Hayball protested, 'But on the line is out!'

'Ah, but this was a very wide line.'

After his unlucky Test at Manchester, Tallon's left little finger, injured in another plunge for a fast ball in the Middlesex match, was so painfully puffy that he could not play in the fourth Test. On his reappearance in the final Test one of his three catches gave Londoners something to remember: his rapid sidesteps and falling capture of Hutton's leg-glance, with the back of his left glove to the ground.

When the fast bowlers swung the ball too far to leg for his footwork and dive to reach it, Tallon often lay outstretched in disgust, on his left elbow, seemingly heedless of how the ball was retrieved from the boundary. Sometimes, through glasses, he appeared to be easing his feelings with pithy comments which a lip-reader might have identified as predominantly in words of four and five letters.

Tallon was not available to tour South Africa in 1949–50. On the shorter New Zealand trip he saved Australia in the unofficial Test by getting seven wickets and making 116 (7 sixes) with batting few men on earth could equal. What pleased him more was that his hands came through the tour unhurt.

For all his high-pressure intensity in the fight, Tallon has humour. In his first Test at Lord's he fooled Compton into running hard by preparing to take a return when nobody was throwing. At Aberdeen his response to an inaccurate leg-break was to signal a wide (over-riding the umpire) and to insist on being given a chance himself to show how leg-breaks ought to be bowled. At Derby, on the morning after the team celebrated having won the Ashes outright, freakish hot weather had many tongues hanging out as left-handed Denis Smith made a new record for the county against Australia in a century partnership with Arnold Townsend. Seldom have eyes been cast more longingly at drinks than at the tray which Don Tallon, as twelfth man, carried on to the ground. Like survivors of a cross-desert trek by the Foreign Legion the players drooped listlessly about the wicket, too far gone to take a step toward the approaching succour. Half-way out Tallon stopped, laid the tray on the grass, knelt behind it and beckoned 'Come and get it.' The crowd of 10 000 saw the humour of it, but the captain was not amused. He sternly commanded the grinning twelfth man to bring the tray to the middle, and reproved him with 'This isn't a circus.'

A wicketkeeper's work is never done.

TALLON, Donald
Born: 17 February 1916, Bundaberg (QLD)
Died: 7 September 1984, Bundaberg (QLD)

Bats: Right-handed, wicketkeeper

First-Class Career
Debut: 1933–34 Queensland v Victoria, Brisbane

M	Inn	NO	Runs	50	100	Ave	Ct	St	Runs	Wkts	Ave	5	10
150	228	21	6034	27	9	29.14	303	129	202	0	–	–	–

Highest Score: 193 Queensland v Victoria, Brisbane, 1935–36

Test Career
Debut: 1945–46 Australia v New Zealand, Wellington

M	Inn	NO	Runs	50	100	Ave	Ct	St	Runs	Wkts	Ave	5	10
21	26	3	394	2	–	17.13	50	8	–	–	–	–	–

Highest Score: 92 Australia v England, Melbourne, 1946–47

ALAN DAVIDSON

Not Exactly the Home of Cricket.
Representing Switzerland:
Davos but No Davo

by Alex Buzo

'**W**hat was it like for you, the first time? Was it all over in a couple of minutes?' a friend once asked. 'Certainly not,' I told him, shocked. 'I stayed the whole day.'

The first time I saw Test cricket was on 9 January 1959 at the Sydney Cricket Ground when England were two–nil down in the 'throwing series'. There were 46 607 people there for the opening day of the third Test, including actors John Mills and Trevor Howard among the cravats and binoculars in the Members' Stand, and Peter May's fiancee Virginia Gilligan, daughter of former England captain, 'What do you think, Arthur?' Gilligan. A school friend and I sat in the 'Bob' stand opposite and saw the matchwinners from the second Test, Alan Davidson and Ian Meckiff, open the bowling. These left-arm pace bowlers were to make quite an impact.

Davo was something of a cult figure at the time, so much so that the publican of a hotel in Flinders Street near the ground advertised it in big neon signs as 'Alan Davidson's Palace Hotel'. It was a crock of the first magnitude: the fine print above the door revealed the licensee to be one Alan P. Davidson, not the A. K. who had pioneered orthodoxy and wicket-taking for the left-arm pace fraternity, much as Rod Laver had given a backhand and dignity to the southpaws of tennis. Davo bowled just like a right-hander, and indeed that's what he looked like in the mirrors of the SCG bars.

Alan Keith Davidson had the classic 15-pace run-up and coiled spring delivery that Harold Larwood and Ray Lindwall had before him, while Meckiff was very much the Voce figure. He looked more like a

---

Alex Buzo, playwright, journalist and author, was vice-captain of the 15As at the Armidale School, and later played for North Sydney Colts, UNSW, Combined Geneva and Metros.

golfer than a cricketer, so it was a bit of a surprise when he began his awkward, ambling run, at the end of which he suddenly hurled the ball at the batsman as if to say 'Oh here, have the bloody thing, and I hope it bites you!' It was impossible to tell if he threw the ball, without a microscopic view of his jerky, angular delivery and its results; the 'chucker' controversy was largely confined to the press box and no one in the crowd even called out 'no-ball!'. Davidson was easier to read; he was all purpose and circular movement, with late swing trawling like a well baited fish-hook, and his attitude to the batsman appeared quite different. He seemed to be saying 'This is what a cricket ball looks like. I think you should know that.'

During the 'Lindmill' days, there was a similar duopoly, with the silky action of Lindwall providing a complete contrast to the short run and sudden, petulant sling of Keith Miller. You would think that cricketers all over the country would be imitating Lindwall, Larwood and Davidson rather than Miller, Meckiff and the late Bill Voce, but you would be wrong.

It was the fashion then for young school players to imitate older school players who took their cue from Test cricketers. When I was at my first school I loved tennis, hated golf and felt ambivalent about cricket because I could never work out whether I should bat or bowl, and if the latter, what sort of action I should adopt. In the first XI, Dent and Lawrie were identikit Davidson and Meckiff figures, with Dent being even more fluent and perfect in his action and Lawrie having even more of an 'I fling dung' demeanor.

Not every cricketer lived up to his image, of course. Davidson was supposed to have an immaculate length and was called 'the Claw' because of his fielding prowess. Meckiff was considered a wild card, an erratic left-arm bowler and no great shakes in the field. The third Test in 1959 began with the defence-oriented Trevor 'Barnacle' Bailey being dismissed lbw by Meckiff, who then caught the other opener, Arthur Milton, off a Davidson full toss. Nevertheless, over the series and over the years, you would have to say that Davidson was a smooth man whereas Meckiff was hairy.

When I was shipped off to my second school, it was on the *Oronsay* and the school was in Switzerland. At least in the meantime there was shipboard cricket, a series of matches played between the passengers and the crew. Constraints of space on the deck only allowed for a four-metre run-up, so I had to streamline everything and concentrate on the delivery stride. There was no room for imitations and I ended up with an action that enabled me to make the best use of what talents I had. No longer smooth or hairy, I had five o'clock shadow and I was finally ready to play. Unfortunately the country I was headed for was not exactly the home of cricket.

Switzerland has many educational establishments, but the International School of Geneva is the best known, and it was there on a glorious day in April that I found a musty cricket kit in a dungeon next to the 'vestiaire', as the changing rooms were called. I dragged it outside and began to unpack the stumps and pads, oblivious to the stares and shudders of the other students and the staff, some of whom were refugees from the British class and sport system.

Soon we were playing practice matches on sports afternoon with some pretty fair cricketers who came from Iran, Ceylon and other places on or near the Empire trail, including a spinner from Manly Boys' High called Stuart Romaine. One of the best was a Welsh student, Peter Grundy, who had fallen in with some Gauloise-smoking decadents in the Upper Sixth, some of whom were 19 or 20. The smell of linseed oil soon brought him back to the fold, however, and to the amazement of his friends he practised long and hard. They gave up on him and scooted off on their Lambrettas, probably to drink absinthe.

This kind of elitism was quite common at Ecolint, as the school was known, and there were lots of children of the jet set hanging about or forming hierarchies. Rita Hayworth's daughter Yasmin Khan was a 12-year-old femme fatale, Hardy Kruger's daughter Christine was tall, blonde and unattainable, while Charlie Chaplin's saturnine son Michael was as silent as his father's films. A Eurasian heiress was part of this crop and I was fervently in love with her, so I was pleased when she sat down to watch one of our games. Maybe I'll get to her through our shared Commonwealth heritage, I mused hopefully. In the event, I tripped and fell trying to retain the strike, and soon after Carnee got up and left. The next day she looked at me with a mixture of pity and disdain (60–40 for pity) in the big dark eyes and I realised I had the job ahead of me. There was no such thing as racism in the jet set, but there was no such thing as love, either.

With Peter Grundy on loan from the Gauloisie, the headmaster's son hitting them in the middle and a good Canadian wicketkeeper, we were putting together a reasonable team. Feeling confident, and wanting to raise the school's profile, we issued a challenge to the Geneva Cricket Club, the expatriates' stronghold. They could not play us – fatally – until the last week of term, when most families had booked early holidays. In the case of Stuart Romaine, his parents had arranged a social occasion on that day. A social occasion! He added, quite unnecessarily, that he wasn't really Australian; he was born in England, spent just a few years in Manly and appeared to know more about Davos than Davo. In no way did he model himself on the man of 15 paces.

The good Canadian wicketkeeper had to attend several social occasions back in Canada, but someone's Uzbekistanian cousin from Berlin would play, I was told. I put him at long-stop, where he was the busiest player on the field. As he didn't speak English, I relayed instructions through first slip, who spoke a bit of German. Unfortunately Peter Grundy's Trueman-derived run-up proved too long and he sprayed the new ball all over the place, so there were more than a few Teutonic oaths heard during that raw and gloomy afternoon. The headmaster came down to watch his son get a duck in one of many umpiring fiascos and the challenge of our Young Guns was turned aside. Stuart Romaine, whose son is now a county cricketer, arrived in civvies towards the end and said it was a pity he wasn't able to turn out and provide some much-needed spin in the attack.

Although Ecolint v Geneva had been a debacle, I was picked, in the summer of 1962, at the age of 17 years and 11 months, to enter man's estate and represent Switzerland in 'international' one-day games against the British armed forces team from Paris. I pleaded briefly for Peter Grundy to be included, but I was the only student they wanted. Did I abandon my friends for the beer-swilling world of the international cricketer? Yes I did!

'What on earth is someone your age doing with all those wrinkles around your eyes?' asked the wife of one of the players and I mumbled something about 'days in the sun' as we assembled on a cool day in late

June. The oval where we played was in fact a circle, a general purpose athletics field where we rolled the grass down and pegged out a coir mat. The Swiss looked at us with a mixture of pity and disdain (80–20 for disdain) as we warmed up, with Mont Blanc and associated alps forming a novel backdrop to the summer game. A light rail line ran along the northern end and when a train went past you would see all these pale faces giving out with a Swiss Stare (I'm convinced that's what they use to get holes in their cheese). For the average citizen of Geneva, this bizarre cricket business was further proof that 'les anglais' were mad.

The English batsmen I had seen on that first day at the SCG had included an overawed debutant called Ted Dexter, who made no contribution, the gentle persuader Colin Cowdrey, who coaxed the ball into gaps and probably sent flowers in the morning, and the punishment machine, Peter May. The precise and pointy-faced May had the best technique of any batsman I had ever seen, and his driving was straight and severe. He only made 42 that day, but they were 42 of the most ominous and sadistic runs I had ever seen and his dismissal brought gasps of relief from the crowd. In retrospect, that was the moment when the Ashes began to look safe, but the collective subconscious noted it at the time.

The captain of the Geneva team was the same age as May, had been to the same university (Cambridge) and came from the same school of thought. Technically perfect when batting, it turned out that was all he did. Like PM he didn't field as such and didn't even bowl at practice, but this was no act of hero-worship like my friend Grundy's borrowing of the long run-up of Freddy S.Trueman. It was an introduction to the English phenomenon of 'The Batsman Who Just Batted'. May was later to ascribe the loss of the 1958–59 test series to the fact that there were too many players in his team making their last tour on the big hard grounds of Australia (code for 'they fielded like statues').

I was young, hyperactive and from a hot climate and I loved running about and 'foxing' balls and diving for catches, so they let me do it. I opened the bowling and they kept me on for hours until I had taken 3/85. If there hadn't been so many dropped catches, mostly courtesy of the only other Australian in the team – genial, fortyish Dr Carter of Adelaide – then I would have taken about 7/ 35, but you can't alter Test records.

We had a close win, lost the second, and then fronted for the third on a sparkling day in July. 'Don't drop it so short this time,' ordered The Batsman Who Just Batted and gave me the new ball. An hour later

I had taken 5/6 against a disorganised, cat-on-hot-bricks opposition, bowling fuller and faster in the crisp air. The Armed Forces captain, who was in fact a major, spent a lot of time at the non-striker's end looking most displeased. 'Two of those wick-its fell to *eau verre* pitched bawls,' I heard him say to the umpire.

That night in the gallery outside the Cafe Movenpick, Carnee walked past nodding vaguely at me. The sound of her echoing heels brought the five-for-sixer back to earth. I never saw her again.

We won the fourth and final 'Test' easily, with my only contribution being an unexpected 32 with the bat, and then I got the news that I was being shipped home to sit for a 'post' to get into university. Reality struck when I fronted up to the wizened coach of North Sydney on a baking day in October. He was called Jimmy Hannan, as indeed a lot of people were in those days, and I asked him if I could join the club. 'Where've you been playing?' he asked. 'I've just represented Switzerland,' I answered, aiming for a note of objectivity. He looked at me with a mixture of disgust and disdain (95–5 for disgust) and said 'Switzerland! Not exactly the home of cricket, is it?' I spent that season, 1962–63, playing for North Sydney Colts as a batsman while Europe froze in the coldest winter of the twentieth century. The voyage of identity and image, if that's what it was, had well and truly ended.

What happened to Carnee? Reader, she married a doctor and they play lots of golf.

NOTE: Alan Davidson retired at the end of the 1962–63 season.

DAVIDSON, Alan Keith
Born: 14 June 1929, Lisarow (NSW)

Bats: Left-handed
Bowls: Left-arm fast

First-Class Career
Debut: 1949–50 New South Wales v South Australia, Adelaide

M	Inn	NO	Runs	50	100	Ave	Ct	St	Runs	Wkts	Ave	5	10
193	246	39	6804	36	9	32.86	168	–	14048	672	20.90	33	2

Highest Score: 129 Australians v Western Province, Cape Town, 1957–58
Best Bowling: 7/31 New South Wales v Western Australia, Perth, 1961–62

Test Career
Debut: 1953 Australia v England, Nottingham

M	Inn	NO	Runs	50	100	Ave	Ct	St	Runs	Wkts	Ave	5	10
44	61	7	1328	5	–	24.59	42	–	3819	186	20.53	14	2

Highest Score: 80 Australia v West Indies, Brisbane, 1960–61
Best Bowling: 7/93 Australia v India, Kanpur, 1959–60

JACK GREGORY

Loved by the Camera

by Gideon Haigh

The camera loved Jack Gregory. Photographers of his day had still to conquer the distance between boundary and pitch, but Gregory's expansive, vibrant cricket reached out to meet them, advancing, radiating from the middle.

There's a famous image of him in his delivery while practising at Lord's: the front leg hanging in mid-air, the right arm at the bottom of its swing, the left arm aloft. The body's slight backward tilt lends him a palpable energy. Another picture features him batting at Sydney a few years later. With the completion of a drive, the hands have ended up over the right shoulder. The force of the stroke has turned Gregory's trunk to face down the wicket, although the ball is disappearing through mid-off, and the front foot hovers just off the ground. Here again is energy, a glad, spontaneous vitality. To enhance the breezy naturalness, Gregory is bare-armed, bare-headed and gloveless; indeed, we have it on Ray Robinson's authority that he even scorned a protector.

Not so long ago, I chanced on another photograph I'd never seen before, on the front page of a copy of Sydney's *Referee*. It was Gregory taking a slips catch, and a blinder, too: he is parallel to the ground, the ball snug in an outstretched right hand, while wicketkeeper Hanson Carter casts a startled glance over his right shoulder. More than 70 years have elapsed since Jack Gregory played cricket. It was hard to avert my eyes. Eighty years since his first breathtaking feats, age hasn't wearied him; photographs show Gregory as he was, the most magnetic and expressive player of his day.

Gideon Haigh is at work on a much-needed biography of Jack Gregory's captain, Warwick Armstrong.

Bradman, incidentally, thought the world of 'vital and vehement' Gregory. 'His bowling in the early days was positively violent in its intensity,' opines the Don in *Farewell to Cricket*. 'His whole attitude towards the game was so dynamic, his slip fielding so sensational, his brilliant batting so pleasing … that thousands would flock to see Gregory play anywhere at any time.'

Another who 'venerated' Gregory was, oddly enough, Harold Larwood. 'Gregory's bowling was the essence of savagery,' wrote Bradman's chief nemesis, 'his great kangaroo leap at the last instant presenting an awesome sight to any batsman.' It is surely something to have both Bradman and Larwood in a corner on any subject, yet admiration of Gregory united them.

An arresting feature of Gregory's career is that it might easily never have happened. Father Charles had played for New South Wales, uncles Dave and Ned for Australia, the former as captain in the inaugural Test match at Melbourne in March 1877, the latter becoming the architect for the Sydney's Cricket Ground's famous scoreboard (disused today, it still peers furtively over the brow of the old Hill). Another uncle, Albert, was renowned for owning Australia's most comprehensive cricket library. And cousin Syd had 10 months before Jack's birth relieved England of the first Test double century on Australian soil.

Yet Jack the lad evinced no particular aptitude for cricket. He captained Shore's first XI in 1911 and 1912, but as a batsman, and impressed at least as much as a hurdler and first XV rugby player. On leaving school, he went jackerooing in Queensland; a source, he wrote later, of deep disappointment to his family. By 20, he cut a striking figure: six feet three inches tall, bronzed, blue-eyed and rugged. In portrait photographs, he has an air of alertness bordering on impatience, as though in a hurry to be elsewhere. But it was not to be playing cricket.

Cricket's prospects of claiming Gregory dwindled further when he enlisted as an artillery gunner in January 1916. He served in the 7th, 10th, 11th and 23rd Field Artillery Brigades and 3rd and 4th Division Artillery Brigades, undertaking two tours of France. He played regimental cricket, and there first toyed with fast bowling: the legendary Charlie Macartney first met Gregory in an inter-unit game on a matting pitch at Larkhill, Salisbury Plain, and remembered him for ending the match by hitting a batsman in the eye with a lifter. But otherwise Gregory's off-duty recreational energies were devoted to winning the hurdles over 120 yards, the sprint over 100 and his unit's tennis championship.

With peace, however, came the notion, mooted by the MCC grandee Pelham Warner, of a touring cricket team selected from AIF ranks. So much of the services' recruiting effort had been aimed at sportsmen that it was heavily endowed with cricketers, and a number of unofficial internationals had already been staged between England and an ersatz Dominions XI. Players were invited to join training sessions preparatory to selection at The Oval; Lt J. M. Gregory was one.

Quite why Gregory should have featured among invitees is unclear. Before enlisting, he'd played exactly one game in Sydney first-grade. According to historian Ron Cardwell, the summons was on the recommendation of another officer in Gregory's unit, former New South Wales Shield batsman Frank Buckle. Gregory himself heard that his invitation came direct from Warner, who'd watched him play in a social match in which Gregory played for the Artillery Officers' School against Red Cross, and intuited latent ability from the family name. In the event, the 24 year old was the last of the touring XVI picked, and then largely on the basis of physique; if he couldn't play much, it looked like Gregory could learn.

In hindsight, the AIF team was a powerful one. Lance-Corporal Herbie Collins, who became its captain, went on to lead Australia. Corporal Bert Oldfield, Captain Clarence Pellew and Gunner Johnny Taylor would serve under him as Test men. Then there was Gregory himself, all his cricket ahead. Yet at the time, their quality was unknown, their resilience unascertainable. Some had endured very hard wars indeed: Oldfield had spent five months in a military hospital with shell-shock, while Captain Bill Trenerry had been wounded twice and Lt Charles Kellaway no fewer than four times. And after scraping into the team, Gregory advanced by accident. Early on, he reported having cut his hand by stepping on it at fine leg. He was ribbed mercilessly; he was nicknamed 'Pavlova', an ironic reference to the dancer, while Collins commented that he had all the elegance of a tank rolling into action and ruefully directed him to convalesce at slip.

To universal surprise, however, 'the long'un' proved a close catcher of uncanny reflex and reach; scorer Bill Ferguson likened his arms to an octopus' tentacles, 'only they seemed twice as many and twice as long'. Impressed, Collins tossed him the ball when the leader of the team's attack, Captain Cyril Docker, broke down. It was like removing a genie from a bottle. In the tour's third match, against Cambridge

University at Fenners, Gregory claimed 6/68, and in bowling two batsmen didn't simply disarrange the stumps but knocked them flying like ninepins. On a benign surface at Lord's a few days later, he struck the chest of Middlesex's Mordaunt Doll so hard that the ball lifted the batsman off his feet, before trickling cruelly on the stumps. Doll departed. Gregory had arrived.

Gregory would bag 178 wickets at less than 17 on that trip, and collect 1352 runs at 31. But a recitation of his successes wouldn't

convey the force of his initial impact. Here was a mediocre grade cricketer, three years at war, suddenly transformed into a self-taught fast bowler, hitter and catcher. And he was dramatic. Oldfield described his run as 'ungainly', for his stride was immense, and his boots so voluminous that team-mates could fit their own shod feet inside them. The action climaxed in what soon became known as a 'kangaroo hop' in the delivery stride, and was completed with a follow-through that rolled like a tsunami halfway down the pitch. The effect of Gregory's hyperkinetic exertion, however, was fearful. Writing 55 years later in *Wisden*, Sir Neville Cardus insisted that Gregory 'ran some 20 yards to release the ball'. In fact, Gregory's approach was only 15 yards, 12 paces; it simply 'seemed' longer.

As the ball descended from almost eight feet, it could do almost anything. When he pitched up, Oldfield thought, Gregory swung the new ball as much as any bowler he ever took. When he pitched short, Collins remembered, the ball seemed to whoosh like a mortar. For he was unbelievedly, inexhaustibly quick. Wrecking the stumps of a South African batsman called Phillip Hand in Johannesburg on the AIF tour's homeward leg, Gregory sent a bail flying 46 yards.

Gregory's batting, initially primitive, always uninhibited, also developed on that AIF tour. He scored his maiden first-class hundred against Northants, and was eventually trusted to open the innings.

Then there was the fielding, infallible at slip, electric anywhere. Against Natal at Durban on the first three days of November 1919, Gregory harvested 9/32 and threw the last man out for good measure.

When the AIF team landed in Melbourne two months later, Gregory was the object of insatiable curiosity. Games were arranged to test the mettle of Collins' now-celebrated cohorts. At his first Australian gallop, Gregory claimed 7/22 against Victoria, bowling flat out on a rain-affected Melbourne surface. A fortnight later against New South Wales, opening both batting *and* bowling on the arena adorned by his uncle's scoreboard, he scored 122 and 102, took eight wickets and three catches. In 80 years since, no one has even approximated such a feat, let alone paralleled it.

Johnny Douglas's English team, which toured the antipodes the following season, must have sensed what it was in for. And, in 1920–21, Australian cricket had a pitiless edge: new captain Warwick Armstrong was a leader who took the tact out of tactics and, with home Tests of the time played to a result, beaten teams had nowhere to hide. The hosts won all five contests and, if Gregory did not completely dominate the rubber, that was only because Armstrong had such a constellation of talent at his disposal: the left/right opening alliance of Collins and Bardsley, the hawk-eyed Macartney and the googly guru Arthur Mailey among them.

As it was, Gregory would almost certainly have been man of the series, had such awards been in vogue. No Australian has approached his 7/69 and chanceless 100 in 137 minutes in the second Test at Melbourne over the New Year. For good measure, he also intercepted no fewer than 15 chances. Sir Jack Hobbs said Gregory stood closer than any slips catcher of the time, and was unmistakably ravenous for the ball; sometimes, when Mailey loosed his wrong'un, Gregory would take a couple of giant strides from his normal post and materialise, like an apparition, at leg slip.

Gregory formed two vital strategic alliances during this series. The first was with his captain. The prickly Armstrong was a figure more respected than admired by contemporaries; sooner or later, he seems to have antagonised most opponents and more than a few comrades. Yet Gregory revered the vast Victorian, referring to him in two very rare articles some years later for *Sporting Globe* as 'my ideal cricketer' and 'the greatest of my time'.

Gregory also aligned with another cricketer from Victoria, although originally a tinsmith's son from Launceston, Ted McDonald. Like

Gregory, McDonald had begun cricket as a batsman, before discovering a natural gift for bowling fast; the great Englishman Frank Woolley thought him speedier even than Larwood. As a combination, they were fire and ice. Where Gregory's approach shook the earth, McDonald's flowed like a river. While the former enjoyed the wind at his back and swung the ball mostly away, the latter didn't mind breasting a breeze and possessed a sinister backbreak. To Cardus, Gregory was 'atomic-powered', McDonald 'Satanic'. On one key question, however, Gregory and McDonald were as one. As McDonald's future Lancashire team-mate Cec Parkin put it: 'He always maintains ... that there never was a captain to equal Warwick Armstrong.'

McDonald actually achieved little in the three Tests of that 1920–21 Ashes series, and had reason for gratitude to Armstrong at its conclusion; the captain insisted on his selection to partner Gregory for the forthcoming tour of England. It was a ground-breaking recommendation. Hitherto, the concept of entrusting the new ball to pace at both ends had been almost unknown; the great Australian pacemen of yore had been solo venturers (Fred Spofforth, Ernie Jones, Tibby Cotter), usually sharing the new ball with a medium-pace bowler or even a spinner. With Gregory and McDonald, speed was now in the ascendant; now, in fact, and evermore.

Neither Gregory nor McDonald fit the contemporary fast bowler's mould of histrionic aggression, and of a general love of attention. Gregory was anything but a limelighter. As Armstrong's Australians crossed the continent to board the England-bound *Osterly* in Fremantle in March 1921, the train had to stop in country South Australia for a civic reception at Quorn. As manager Syd Smith addressed the crowd, a cry went up for a word from Gregory and a posse of locals boarded the train in search of him. The first player they encountered was Gregory himself but, in those days when news was vested in word rather than image, he went unrecognised. Thinking quickly, Gregory confided that the man they sought had slipped off the other side of the train, sending his admirers off in comic pursuit.

Bradman noticed that Gregory could never be drawn to discussing his on field accomplishments, though unfailingly generous-hearted toward younger team-mates. Larwood, so exhilarated by Gregory's bowling, also found him the gentlest of men away from the fray: 'Off the field you could not meet a more friendly and amiable chap.' Leery of the press after once being misquoted, the only interview he granted was a most reluctant one in the year before his death, an aspiring cricket writer called David Frith driving 200 miles on the off-chance of catching him in his shack at Narooma on New South Wales's south coast, and coaxing him into a few quiet reminiscences. There were no visible trophies or mementos. 'Here,' recalled Frith, 'was a cricketing Garbo.'

McDonald, likewise, was a self-contained character with little small talk, among strangers as inscrutable as a cigar-store Indian; Ronald Mason thought that he 'harboured in a not very approachable personality a genuine vein of genius'. His energy seemed almost supernatural. Even bowling at his fiercest, Oldfield recalled, he did not seem to perspire. On one occasion, he arrived late for a day's play, drained a glass of water, took a couple of drags on a cigarette, and bowled unchanged till lunch.

Yet that summer of 1921, these quiet assassins sapped English spirit where bombs dropped on London from the Kaiser's Zeppelins had failed. In the first innings of the first Test at Trent Bridge, Gregory had Donald Knight caught behind then bowled Ernest Tyldesley and Patsy Hendren in one hectic, breathless over. In the second innings, he bowled Tyldesley again, this time off his head. No Man's Land had been recreated over 22 yards of turf.

For the second Test at Lord's, England picked a batsman called A. J. Evans: a good player, and a courageous man. As a pilot during the Great War, he'd won the Military Cross and bar. As a POW, he'd organised escape attempts of such reckless derring-do that he'd been persuaded to pen a book, *The Escaping Club*, describing how his mother had sent him maps and compasses concealed inside cakes and jars of anchovy paste. Yet on the day of his Test debut, a team-mate remembered: 'He was so nervous that he could hardly hold his bat, and his knees were literally knocking together … His nerve had gone and the first straight ball was enough for him.'

Australia won those Tests, and the next at Leeds, to retain the Ashes, and against the counties waged a reign of terror. Even Wally Hammond, then a rising star with Gloucestershire on the brink of a brilliant 30-year career, had not the stomach for the fight: 'Jack Gregory had cultivated a fearsome stare and gave me the treatment. With knees trembling and hands shaking, I was relieved when he bowled me first ball.'

It was Armstrong's turn for gratitude. No Australian touring party has won more first-class games. Gregory and McDonald claimed 116 and 138 wickets in England respectively, all at the pin's fee of 16.6 each. In 27 matches, Gregory also accumulated 1135 runs at 36.6 and hauled in 37 catches; no Australian all-rounder has performed such a 'double' since. En route home via South Africa, he then annexed the honour of the fastest Test century, belting 34 from his first 12 deliveries, and cruising to three figures in 10 minutes over the hour. Those who regard packed international schedules as a feature only of the jet age should inspect Jack Gregory's figures in the first three years of his cricket career: 80 first-class matches on three continents for more than 4000 runs at almost 40, and 400 wickets at 17.

Perhaps it was too much. On his return home, Gregory foreshadowed retirement, and his intention of returning to the rural life he'd left six years before; his right knee was by now constantly painful and inflamed.

In the event, he found a job with a Sydney sheet metal manufacturer, Kavanagh & English, and submitted to a surgeon removing a cartilage from the afflicted joint: an operation at the time from which recovery was never total. Indeed, despite being an absentee from the next two domestic seasons, Gregory was seldom the same. On occasion, he offered glimpses of his former threat, once breaking the shoulder of Arthur Richardson's bat in a Shield match at Adelaide Oval as he had him taken at slip. More often, he was merely a good bowler rather than a great one.

By coincidence, his admirers Larwood and Bradman were both present when Gregory's knee finally buckled during the Brisbane Test of December 1928: Larwood batting in his first Australian international, Bradman making his Test debut. As Gregory dived headlong for a return catch, his knee bore the brunt of the fall. Larwood recalled the Australian's tears 'not from the pain of the injury, but from the realisation that he could no longer play the game he loved'. Bradman recorded Gregory's words when he was carried to the dressing room: 'Boys, I'm through, I have played my last game.'

A photograph exists of the moment Gregory was maimed; as I said, cameras were seldom idle in his presence. Two features compel attention. Larwood's bat has shattered at the shoulder; a final attestation of Gregory's force. And Gregory's prone figure lies more than halfway down the pitch; a last intimation of his athleticism. Jack Gregory was right; he never played again. But, at a glance, he continues to come alive.

GREGORY, Jack Morrison

Born: 14 August 1895, North Sydney (NSW)
Died: 7 August 1973, Bega (NSW)

Bats: Left-handed
Bowls: Right-arm fast

First-Class Career

Debut: 1919 AIF v Robinson's XII, Attleborough

M	Inn	NO	Runs	50	100	Ave	Ct	St	Runs	Wkts	Ave	5	10
129	173	18	5561	27	13	36.52	195	–	10580	504	20.99	33	8

Highest Score: 152 New South Wales v New Zealanders, Sydney, 1927–28
Best Bowling: 9/32 AIF v Natal, Durban, 1919–20

Test Career

Debut: 1920–21 Australia v England, Sydney

M	Inn	NO	Runs	50	100	Ave	Ct	St	Runs	Wkts	Ave	5	10
24	34	3	1146	7	2	36.97	37	–	2648	85	31.15	4	–

Highest Score: 119 Australia v South Africa, Johannesburg, 1921–22
Best Bowling: 7/69 Australia v England, Melbourne, 1920–21

CLARRIE GRIMMETT

The Master Craftsman

by Ashley Mallett

Clarrie Grimmett was the master craftsman of the spinner's art. He did not have what Bill Brown calls to memory about Bill O'Reilly's bowling, possessing neither O'Reilly's 'unrelenting hostility', nor Shane Warne's supreme power of purchase on the ball. However, Grimmett ranks high in the list of all-time greats because of his extraordinary will to succeed, allied with unerring accuracy and the patience of Job.

Grimmett was cricket's version of a stalker. He watched and he waited. He was the wicket fox, perhaps cricket's supreme hunter of batting scalps. He never took his eyes off his prey. He looked for the slightest hint of a weakness. Had he played in another era Grimmett would have quickly picked up on Ian Botham. Botham liked to chat, so Clarrie would have totally ignored him. He traded on the psychological edge. Then again, Botham, like his Somerset team-mate, West Indian Viv Richards, who battered all manner of bowlers, struggled against even the ordinary leggies. Grimmett would have dealt with them easily.

Unlike his old mate O'Reilly, with Clarrie there was no gangling approach or demonstrative whirling of arms – Grimmett approached rather like a timid cat on thin ice. His tread was so light it told you he had a suspicion that the ground might give way at any moment. He crouched low, like an arthritic cat that had lost its rhythm of youth but was preparing to pounce anyway. Any batsman facing Grimmett first time could be forgiven for thinking that there was no menace about this little fellow. Yet all the while, Grimmett's mind worked overtime. There was no great surge of energy through the crease as there is with Warne. Grimmett crept up on you and once he attached himself to a

Ashley Mallett's biography Clarrie Grimmett: the Bradman of Spin *was published in 1993.*

batsman the poor fellow could not shake him loose until it was time to depart for the pavilion. Even then Grimmett's ghost sat on the batsman's shoulder. Grimmett wheeled away and he schemed. He removed batsmen from his presence with stealth and cunning. He built the pressure with persistence and subtle changes of pace.

O'Reilly wore his heart on his sleeve and crashed his way through a batsman's armoury with quickish leg-breaks which pitched and spat venomously like an angry snake. Warne relies on a natural hard spun leg-break which dips wickedly. His arc would please Grimmett, for it is usually above the level of the batsman's eyes.

Clarrie Grimmett lived and breathed cricket. He literally pored over its history and culture with the sort of meticulous enthusiasm you'd expect from a committed anthropologist. Grimmett studied how a ball swung and how it spun. He could tell you precisely where you would need to take up your stance in the cosmos to see the spinning Earth as a leg-break or wrong'un. Statistically speaking, Grimmett's bowling record is Bradman-like, for in 248 first-class matches – from 1911 to 1940 – Grimmett took a bag of five wickets or more per innings 127 times. In 37 Tests he took 216 wickets at 24.21, taking bags of five wickets or more on 21 occasions. His record is astounding, for in 105 matches for South Australia, Grimmett took 668 wickets – 513 in 79 Sheffield Shield matches (504 for South Australia and 9 for Victoria). On ten occasions Grimmett took 50 or more first-class wickets in an Australian season. 59 (1924–25), 59 (1925–26), 71 (1928–29), 82 (1929–30), 74 (1930–31), 77 (1931–32), 55 (1932–33), 66 (1933–34), 58 (1934–35), 73 (1939–40). Next best is Dennis Lillee who achieved the feat on six occasions, then comes Chuck Fleetwood-Smith, Bill O'Reilly and yours truly, each of us reaching the 50 wickets in a season on five separate occasions.

A student of the game with an undying passion to listen, learn and absorb, Clarrie was 'working' on a 'wrong wrong'un' when I first met him back in 1967. Clarrie's new mystery ball was the leg-break spinning out of his hand which seemed perfectly positioned to deliver a wrong'un. I had written to Grimmett, asking him for help about my bowling. I explained that I was technically okay, but as well as I bowled I didn't seem to get many people out. Despite my lack of success someone must have seen a glimmer of ability for I was made 12th man twice for Western Australia in the 1966–67 summer. I felt I could bowl and was a talent, but I was more like the doctor who explained to a grieving relative that while the operation was a total success, the patient died.

When I enquired at the Grimmett front door, Elizabeth Grimmett directed me to the back garden and pointed at the top of a huge pepper tree. 'Clarrie's up there,' she said, shielding her eyes from the early morning sun. Clarrie finished sawing off a high branch and suddenly dropped into my world. His face lit up and we shook hands. Clarrie grabbed his 'Jack Hobbs' bat and indicated that I use it to strike the ball inside a stocking attached to string and suspended from a branch of the pepper tree. I decided that any protest was useless. Here I was having travelled to Adelaide from Perth for him to critically analyse my bowling, not my batting. Grimmett said, 'There was a young man whom I taught the late cut on the ship going to England in 1930 ... and young Don Bradman was a fast learner!' I struck two balls and Clarrie said he had seen enough.

He then invited me to bowl to him. Here was the 76-year-old spinning gnome of legend standing there at the wicket of his full-sized, lovingly prepared turf wicket. He wore no pads, no protection of any kind and his eyes sparkled behind black horn-rimmed glasses. I delivered two balls, each met the middle of his Jack Hobbs bat. He called me down the pitch. 'Now son, give up bowling and become a batsman!' He added that he could play me blindfolded. I called his bluff and he tied a handkerchief over his glasses. My next ball met the middle of his Jack Hobbs bat.

When he stopped laughing the old man proceeded to deliver the best coaching lesson I've ever heard, up until then and since. He talked about flight above the level of the eyes. He talked about change of pace, breaking the batsman's rhythm. Clarrie took care to explain what he meant. He walked me through his theory, then constructed an extraordinary contraption across the pitch to ensure that my deliveries would arc over the line (or the batsman's eyes) before landing. He made me realise that to a spin bowler it was not where the ball pitched that was the key, it was how the ball was arriving.

Clarrie was both blunt and sensitive. His sensitive side harked back to his early days in New Zealand, the very day he bowled for Wellington on Basin Reserve against the touring Aussies and his hero, Victor Trumper – the year: 1914.

They toured England together in 1926 and eventually Grimmett, 'the miser', took over from Mailey, 'the millionaire': such descriptions referred not to their fiscal status, but to their attitude regarding runs taken from their bowling. It was nothing for Mailey to purposely bowl a high full toss. Clarrie was meaner than the most territorial of junkyard dogs. He wouldn't concede a single to a good player to attack a lesser light. Clarrie always backed himself to dismiss the best of them all, like the day in Adelaide in 1937 when he played in his own testimonial and clean bowled Don Bradman for 17. When Clarrie bowled Bradman he was jumping about excitedly, not thinking that Bradman's dismissal would have certainly impacted on gate takings.

'I did it, I did it! I told you I could get him,' Grimmett beamed.

The stern-faced Richardson said, 'Ease up, Clarrie. You've just cost us a thousand quid!'

Born in Dunedin, New Zealand, on Christmas Day, 1891, Clarence Victor Grimmett learnt his early cricket playing impromptu games on the Basin Reserve, after the family moved to Wellington when he was a toddler. At Mount Cook Boys' School, young Grimmett was, according to good judges, developing into a fine fast bowler. The school's cricket coach was F. A. 'Dimp' Hemplemann, a teacher with a quick mind and a firm hand. He ran a hard school in the nets. At the end of a two-hour session all the bowlers had to finish with a succession of six balls. Clarrie bowled his over and tired but happy at the thought of a rest he started to walk away.

'Ah, wait on there Grimmett. Give me another six balls,' Hemplemann ordered.

Another six balls? Clarrie was spent. But when the order was from Hemplemann, all of the students followed the order to the letter. Grimmett moved in determinedly and by a curious mix of fatigue and mischief, Clarrie readjusted his grip and sent down a perfectly pitched leg-break. It curved in, landing on the line of leg, then whipped across to beat the right-hander's outside edge.

Hemplemann beamed. 'Mr Grimmett, that is it. From now on you will bowl leg-breaks; only leg-breaks. Remember, Mr Grimmett you are now a leg-spinner.'

Clarrie had only bowled one ball. It was a brilliant leg-break, but it could have happened by chance. Everyone bowls a 'pearler' now and again. He used to practise his leggies with the Harris brothers on the ridge and furrow turf at Basin Reserve. Bowling this stuff to good players on true wickets – now that might worry Clarrie more than his opponent. Clarrie worried about the next school match. He was Mount Cook's 'demon' fast bowler. Mr Hemplemann was both coach and umpire. Just as Clarrie began to measure his run, Mr Hemplemann was called away to the docks. Clarrie lengthened his run and charged in. He bowled like the wind and took 7/3, thus enhancing his reputation as a demon fast bowler.

Next match was against Wairarap School and Hemplemann was umpiring. Clarrie handed him his cap, bemused at the field Clarrie's skipper had set for him: three slips, gully, third man, fine leg. He heard Clarrie's captain urge: 'Let's see how fast you can bowl, Grimmett!' To the amazement of all, other than Hemplemann and Grimmett, Clarrie's first ball was a highly tossed leg-break; it landed and spun prodigiously. He took 6/5 in the first dig and 8/1 in the second. Clarrie Grimmett never again needed prompting to bowl leg-breaks.

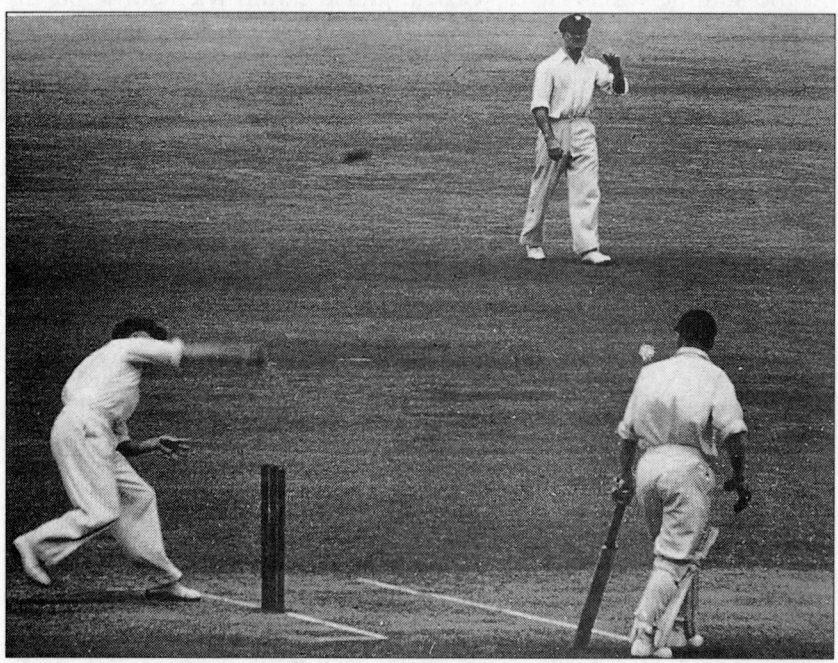

Clarrie played first-class cricket for Wellington, teaming with the old Aussie left-hander Jack Saunders, who toured England with Joe Darling's celebrated 1902 Australian team. In 1913–14 Clarrie was 'reserve' for the New Zealand team about to tour Australia, but no one fell ill and Clarrie stayed home. Clarrie dearly wanted to play Test cricket and at that time New Zealand did not have Test status, so at the age of 23 Clarrie packed his swag and headed for Sydney.

There he joined Sydney, after Paddington turned him down because he lived out of its district. The young Herbie Collins was a member of the Sydney A Grade team at that time, but Clarrie's debut was in the club's Third XI. What a psychological fall from playing with Wellington against Victor Trumper a few weeks before! Nonetheless he took 12/60 in his debut match for the thirds and was rushed into the seconds the next week. He stayed in the seconds until Dr Willcocks fell sick and Clarrie was picked to play in the As against Arthur Mailey's Redfern team at the SCG. In 14.2 overs of fabulous spin bowling, in which Grimmett teased and mesmerised his opponents, the little gnome of turn took 7/32. Mailey grabbed 3/45 in 12 overs in reply, before Clarrie completed his demolition of Redfern with a second-innings haul of 5/33. Mr Hemplemann and Jack Saunders wired their congratulations.

The Great War continued preventing any big cricket being played. In the summer of 1917–18, Clarrie joined South Melbourne on the advice of Jack Saunders. Grimmett stayed in Victoria for seven years, before his final move to Adelaide, which he found to be his haven for the unwanted and the staging post for England. Just after the Great War ended, Clarrie was picked for Victoria to play against New South Wales in Sydney. He played under Edgar Mayne who was no great shakes in understanding how to utilise spin bowlers.

When Grimmett finally played for South Australia his first match was against Victoria. He took five wickets against his old state, included in that bag was none other than Edgar Mayne. Grimmett rubbed in his little win at a rest-day roast. He purloined the skeletal head of a sheep and slammed it into Mayne's soup dish, 'There you are Mr Mayne, your head on a platter: caught and bowled!'

In 1919, Clarrie's Victoria played at Goulburn on the return journey. On the hill was the youthful Bill O'Reilly, aged 14, who was intrigued by the name 'Grummett' which went up on the scoreboard. O'Reilly thought his 'Grummett' must be pretty good to be batting in front of the likes of Vernon Ransford, Jack Ryder, Les Keating, Basil Onyons and Phil Le Couteur. Years later O'Reilly and Grimmett, whom the Tiger always referred to as 'Grum', became the greatest spin combination of them all.

Clarrie left South Melbourne and played for Prahran. There he continued to collect wickets en masse, but state matches were few and far between. His determination to become a great bowler was evident in that he fashioned a turf wicket in his backyard and each Sunday his version of 'rest' was to bowl to such luminaries as Bill Ponsford and Matt Ellis. Clarrie trained a little black and white fox terrier to fetch the balls for him as he practised alone, ever spinning, ever scheming. Ponny once said to Clarrie: 'That dog of yours – Joe Grimmett – will be famous one day, Clarrie. Mark my words.'

Every now and again Clarrie would be picked to play for Victoria. He played against the touring Englishmen in 1920-21, but suffered a split finger in attempting to take a hot return catch from Jack Hobbs and was relegated to grade cricket again. His dream to play Test cricket never wavered in Clarrie's heart. His belief remained strong despite the knockbacks and the Victorian selectors' seeming indifference. The years skipped by. All the time Clarrie practised and schemed. Most years he took in excess of 50 grade wickets. The likes of Ponsford knew how good Clarrie was, but the Victorian selectors continued to ignore his claims.

Vic Richardson, the South Australian captain, was growing heartily sick of South Australia spending days in the field due to an impotent attack. For years he had heard glowing reports of this little fellow Grimmett, who bowled to Ponsford on Sundays and had a dog trained to fetch the balls for him. Richardson wanted a good spinner and he thought about Clarrie. He spoke to Clem Hill, the ex-South Australian and Test great, about Grimmett and Clem had a good look at Clarrie bowling in a match in Melbourne. Clem reckoned the Grimmett of 1923 to be the best leg-spinner in the land. He recommended that South Australia try to secure Clarrie's services for the following summer. Adelaide Cricket Club sounded Clarrie out, then right out of the blue Grimmett was selected to play for Victoria. The match was against South Australia in Adelaide. Here was a double chance: to look about Adelaide, his potential new home, and to show everyone his skill in big cricket. Grimmett took 1/12 and 8/86 – his one and only Sheffield Shield match for Victoria.

In May, 1924 the Grimmetts – Clarrie, his wife, Elizabeth, son, Vic and the dog, Joe – arrived in their new home, Adelaide. He took five wickets in his first grade match for Adelaide against Richardson's Sturt. Clarrie was rushed into the state team and took a steady stream of wickets, impressing everyone with his calm under pressure and the relentless pressure he maintained over the batsmen. In the return match with New South Wales, Clarrie took a second-innings haul of 6/103 to help South Australia to its first victory in a Sheffield Shield match since 1914. Grimmett had taken bags of five wickets in every match leading up to the last Test match of the 1924–25 season in Sydney. Clarrie, at the age of 33, was picked alongside Arthur Mailey, and Alan Kippax was the other Aussie making his Test debut. Clarrie, with an unconquered 12 in Australia's first innings of 295, then saw Bert Oldfield take a magnificent catch down the leg side to get rid of Hobbs for a duck off the bowling of the energetic Jack Gregory.

Clarrie was given mid-off and he was soon in the action, swooping on an Andy Sandham drive, which the Surrey man hit between mid-off and Tommy Andrews at cover. Clarrie had moved swiftly with the stroke, anticipating its direction. He stooped and conquered with a smart throw to the bowler Gregory covering the stumps at the non-striker's end. Sandham was run out for a duck. Clarrie had made an early mark, displaying his baseball skills with pace to the ball and a swift, flat throw. Clarrie's old Sydney team-mate Herbie Collins was the Test skipper. With England in trouble at 4/89, Collins threw Clarrie the ball. Grimmett had a weathered, almost wizened, appearance.

His approach was akin to the unlikely combination of Johnny 'Cho' Gleeson and Groucho Marx. There was a paradoxically casual urgency about it all: an ungainly run-up, the body losing height as it neared the delivery point. Clarrie's body seemed to crouch even lower as the arm came over, none too high, although he insisted his arm was as high as the next man. He didn't drag, as did Richie Benaud, who also lost height at delivery. Grimmett came to his full height at the point of delivery, propelling the red sphere unerringly on its way, dipping deceptively and inevitably to deal with his nervous foe.

But this first ball in Test cricket was against Frank Woolley, the tall left-hander who stood as straight-backed as any Grenadier guard. Woolley was a batting aristocrat: a batsman of great style and presence. He caressed the ball, dismissing it from the wicket with precision and timing, rather than hammering it with brute force. Grimmett needed to be on his mettle, for Woolley was a formidable foe. Grimmett's first ball was on song. Woolley came forward like Kent's Fuller Pilch of old, 'very commanding, extremely forward'. Woolley smothered the spin and sent the ball to Collins at mid-off. Collins nodded to Clarrie as if to say, 'that's got rid of the nerves. Now *we* bowl!' Woolley was looking for the wrong'un. Clarrie was banking on it. He knew that if he tossed a ball higher and wider Woolley might well suspect a wrong'un and launch into a drive, effectively hitting 'with' the spin away. The width of delivery would free his arms giving him room to hit with great freedom. However, Clarrie knew that for Woolley to have such freedom of movement, he might then forget to cover any gap between bat and pad. A wrong'un was not a worry, but the stock leg-break, that was a different matter. Clarrie did toss one up – invitingly wider than the others. Woolley's eyes lit up. He prepared to drive, but the ball swerved away in flight, then upon pitching it spun back, alarmingly. Woolley was fully committed. He lunged at the ball and almost overbalanced, but it was all too late. The Grimmett leg-break had found the gap between bat and pad and the ball sailed through the huge gap to hit Woolley's off-stump. It was Grimmett's first Test wicket.

Grimmett took a match haul of 11/82 (5/45 and 6/37) to completely dominate the game. In the second innings he had Hobbs stumped and further satisfaction to be given the ball ahead of Mailey. In fact, Mailey bowled only five overs in the match for a return of 0/13. Clarrie was Adelaide's latest hero.

In 1930 it was Grimmett and Don Bradman who held the limelight. Richardson maintained that Grimmett was every bit as valuable as Bradman in that 1930 campaign, although it's tough to argue against Bradman, who, at the age of 21, tore the heart out of the England attack, hitting 2960 tour runs at 98.66, including 974 runs in the Tests at 139.14. Grimmett took 142 wickets at 17.09, including 10/37 against a strong Yorkshire XI and a record-breaking 29-wicket haul in the Tests. He had wonderful battles with the new England master Wally Hammond, a great, hard hitting batsman, who could collar the very best of attacks.

With O'Reilly, Grimmett struck fear into all batting combinations from 1934 when they really came into their own as a brilliant spin combination, despite having been first pitched together as early as 1931–32 against the South Africans.

Perhaps the Irish lass who wrote to Clarrie during his brilliant 1930 tour gives us an insight into Clarrie's impish character:

You remind me of Puck or Punch for you are rather tiny, aren't you? Or some sort of Irish Leprechauns, that live at the bottom of Lakes Killarney – dear little folk they are, but all alive, and up to mischief. You know you would make a cute little Irishman. This letter is to wish you luck with the ball. I would like to read of you doing something really startling. Can't then I read of Grimmett breaking all records – Bradman becomes boring – even all the schoolgirls know of Don Bradman, who does seem to be a bit of a darlin' but – I began this because I had nothing to do, now I have nothing to say …

Ida Burke's letter must have inspired Clarrie, for one week later the impish little trickster of her imagination dismissed Percy Holmes, Herbert Sutcliffe and Maurice Leyland on the way to taking 10/37 against Yorkshire at Bramall Lane. Like the Leprechauns of Ireland, Grimmett revelled in mystery. He was always working on a new sort of ball. He invented the flipper, but so wanted to perfect the ball that he waited 12 years before he bowled it in a match. At the SCG in 1940 Grimmett took two New South Wales wickets on the trot with his flipper. The two New South Wales players were Test men Sid Barnes and Arthur Chipperfield, both went back and were trapped dead in front, lbw.

On the SCG Hill that day was a cricket-mad 10-year-old kid named Richie Benaud. Clarrie taught the flipper to Cec Pepper, he taught Bruce Dooland and he taught Benaud. Years passed and no one else had a decent flipper until Warne learnt the craft from then AIS Cricket Academy Head coach, and former Victorian batsman, Jack Potter. Potter used to dabble with Jack Iverson-type finger flick deliveries and the flipper. Warne found out how, and the world's best batsmen soon knew its deadly effectiveness.

O'Reilly revered Grimmett. One of the last pieces of writing O'Reilly ever penned was about Grimmett:

Clarence Victor Grimmett, my revered workmate, was the greatest leg-spin bowler I have ever seen. He sized a batsman up in a few deliveries, and concentrated on bowling straight at the stumps and landing the ball in a chosen awkward spot which demanded expert use of batting feet. He never resorted to 'loop' as onlookers call it, but he was an expert in overt changes of pace, which was the very backbone of his undisputed claim to have been the greatest of his tribe.

Clarrie Grimmett's self-belief was inspirational. He never gave up. Australian cricket is eternally grateful that Clarrie kept plugging away. He deserves an exalted place in Test history.

GRIMMETT, Clarence Victor

Born: 25 December 1891, Caversham (NZ)
Died: 2 May 1980, Kensington (SA)

Bats: Right-handed
Bowls: Right-arm leg spin

First-Class Career

Debut: 1911–12 Wellington v Auckland, Wellington

M	Inn	NO	Runs	50	100	Ave	Ct	St	Runs	Wkts	Ave	5	10
248	321	54	4720	12	–	17.67	139	–	31740	1424	22.28	127	33

Highest Score: 71* South Australia v New South Wales, Adelaide, 1928–29
Best Bowling: 10/37 Australians v Yorkshire, Sheffield, 1930

Test Career

Debut: 1924–25 Australia v England, Sydney

M	Inn	NO	Runs	50	100	Ave	Ct	St	Runs	Wkts	Ave	5	10
37	50	10	557	1	–	13.93	17	–	5231	216	24.22	21	7

Highest Score: 50 Australia v England, Manchester, 1930
Best Bowling: 7/40 Australia v South Africa, Johannesburg, 1935–36

LINDSAY HASSETT

The Missing Years

by Laurie Clancy

Those who have examined the cricketing career of Lindsay Hassett will always ask themselves the same question more commonly asked about Bradman, though Bradman at least tasted a few years of cricket before the war: what would his career have been like had it not been for the war?

In the case of Hassett it is an even more poignant question for two reasons: the war coincided exactly with what would probably have been his most productive years, but as well as that he emerged from it a completely different and much less exciting batsman, though an extremely accomplished one.

In typically philosophical mode, Hassett himself claims not to regret missing his best years. He wrote in a speech given during the Commemorative Test, 'I had a rather uncommon Test career. I played my fourth Test match at the age of 24 and my fifth when I was 33. The war stole eight of the best of my cricket years but, on reflection, I doubt whether I was the loser. The brief period I spent in the company of the members of the Services team, and the cricket we played, provided me with a rare and very special quality of enjoyment.'

Hassett was one of nine children (including six sons) of a Geelong real estate agent. He learned to play at Geelong College, where he was captain of cricket and football. He was the Victorian Public Schools tennis champion in 1931, a top-grade squash player and in five years at the College scored 2191 runs in 41 innings, with five centuries. His brother Harry was an interstate tennis player while Dick played cricket for Victoria as a googly bowler.

Laurie Clancy is a critic, novelist and long-standing skipper of the Parkville People's XI, and producer of such cricket festivals as Writers v Artists, *and* Meanjin v Overland.

Hassett burst onto the scene at the age of only 17 with a brilliant innings of 147 for a Victorian Country XI against the West Indian tourists of 1930–31, the only century scored in the match. He made his debut for Victoria shortly afterwards and after a shaky beginning, at the age of 22 he became a regular. His international career began with a not-out century against a New Zealand team in pre-war days before he was selected for the 1938 tour of England at the age of 25. On tour he played superbly in the County matches, finishing with 1607 runs at 50.21, third only to Bradman and Brown, though his Test record was less distinguished. But he did play a fine, aggressive innings, full of boundaries, at Leeds – 33 runs after Australia, chasing only 105, had lost Brown, Fingleton, Bradman and McCabe.

During what would have been the 1942–43 season, Hassett was organising matches in the Egyptian desert between Australians and other combinations. The success of the team led to the idea of an Australian Services team. Hassett was appointed captain under difficult circumstances. He had refused a commission based on his services to cricket during World War II. This would have strengthened his case for the captaincy. The RAAF men in the side resented him, believing that their legendary war hero Keith Carmody, another player who showed a fine tactical sense in captaining Western Australia later, deserved it. Hassett remained calm, ignoring the inter-services friction. He took his team for a series of one-day village matches. 'Hassett,' said one commentator, 'led his players in some hilarious post-match singing sessions, usually balancing his tiny frame on top of a beer keg while he conducted them through "Down Came a Blackbird", "The Desert Song" or "Champagne Charlie". Hassett's speciality was his rendition of "There's a Bridle Hanging on the Wall", which he finishing wiping mock tears from his eyes, gazing mournfully at a handkerchief tucked over a clock or pot to represent the bridle.'

In the Victory series, Hassett was the only player with Test experience; there were six state players and four who had not gone beyond grade cricket. It played a 20-match tour of England, including five unofficial Tests, from 19 May to 15 September before going on to India, Ceylon and a tour back home. These so-called 'Victory Tests', with the Australian side formed out of the former RAAF and AIF sides, drew large and steadily increasing audiences. In a speech at the end of the series, Hassett commented, 'This is cricket as it should be. These games have shown that international cricket can be played as between real friends – so let's have no more talk of "war" in cricket.'

After captaining the Australian Services side in 1945 Hassett returned to international cricket, but his style according to observers had changed markedly. A shrewd observer, A. G. ('Johnnie') Moyes claimed that he played much more cautiously, forsaking brilliance for mere steadiness. In a side of Bradman's quality this was hardly necessary. Moyes wrote of him, 'Later on, when Australian batting had lost much of its soundness and assurance and had become so fallible, his determined and competent defence was often of the utmost value; but even then one could not escape the thought that a man so richly endowed with talent could have lived by controlled attack, and by doing so would have made it easier for those who followed.' Moyes even argues that he put pressure on players lower down the order such as Harvey and Miller because of his slowness, though from all accounts both those players tended to be pretty impetuous anyway. Moyes dismissed the theory that Hassett was batting to instructions and remained puzzled by the change in tactics but perhaps the reason is as simple as the answer Hassett himself gave to Neville Cardus, who challenged him after a particularly boring innings in Adelaide: 'Wore out!' he said. 'Just plain worn out.' Hassett himself seemed to be ambivalent later in life about his change in tactics. One day, commenting on radio, he admitted that he might have been too conservative and advised the young Norman O'Neill not to make the same mistake.

Hassett was overlooked as captain for the 1946 New Zealand tour in favour of Bill Brown; he received only one vote. Bradman had fully expected Hassett to succeed him after his retirement, but when the selectors sat down to choose the team to tour South Africa in 1949–50 he won the position only very narrowly, seven votes to six, over Arthur Morris who had no experience of captaincy. Ray Robinson said at the time that the near decision had 'prevented a disgusting act of ingratitude' and that 'once again Hassett's notable achievements with the Services team had been devalued'.

As he had done with the Services side, Hassett took over under difficult conditions, succeeding the greatest batsman of all time and with a side that was clearly declining in ability, but he quickly made his mark. When commentators talk about the great postwar Australian captains, the usual candidates are Benaud, Ian Chappell and Taylor, but there is an argument for Hassett being right up there with them. As well as the contrast between his pre- and postwar batting, the other great contradiction of his career is that between his scrupulous sense of fairness on the field and his tactical brilliance and ruthlessness.

Examples of his personal integrity and sense of fair play abound. When Freddy Brown won the toss in the third Test of his Australian tour Hassett was quick to pat him on the back. In a Test match against South Africa, when Australia was in dire need of a wicket, he called back a batsman who had been run out; he wasn't sure but he thought he might have impeded him. In a match against England he refused to run Denis Compton out after he dropped his bat. Sam Loxton tells a

story of when, as twelfth man for Victoria, he brought out the drinks as usual. Again, Compton was involved, batting on 99. Hassett waved him back. The next over Compton got his century and Hassett signalled Loxton to bring out the drinks. 'Lad,' he said, 'You never bring drinks onto the ground when a bloke is on 99.' It is no surprise that when Hassett retired from ABC commenting he expressed his dislike for what the game had become. When the itinerary for the West Indies tour of Australia was announced and it was revealed that they would play only one first-class match before their first Test he was public and vociferous in his protests.

And yet he is arguably the greatest of all Australian captains as a tactician. Two famous examples can suffice. In the first Test in Brisbane during Freddy Brown's tour, Australia batted first in perfect conditions and was dismissed for a dismal 228, with only Harvey succeeding with 74. Rain poured down all the next day, turning the wicket into a treacherous minefield, and in an extraordinary day's cricket 20 wickets fell. Brown declared at 7/68, still 160 runs behind, in order to get the Australians in, but then Hassett turned the tables on him by declaring, much to Brown's amazement, at 7/32. By the next day there wasn't much to worry about in the pitch but by staring at it suspiciously and bringing his fielders in close Hassett bluffed all the Englishmen except Hutton and won the match narrowly.

The second example that has passed into folklore is the third Test in South Africa. On a sticky pitch that saw Australia dismissed for 75, 236 runs behind, Hassett instructed his bowlers to get Nourse out but no one else. As the pitch slowly dried, the Australian attack bowled outside the stumps to a deep-set field that conceded only singles and again the tactic was successful. He was not afraid to anger Keith Miller just before the first Test in South Africa. When Miller came out to bat, Hassett ordered Jack Iverson to stop bowling. He knew that when Victoria played New South Wales in the Sheffield Shield final, as they almost invariably did in those days, Iverson would be one of his key weapons and he didn't want Miller and Morris to gain practise in reading his spin.

During the 1948 tour Hassett was captain in Bradman's absence in the match against Yorkshire. Frustrated by Bradman's edict that the side could not be changed and without a spinner on what was transparently a spinner's wicket, Hassett suggested to Bill Johnstone that he try his hand at bowling leg spin around the wicket – and thus a new career was born.

At the same time he was a renowned prankster and raconteur who could always see the absurd side of cricket. It was Hassett who was blamed for installing a muddied goat in the room O'Reilly shared with McCabe during the 1938 tour. The next day he came back with a hedgehog but the doors had all been secured. At the end of the Victory Tests, which attracted hundreds of thousands of pounds for British charities but for which the players received only their meagre military salaries, Hassett made a famous and much-quoted speech celebrating the end of the war which began, 'Never have I seen so many ugly men at the cricket' – stray boos – 'nor so many beautiful women.'

Among other anecdotes, Hassett tells a story about dropping Cyril Washbrook twice in the deep off Lindwall. After the second miss he borrowed the helmet of the local policeman and stood waiting for the catch. He claims that everyone laughed – except Lindwall. Another example of his humour was his protecting Bill Johnstone at No. 11 by declaring, so that Johnstone won the batting averages for the tour – once out for 102 runs.

Emeritus Professor of English at La Trobe University, Derrick Marsh, remembers almost playing against Hassett in the first match of their South African tour against Free State. He had been placed on stand-by as their opening bowler was a doubtful starter, but unfortunately in the end was not needed. The South African captain won the toss and being a chivalrous man invited the tourists to bat first – on the notoriously placid Ramblers wicket, which Len Hutton had wanted to dig up and take around the world with him. Hassett stared at him incredulously. 'I'll go in first myself,' he said. Two overs before lunch he had reached 96 but he then decided he didn't want to make a century before lunch, blocked every ball and went in on that score. The first ball after lunch he pulled for six, and he then gave his wicket away.

Professor Marsh says of the match, 'Obviously the Aussies could take it all very lightly and could afford to be generous, but they didn't treat us with contempt, rather with genuine friendliness. In his quiet way, Hassett was one of the nicest. He was really funny, and a master of the dead-pan one-liner. When we took them out on Sunday to a place on a river for a day in the country, they cheerfully joined in an impromptu cricket match on the lawns with the local kids. Most of them were ex-servicemen, and I think still delighted to have survived the war. Also, I think, it was their first tour without Bradman, and they found touring under Hassett a much more relaxed business.'

Hassett was one of Australia's greatest-ever cover and outfieldmen. He is the only Australian to have made 10 Test centuries after the age of 33; even Bradman only managed eight. Despite missing his best years, on retirement he had the largest number of centuries in first class cricket by an Australian (59), except of course for Bradman (117). In England, in his fortieth year, he hit two centuries in the Tests and was the finest Australian batsman. He even took on the job of opening. His 10 centuries included four against England, three against South Africa, two against the West Indies, and one (his highest score) against India. Apart from his matchwinning 33, his finest innings was a brilliant century at Old Trafford. Curiously enough, his average for his district club South Melbourne is lower than his Test average; he once made seven successive ducks and contemplated giving cricket away. In 1948 he was named by *Wisden* as one of the five cricketers of the year. Bradman spoke with unusual generosity (for Bradman) of his ability. In *Farewell to Cricket* he wrote, 'A great player and valuable lieutenant as vice-captain. Extremely sound knowledge of game and tactics. Beautiful stroke-player when in the mood – could take charge in crisis, and willing to risk wicket in the interests of the team or the match. Sound defence made him at home under almost any conditions.' After his death he spoke also of his total loyalty, a fact confirmed by his wife who said that he would never allow a word to be spoken against the Don. He was also the finest player of Bill O'Reilly in the world,

HASSETT, Arthur Lindsay
Born: 28 August 1913, Geelong (VIC)
Died: 16 June 1993, Batehaven (NSW)

Bats: Right-handed
Bowls: Right-arm medium

First-Class Career
Debut: 1932–33 Victoria v South Australia, Melbourne

M	Inn	NO	Runs	50	100	Ave	Ct	St	Runs	Wkts	Ave	5	10
216	322	32	16890	74	59	58.24	170	–	703	18	39.05	–	–

Highest Score: 232 Victoria v MCC, Melbourne, 1950–51
Best Bowling: 2/10 Australian Services v Ceylon, Colombo, 1945–46

Test Career
Debut: 1938 Australia v England, Nottingham

M	Inn	NO	Runs	50	100	Ave	Ct	St	Runs	Wkts	Ave	5	10
43	69	3	3073	11	10	46.56	30	–	78	0	–	–	–

Highest Score: 198* Australia v India, Adelaide, 1947–48

something even O'Reilly acknowledged, spotting his wrong'un easily and hoisting him impudently back over his head. Spectators used to taunt the big man by threatening to bring Hassett back.

He was a more than useful bowler as a schoolboy and once took 5/31 against New Zealand but he remained self-deprecating about his bowling. Asked once about it by a fellow commentator on radio, Hassett admitted that he used to bowl a bit, then added dead-pan, 'I was always surprised at the speed with which the ball came off the bat.' In the fifth Test in the 1953 tour, when it was clear that Brown's side had finally broken England's drought, Hassett brought himself on to bowl the last over, and convulsed with laughter. He held 170 catches and apart from that memorable afternoon with Washbrook rarely dropped one. Ray Robinson claims that he never saw Hassett drop a catch until he was 35 years old.

Hassett had his testimonial match at the MCG in January 1954 and, free from the responsibilities of Test leadership, rediscovered all his old fluency, scoring 126 runs in only 107 minutes. In that match (in which Miller scored centuries in both innings) 49 454 attended over four days. Hassett went out of first-class cricket with 126 and a cheque for £5503. He captained Australia in 10 matches against England, winning 4 and losing 2. Hassett was a commentator on ABC radio until 1981 before retiring to live the life of a fisherman and raconteur at Bateman's Bay. He died in his 80th year, shortly after undergoing heart bypass surgery.